£55

National Theatres in Context

National Theatres in Context:

FRANCE, GERMANY, ENGLAND AND WALES

ANWEN JONES

UNIVERSITY OF WALES PRESS
CARDIFF
2007

Published by the University of Wales Press

University of Wales Press
10 Columbus Walk
Brigantine Place
Cardiff
CF10 4UP

www.wales.ac.uk/press

© Anwen Jones, 2007

The right of Anwen Jones to be identified as the author of this work has been asserted in accordance with the Copyright, Designs and Patents Act 1988.

All rights reserved. No part of this book may be reproduced, stored in a retrieval system, or transmitted, in any form or by any means, electronic, mechanical, photocopying, recording or otherwise, without clearance from the publisher.

ISBN 978-0-7083-1917-8

British Library Cataloguing-in-Publication Data.
A catalogue record for this book is available from the British Library

The publishers wish to acknowledge the financial support of the Higher Education Funding Council for Wales in the publication of this book.

Printed in Great Britain by Cambridge Printing, Cambridge.

I dad, i ddiolch am dy gyngor a'th garedigrwydd
ond yn bennaf am y fraint o'th gwmni.

Contents

Foreword	ix
Acknowledgements	xiv
Introduction	1
1 The French national theatre: courting the crowd	15
2 The stage of the German nation: twin developments	47
3 The English national theatre: O brave new world, That has such people in't	90
4 The National Eisteddfod, the national pageant and the Welsh national theatre: friends or foes?	129
5 Fragmented reflections and shattered fragments: the mirror image of Welsh national life?	156
6 Changing old lamps for new: private patronage gives way to public subsidy	182
Conclusion	213
Notes	217
Index	257

Foreword

In May 2003, the second Welsh general election was held and the Welsh National Assembly began its second term of office under a new Labour government. In March of the same year, a new Welsh-medium national theatre was launched in Wales. Its first performance was announced in Alfred Hickling's report, 'Played in Wales'[1] in *The Guardian*. Hickling noted that Michael Bogdanov, who had recently outlined his own proposals for a Welsh national theatre under the auspices of a ministry of culture and a national charter, felt that the launching of Theatr Genedlaethol Cymru[2] should not have preceded a process of decision-making with regard to the future of English-language theatre in Wales. Both Terry Hand's Theatr Clwyd and Bogdanov's own Swansea-based Wales Theatre Company, two predominantly English-medium companies, have been afforded the epithet 'national' at times, but both are equally aware of the limitations imposed by their geographical locations and of their inability, to date, to provide south Wales with a major repertory theatre. The Arts Council's decision in 2000 to fund SgriptCymru, a national company responsible for promoting new stage writing in both Welsh and English in Wales suggested that it sought to foster a bilingual theatrical environment in Wales. However, despite this initiative, and despite Bogdanov's feeling that separating English- and Welsh-medium theatre was a retrogressive step, that step was taken in early 2003 when, having secured a grant of £750,000 from the Welsh Arts Council, Theatr Genedlaethol Cymru was launched. The company put an end to a long period of 'false dawns'[3] by giving its first official performance between 23 April and 29 May 2004 with a touring production of *Yn Debyg Iawn i Ti a Fi*,[4] a play by the contemporary Welsh-language playwright, Meic Povey.[5]

The company's performance schedule to date has striven towards and, more often than not, realized the aims set out for it by its steering committee, including the provision of:

- An exciting and modern theatrical style based on Wales's theatrical tradition and its culture.
- Programmes of work including a variety of genres.
- Training and career development opportunities.
- A good name for the company and for drama produced in Wales on the international stage.
- New work in Welsh.
- Access to the widest possible audience[6] [my translation and adaptation].

Its initial production – an exploration of the interaction between the different members of a traditional Welsh family and their schizophrenic young brother for whom language is a haunting, difficult and abusive battle with the voices in and outside his head – provided a stimulating parody on the difficulties and the drama of the national discourse in twenty-first century Wales, both on and off the stage. The second production – a translation of Shakespeare's *Romeo and Juliet* – was another provocative performance in terms of the linguistic issues it raised and the suggestion that the search for Welsh identity might still be governed by imported values, by a Welsh version of 'good, quality mainstream theatre in the literary tradition from Shakespeare through Ibsen and Shaw.'[7] The third and most recent full-scale production[8] – a Welsh-medium farce, *Plas Drycin*, written by an up-and-coming new Welsh playwright, Gwyneth Glyn – was a humorous exposé of all that is ridiculous in ideas of Wales and Welshness that could be read either as an indictment of the failure of the Welsh national identity to respond to the challenges of the twenty-first century or as a declaration that it was preparing and prepared to do so, with mirth and vivacity.

Whatever our assessment of the quality and kind of Theatr Genedlaethol Cymru's productions and progress – the very existence of a new national theatre company in the second millennium is surprising. Its appearance has stimulated a wealth of debate within and without Wales, conducted to a considerable extent via the internet – the favoured technological tool of a postmodernist era in which the 'world-wide paradox of the simultaneous homogenising impact of consumerism and the fissiparous search for distinct identity has been played out against the backdrop of globalisation'.[9] There is no doubt that the twenty-first century is late in the day for any nation to be launching a national theatre yet the onset of a great national theatre debate in Scotland as the Scots scrutinize their newly established non-building, non-company-based national theatre run on a budget of £7.5 million under the care of its first director, Vicky Featherstone,[10] proves that Wales is not alone in her most recent national theatrical undertaking. What makes the case of Wales particularly interesting is the fact that Theatr Genedlaethol Cymru is only the most recent in a series of national theatrical creations – starting with Lord Howard de Walden's pioneering efforts at the turn of the twentieth century and achieving its greatest success with Cwmni Theatr Cymru[11] in the seventies. The question to be answered is not why a Welsh national theatre has not appeared before now, but rather why the struggle towards the expression of a Welsh national identity by means of a Welsh national theatre continues now.

The focal point and ultimate preoccupation of this book is the search for an explanation of the persistence of the idea of national theatre in Wales in a new millennium in which the nation, having acquired new powers of political expression, faces the task of mediating its national identity to a European community. This is a community founded on a celebration of multi-nationalism, representative of both the insidious insecurities of the postmodern experience of being and the tantalizing freedom that multi-nationalism allows for the manufacture of a long range sense of belonging with other national entities within a European supra-structure.

In order to establish a vantage-point from which the phenomenon of Wales's tireless engagement with the idea of a national theatre may be viewed, the book sketches out the historical background of the idea of a national theatre in Wales within the context of the development of several other national theatres in north-western Europe. By placing this general development within the trajectory outlined by Jürgen Habermas in his influential study of the transition from a medieval to a modern society, the significance of national theatre as a forum for the articulation of a national identity is explored and evaluated with reference to the fast-changing world of capitalism, consumerism and individualism. No attempt is made to provide an exhaustive account of the history of any of the national theatres under survey. The aim is rather to place each national theatre within the framework of the society from which it emerges, more or less organically, and which it eventually comes to reproduce and represent. During this analysis, a historical hierarchy becomes manifest in the sense that different national theatres precede, parallel or even reconstitute the new, liberal public sphere identified by Habermas as the characteristic of a modern society, in which egalitarian, public debate replaces the representation of power by an authoritarian figure such as a monarch. The study begins with the Comédie-Française because it was set up by such a figure, intent on regulating his relations with the nation. Its subsequent history mirrors the political adjustments that shook France and reverberated throughout Europe in the 1789 revolution until it reaches a dignified position of semi-retirement with the contemporary development of a network of regional national theatres in France. The history of the German national theatre begins later and mirrors the development of the liberal, public sphere until it reaches the crisis of the Nazi period from which it emerges weakened and wary of the new challenges presented by the modern, unified Germany of the late twentieth century. The English National Theatre is most interesting for its late start and the laboriousness of its coming into being. The fact that the English National Theatre did not take shape until the onset of the twentieth century – a point by which the new, liberal public sphere had already begun to disintegrate under the pressure of modernist forces – might appear to place it outside the trajectory outlined by Habermas. In actual fact, the English middle classes used their national theatre to reconstruct the conditions of the new liberal, public sphere so that they might discover a freedom and force of expression that had been denied them hitherto.

The three chapters dedicated to a study of the Welsh national theatre reveal that Wales was also a late starter. The Welsh national theatre movement, like its English counterpart, had to re-formulate the conditions of the liberal, public sphere in order to activate interplay between audience, stage and players that provided a constructive response to the challenges of national and international relations in a modern Europe. This task was complicated by the fact that Wales also had to negotiate its relations with that neighbour in a struggle to come to terms with its position of subservience within a British framework that often militated against the aspirations, tendencies and conditions of its own national infrastructure. However, what makes the history of the national theatre in Wales unique is not the fact that it first saw the light of day in the modernist period, but that it reappeared in a post-modernist era – an era beset by the challenges of the paradoxical disintegration of the familiar forms of social interaction and organization and the persistence, if not the accentuation, of the desire to be and to belong. What is most fascinating about the idea of a national theatre in Wales is its refusal to find a resting place, its rejection of an epitaph of any kind and its resurgence in a contemporary time-zone that seems inherently antagonistic to communal, cultural activity of the theatrical or any other kind. As Michael Billington asks, in an era of multiculturalism, 'Who needs a national theatre?'[12] The answer, he admits, seems to be almost everyone. The aim of this book is to provide a context for the answering of another question: not who wants a national theatre but why Wales persists in wanting hers.

Acknowledgements

I would like to thank Mrs Mary Pettman for permission to reproduce Elidir Davies's plans for a national theatre at Sophia Gardens, Cardiff, and Geraint Wyn Parry, the secretary of Cymdeithas Theatr Cymru, for permission to reproduce written and visual material from the Theatr Cymru archive held at the Caernarvon Record Office, Gwynedd County Council Archive.

I would also like to extend my thanks to the staff at the National Library of Wales for their efficiency, good humour and patience and to acknowledge the advice and assistance of Dr Russell Davies and Dr Roger Owen, University of Wales, Aberystwyth. However, the inspiration for this book came directly from my father, Professor Ioan Williams, University of Wales, and although he can in no way be held accountable for its contents, its existence is ultimately attributable to him. I am indebted to him for his constant encouragement and the generosity of his invaluable, professional advice. Two other, less direct but important, sources of inspiration and motivation were Gwyn Williams's *When Was Wales?* and Kenneth Morgan's *Rebirth of a Nation*.

On a personal note, I would like to express my gratitude to Mrs Llywela Jones for every practical assistance offered during the difficult period of writing this book. Finally, I am deeply indebted to Mrs Margaret Williams for her vital support as a proofreader, a babysitter and an ever-reliable check on my somewhat eccentric English. I also thank my husband and children for their forbearance and support.

Introduction

This study traces the debate surrounding the idea of national theatre in modern Europe and its role in the emergence of modern society. In his study, *The Culture of Power and the Power of Culture*, T. C. W. Blanning, discussing the influence of culture on society as a whole, defines national theatre as one of the cultural phenomena of the modern world.[1] He goes on to discuss the nature of this modern world in terms defined by Jürgen Habermas's influential book, *The Cultural Transformation of the Public Sphere*. In a summary of Habermas's main argument, he describes how, in the transition from medieval to modern society, space was cleared for the formation of a new sphere occupied by a body of private people who engaged the public authorities in a debate over 'the general rules'[2] governing human life and relations. This debate was conducted via the cultural media and Blanning identifies theatre, and national theatre in particular, as one of the artistic channels most suited to the task. I would like to suggest that national theatre was not only able to participate in the contemporary public debate in eighteenth and nineteenth century Europe, but that the affinity between its make-up and mechanics and that of the 'public argument'[3] characteristic of that sphere allows it to resurrect and reconstruct a similar discourse at any chosen time or place – past, present or future.

The emergence of a public sphere characterized by its facilitation and promotion of critical discourse might, at first glance, seem to render the idea of nation and, by extension, the idea of national theatre, redundant. If membership of a public body was now open to all private individuals simply on the basis of the effort of communication, did people still need other modes of belonging? The answer proved to be in the affirmative and one of the major concerns that quickly came to the fore in the new, liberal public sphere was nationalism. It goes without saying that national theatre is an appropriate vehicle for the investigation and expression of national identity and feeling, but I will argue that it has particular relevance in this field because the way in which theatre works mirrors the process at work in Habermas's modern liberal sphere – the sphere that has, according to Blanning, dominated European culture ever since its first appearance in the eighteenth century.[4]

In her history of European drama and theatre, Erika Fischer-Lichte argues that the 'fundamental conditions of the very existence of theatre are to be found in the *conditio humana*.'[5] She claims that the basic theatrical situation contains all the constituent factors of the human condition and experience because, in theatre, 'it is always a question of ... the creation of identity and changing identities ... whether as member of a culture, a nation ... a social class ... a family, or as an individual.'[6] Her understanding of the human identity – whether individual or collective – is one based on the primacy of change and her argument regarding the general affinity between life and theatre assumes particular poignancy in relation to modern modes of life and experience. In the fictitious world of theatre, it is *always* a question of the creation and recreation of identity, but in the current manifestation of human society, the principle of change has assumed an extraordinary significance.

Fischer-Lichte's awareness of the fundamental importance of change in understanding modern European identities does not lead her to question the reality of Europe itself but Patrick J. Geary's vision of the volatility of the modern mode of being – set in motion, according to Habermas, by the separation of the Privy Purse from the state budget, government institutions from the court and the development of a professional bureaucracy in eighteenth-century Europe – alerts him to the ambiguities of the concept of territorial classifications. He launches a fierce attack on the pseudo-history that portrays Europe and its member nations as a collection of inter-connected 'stable and objectively identifiable social and cultural units.'[7] His exposure of the myth of a moment of territorial acquisition at which Europe came into being brings Benedict Anderson's probing phrase 'imagined communities' (Anderson, *Imagined Communities*, 1991) to mind. I will argue that national theatre rises to the challenge of modernity because it can 'transgress certain boundaries and cancel out certain differences'[8] in a way that actively sustains both distinctiveness and divergence.

Whilst there is much scholarly disagreement regarding the fundamental nature of nationalism and nations, there does seem to be a general consensus that the phenomenon itself originated in its most self-conscious and objectively definable form in the eighteenth century. Johann Gottfried von Herder was one of the first philosophers to think and talk of nationalism in terms that remain relevant today. Whilst his terms of reference were not confined to Europe (he conceived of nations in terms of the human race in general) it was he who introduced the concept of the 'national soul.'[9] This idea held its validity for Ernest Renan a century later, when he claimed that a nation was a 'spiritual principle.'[10] This spiritual entity, he argued, was made up of two things: a common possession of a rich legacy of memories and a creative act of consent to co-habit and continue to value a shared heritage.[11] The fact that Renan, one of the great heroes of the materialistic and mechanistic world of the nineteenth century, talks of a nation in such romantic and arguably religious or, at the very least, spiritual terms highlights both its magnetism and the difficulties inherent in articulating its allure in an objective fashion.

Renan's references to a shared heritage and a legacy of memories do go some way towards signalling the importance of culture as one of the constituent parts of the national whole and E. J. Hobsbawm pinpoints the period between 1780 and 1840 as the heyday of a widespread European cultural revival centred on the re-discovery and promotion of peasant and folkloric traditions.[12] Long before this and despite their differences both Herder and Hegel had expressed a common awareness of the interdependence of culture and nation. Herder talked of distinct modes of representation peculiar to particular peoples, conditioned or created by their spatial and temporal environs and their mode of living, handed down from father to son in the form of an inherited mythology. Hegel also referred to the way in which art, religion and philosophy come together to make up a people's cultural fabric by their articulation of a 'particular, historically conditioned expression of the general human aspiration for perfection and ultimate truth'.[13] The way in which Hegel dignifies the process of accumulating the cultural clout necessary for the formation of a collective identity by means of its association with humanity's general aspiration towards perfection and truth is particularly interesting. Otto Bauer talks in similar terms of the ennobling effect of appreciation for a national work of art, in the sense that it teaches a love for the nation that has produced it. He also emphasizes the pivotal role played by culture in the process of identity formation when he comments that a nation is 'never simply a natural community'[14] brought together by common factors such as place, ethnicity, language or race, but always also a cultural community.

Culture clearly plays an important role in the construction and continuance of nations, but Julie Stone Peters suggests that neither cultural identities nor the cultural inheritances that make up those identities are fixed and that we are, in fact, able to change the material we have inherited.[15] Whereas Patrick Geary would claim that changing an inherited past was a negative act of virtual re-construction, Peters argues that it is a positive and indeed an essential part of identity formation and articulation. Miroslav Hroch is similarly unafraid of cultural self-creation as Geary would term it because he is convinced that the nation exists a priori and is not simply the product of 'national consciousness, nationalism, the national will and spiritual forces'.[16] In fact it is Hroch's conviction that the nation itself does not need culture or anything else to support its existence that makes him at ease with the idea that culture may be called to the service of nationalism.

Geary and Hroch clearly respond differently to the idea of cultural invention – the former with suspicion, the latter with enthusiasm. Neither is alone in recognizing an element of fabrication, or at the very least imaginativeness, in the history of nations. In recognizing the link between the accumulation of a national heritage and the strength of national identity, Renan reflects that 'forgetting, and, I would even say, historical error are an essential factor in the creation of a nation, and thus the advances of historical study are often threatening to a nationality'.[17] It is this historical error to which Geary refers when he claims that early medieval historians are drawn into a nationalist debate and become agents in the creation of a pseudo-history that assumes the genesis of stable, objectively identifiable social and cultural units in denial of the realities of mass migration and the ambiguities of national character. In her efforts to construct a theory of urbanization, Christine Boyer argues that attempts to map and compartmentalize cities into areas, zones or departments betray a similar search for stability albeit at a different level. She cites the attempt to provide Paris with a 'new rational geography'[18] in the late eighteenth century as a specific example of this trend and claims that a certain street crier's game of the same era based on the activity of Paris street criers, provides an entertaining, artistic replica of the general desire to offer a 'stable and mappable representation'[19] of a city in flux. What Geary argues is that the mapping of national territory – facilitated by historians who talk and write of the links between nations and particular land parcels as if these links were forged in permanence at a particular fateful moment – is a deceitful or, at the very least, a wrongheaded attempt to stabilize the constant movement of peoples and boundaries that constitutes the very life and soul of modern Europe. Anthony Smith seems more prepared to follow Walker Connor in his acceptance of the importance not of factual but of 'felt history'[20] in understanding the concept of a nation. Nevertheless, Geary can only see this western tendency towards historical fabrication as a pernicious weapon enabling military and political leaders to claim that they represent ancient traditions of peoples so that they are excused from justifying their relations with the people whom they are moulding at any given moment of contemporary history.

According to Geary, contemporary nationalists think of history in a static and linear sense and as part of this reductive process they define a moment of 'primary acquisition' at which their chosen nation, 'first arriving in the ruins of the Roman Empire, established their sacred territory and their national identity'.[21] He is confident that all attempts to anchor ethnicity are doomed to failure because it is ultimately a creation of the human will, existing 'first and last in people's minds'.[22] Nevertheless, many people and peoples demonstrate a strong attachment to their country that forms an indelible part of their idea of themselves and others. The idea of a homeland finds articulate expression in all sorts of artistic media and the connection between people and the land that nurtured them and to which they return in death (at least in the case of conventional Christian burial traditions) is as difficult to deny as it is to rationalize or explain. Both Otto Bauer and Johann Gottfried von Herder discuss the link between human identities and territorial environments in a comparable vein, referring to man's effort to harness and manage the forces of nature in order to sustain human life and civilization. Bauer accepts Marxist the-ories regarding the emergence of the nation as part of mankind's struggle with nature and Herder claims that peoples are fashioned according to the conditions of their country. 'Their body', he says, 'their way of life, and the pleasures and occupations to which they have been accustomed from their infancy, and the whole circle of their ideas'[23] are all products of their relationship with the soil. Deprived of their country, he argues, they are left with nothing. This view evokes the ideology voiced by Gottfried Ephraim Lessing – one of the pioneers of Germany's first national theatre – in his discussion of theatre as an artistic medium that reveals to its audience not 'what this or that man has done, but what every man of a certain character in certain given circumstances would do'.[24] In the context of national theatre, we might conceive of 'character' as national character and 'given circumstances' as the spatial and temporal environs outlined by the playing space in its relation to the geographical reality and idea of the nation itself.

Whilst Geary is adamant that historians of the Middle Ages are wrong in their attempts to think geographically because the ethnically homogenous territorial state does not in fact exist, Gertjan Dijkink puts a different point of view. Dijkink claims that it is almost impossible to separate a discussion of national identity from that of geopolitical visions. He goes on to identify these visions as any idea concerning 'the relation between one's own and other places, involving feelings of (in)security or (dis)advantage (and/or) invoking ideas about a collective mission or foreign policy strategy'.[25] According to Dijkink, a geopolitical vision requires 'at least a Them-and-Us distinction and emotional attachment to a place'.[26] Habermas's definition of the interaction between new social movements and established institutions as attempts to carve out some 'autonomous space for identity articulation'[27] expresses his conviction that the act of laying claim to a particular space is a necessary part of the process of defining and understanding the self. The need to establish one's own identity in a subjective sense is clearly important to the health of the individual and the community within which he or she functions, but the need to identify a territorial base that is a vantage point for constructing visions of the outside world is an equally important part of this process.

Robert J. Kaiser refers to this phenomenon as the territorialization of national identity and describes it as the promotion of an idea of the nation as an unchanging entity rooted to a particular place.[28] Ironically, as actual places become less rigid and more flexible, Kaiser feels that concepts of culturally and ethnically distinct places become more prominent and that the idea of an ethnic homeland, 'imbued with an emotional, almost reverential dimension'[29] still holds its force in an era of globalization and transnational migration. It is probably fair to say that it is the way in which territorial attachments are manufactured that perturbs critics such as Kaiser and Geary, as opposed to the phenomenon of emotional attachment towards a father or motherland in itself. These places, Kaiser warns, are often depicted as neutral and eternal places, but this is in fact never the reality. Geary illustrates similar concerns by describing a case in which a venue is hijacked and, as he would put it, place is played for politics. He cites the way in which, on 28 June 1989, Slobodan Milošević organized an assembly of over a million people on the 'Kosovo polje' or 'Blackbird Field' where, on the same date in 1389, the Ottoman Turks had defeated the Serbian army. This attempt on Milošević's part to legitimize the Serbian claim to this territory on the basis of their relation with the ancient Illyrians indigenous to the region, in the face of the reality of a current Albanian majority, is the kind of ideological territory occupation that alarms Geary. One might well argue that part of the significance of commemorative sites is their capacity to offer the permanence of place to passing historical events. However, Geary evidently feels that a manipulative use of history and the ceremonial occupation of space for political ends are different aspects of the same fundamentally deceitful activity.

Geary's concerns might well be justified by the harrowing geopolitical vision that achieved a particularly disturbing and spectacular embodiment in the highlight of Hitler's cultural programme – the Nuremberg rallies. Hans-Ulrich Thamer offers an incisive discussion of this terrifyingly effective process of transforming place into politics. The Nuremberg rallies, he claims, were orchestrated with great care in order to articulate the support of the masses for Hitler's political programme. They occupied a specific place in the calendar year and Nuremberg itself surrendered its former character in favour of its new identity as the stronghold of and showpiece for the German Nazi party. In this case it was not a question of a basic and instinctive response to personal or communal history, manifest as affection for one's birthplace, but rather the artificial birth of a place that was to become a national symbol. Nuremberg became a national historical site that glorified a contemporary political force rather than commemorating some aspect or other of the country's past. According to Thamer, the rally was carefully stage-managed so that it became the stage for the production of a Führer-cult. Hitler himself was the 'leading actor and point of reference for both the architecture and the processions ... symbolically bringing the people together in an emotionally elating, communal experience'.[30] If we look at the terms used by Thamer in his discussion of the nationalization of the masses, we note the similarity between his descriptions of the rituals and ceremonies of the Nuremberg rallies and the workings of theatre itself. The theatrical terminology employed by Thamer highlights the performative aspects of the political, social and quasi-artistic activities at the core of German mass representation and domin-ation during Hitler's regime. He also notes that the staging of these spectacles was designed to utilize the fact that the highpoint of bourgeois nineteenth-century festival culture was national celebrations. His feeling that in a nation state headed by a dictator these ritual events inevitably came to be led from above recalls Habermas's similar impression of the way in which art and artistic occasions in fifteenth-century France were bound to the service of social representation.

The Nuremberg rallies staged a political statement and in so doing created both a company of political actors and a national and political public. They did so by the use of spectacle, performance both exhibitionist and participatory, aimed at transforming 'the crowd into a coherent, political force'.[31] The rallies were subject not only to scrupulous planning but to revision and the programme for such debriefing might well have been a format for the study of national theatre: first, 'to analyse their rituals as an expression of political aims and as a means of influencing the masses'; secondly, to 'enquire as to what effect they had on their audiences'.[32]

The discussion of nationality within a cultural context or in terms of affiliations towards land or territories is common, but many thinkers on the subject conceive of the nation from an obliquely or overtly political viewpoint. Renan demonstrates a political understanding of the idea of nations and nationhood when he pays tribute to his homeland for its spectacular declaration that 'a nation exists by itself'.[33] In his study, *Nations and Nationalism,* Eric Hobsbawm voices agreement with K. Renner's assessment of 1789 as the point at which the French people emerged from a state of hibernation typical of a 'passive people'[34] to become a political nation. The French Revolution may well have postulated an overtly political idea of nation and nationalism, but it is worth noting that its political drive was a general concern with the assertion of basic human rights. Alexis de Tocqueville makes an oblique comment on the cosmopolitan character of the revolution when he advocates modes of belonging such as nationalism as positive social forces. He sees social ties of all kinds as attachments that save the individual from the egotism and self-promotion encouraged by despotism by means of its renunciation of 'all common passion, all mutual needs, all necessity of understanding one another, all reason to act together'[35] [my translation]. Geary also notes his impression of revolutionary nationalism as a force that generally focused on a willingness to support a common good and an acceptance of the laws and liberties of the republic rather than the promotion of any ethnic, geographical or linguistic compact.[36] It is interesting to note that Friedrich List also regarded nationalism as a useful, or at least purposeful, social structure in that it represented intermediate interests that lay somewhere between those of individualism and those of humanity as a whole. In this context, a national theatre might well be a particularly valuable cultural tool by virtue of its ability to promote common needs and interests whilst also providing an occasion for communal activity even – or perhaps particularly – in cases where the social and political actuality of everyday life excluded opportunities for this kind of collective undertaking.

In recent times, Ernest Gellner has invested nationalism with an overtly political substance and significance by describing it as 'primarily a principle that holds that the political and national unit should be congruent'.[37] In his exploration of the national identity of place, Gertjan Dijkink pinpoints Europe as the part of the world in which the overtly political concept of the nation state originated and developed.[38] He is referring to the Hegelian notion of the nation state in particular and he would probably agree with

Hobsbawm that the idea of a nation as a unit of territorial, political organization is a crucial aspect of our understanding of a modern nation. Both Gellner and Hobsbawm, however, move beyond the Hegelian idea in their grapplings with nationalism and whilst Dijkink recognizes the importance of the nation state in western concepts of nations, he also observes that it is by now a faltering concept as far as Europe is concerned. Nonetheless, as these commentators look outward beyond the nation state, they find it increasingly difficult to explain the continued existence and persistence of nations and nationalism in twentieth- and twenty-first-century Europe.

Whilst the Hegelian terms of reference have been subject to appropriate review in the light of current experience of twenty-first-century Europe, it is evident that they did herald a fundamental change in the evolutionary history of nationalism. Both Gellner and Hobsbawm pinpoint the period around 1880 as a time of transition. Hobsbawm talks of the birth of an era of European democratization and mass politics and Gellner refers to a radical current of change that swept over Europe as a result of the idea of Progress and the loss of religious faith. Awareness of the nation as a political entity did not involve a fundamental break with the principle of interaction between a nation and its culture but rather proposed that a nation's ethnic, linguistic and cultural make-up should be understood as an inherent aspect of its political identity. Habermas highlights the relationship between these separate strands in the fabric of society when he discusses the representational burden shouldered by culture and cultural products in the Middle Ages. He begins his analysis at the highpoint of this representational culture in fifteenth-century France when the ceremonial style of court life was dictated by the need to manifest the power of the establishment and its primary representatives. He then proceeds to argue that this state of affairs underwent radical change when culture, and the arts in particular, were liberated from this political burden. At this point, culture became freely accessible to private individuals who had to validate it in their own terms since it no longer had any value foisted upon it by external agents.

Habermas refers specifically to drama in this discussion and in so doing demonstrates his sense of theatre as an artistic medium that celebrates plurality and diversity without compromising its own structural unity. He acknowledges the fact that both the Globe in England and the Comédie-Française in France opened their doors to the populace[39] in the seventeenth century, but argues that this selective public – 'a thin bourgeois upper stratum whose members occupied the loges of the Parisian theaters'[40] – did not constitute a mature, liberal public sphere such as would gradually emerge during the course of the next century. This was primarily due to the fact that this theatre-going public still conceived of itself exclusively in political terms: in terms of its relations to princely patronage and prestige. According to Habermas, it was only in the eighteenth century that a fully-fledged theatre-going public emerged. This was also the point at which theatre's unique capacity to respond constructively to the multiplicity of demands created by the advent of this new audience secured its place as one of the most effective artistic agents of the new, liberal public sphere. In fact, Habermas cites the establishment of a permanent national theatre in 1766 as the declaration of the emergence of this public in Germany.[41] The terminology he uses in this context is interesting because it indicates his perception of a link between the fact that this was a national theatre and the fact that it was both permanent and 'public'. Might it be that he sensed that national theatre could provide people with a new sense of belonging in a world where modern egalitarian tendencies were slowly but surely rendering old meanings and modes of being redundant?

If it is plausible that national theatre could provide the kind of public identified by Habermas as the new liberal public sphere, not only with a means of playing out a rational debate central to its interests but with a sense of participation and community – an awareness of belonging – then it follows that it might also be a particularly potent player in the forum of political culture. Peters suggests that theatre offers an 'aestheticized brand of performance, of the way things happen on the political stage'.[42] If we take this comment in its fullest sense, we understand that theatre in general, and national theatre in particular, not only mimics the political actualities of real life, but also functions according to a political format by making its meaning manifest both as an overt and public declaration and as a private, enclosed and individually interpreted artistic experience. In other words, it simultaneously occupies both a quasi-private and an overtly public domain in the experience of those who participate in it either as theatre practitioners of one kind or another or as members of its public. Peters goes on to argue that theatre offers a particular version of orature, those 'performances of the voice and body that serve as cultural inscriptions'[43] and that this process is crucial to cultural self-perception in the modern period. Her reference to cultural inscriptions alerts the reader to the potential for manipulation and exploitation inherent in the theatrical form, particularly in terms of a nationalist agenda. Apparently autonomous works of art are often part of a cultural web designed to perpetrate particular social and political patterns, such as the practice of empire or indeed the practice of nation. Clearly, the manipulation of art for the purposes of promoting imperialism does not always occur on a conscious or deliberate level but results from the fact that the performative principles of the western theatrical tradition are deeply invested in the 'discourse of empire'.[44] Inevitably, they are as deeply invested in the history of modern nations. Geary makes this point in a different context when he accuses the Christian missionary A. T. Bryant, the first man to record a continuous account of Zulu history, of moulding fragments of Zulu traditions into a pseudo-history constructed according to the values and vision of a Judeo-Christian world that mirrored European traditions, quite alien to those of the Zulu people themselves.

Geary does not stop at this but makes his theory of national fabrication the basis for issuing the greatest challenge yet, both to Europe and to its member nations, by arguing that the international community and its constituent nations are all equally fictitious entities. Gellner's conviction that nations are in fact the product of nationalism and Anderson's belief that nationalism can be thought of in an anthropological way as an imagined sense of community, as opposed to a community in real contact, are relevant to Geary's vision to some extent. Historians, Geary claims, collude in duping the public with regard to the nature of European nationalism, both in terms of what kind of interrelativity its policy of interdependence can achieve and what actually constitutes the independence of its distinct nation members. Miroslav Hroch, however, presents an alternative vision of nations as fundamental historical realities. He counteracts the subjectivist conception of nation as a product of national consciousness, national will and spiritual forces with the argument that it is in fact a constituent of social reality of historical origin. The nation exists, he says, and nationalism develops from the existence of the nation. It is, he maintains,

> a large social group characterized by a combination of several kinds of relation (economic, territorial, political, religious, cultural, linguistic and so on) which arise on the one hand from the solution found to the fundamental antagonism between man and nature on a specific land-area, and on the other hand from the reflection of these relations in the consciousness of the people.[45]

Whereas Anderson argues that nations manufacture a sense of belonging based on their perceived relations as opposed to their actual relations, Hroch accepts the evaluations and assessments of the human consciousness as indicative of the reality of a stable set of interactions and a series of objective, social relations. Otto Bauer's assertion that national consciousness is dependent on a close-knit community of character, so that an understanding of how fate and culture have shaped the individual is tied to the concept of one's own ego, is relevant here. Bauer argues that nationality is understood as 'my own way of being'[46] because it is based on the idea of culture as a formal influence on both one's own inner nature and the general character of the community to which we belong. He roots nationality in the relationship between the individual's inner self and the external environment in which he lives and breathes, claiming equal status for both these inner and outer worlds.

Whether we subscribe to Hroch's view on the one hand, Gellner and Geary's on the other, or Anderson's somewhere in between, Hroch's definition of a nation is particularly interesting with reference to definitions of national theatre. A national theatre also provides an occasion for the assimilation of a social group brought together by their participation in a common economic, ceremonial, cultural and linguistic event which investigates the struggle between man and nature on a specific stage-area and reflects this in the consciousness of its audience. I wish to use this adaptation of Hroch's definition to support the argument that the phenomenon of national theatre can, in theory at least, provide an alternative to both Geary's mythical and Anderson's imagined national and international communities. National theatre is an ideal place for rational public debate, national or otherwise, in a modern age because it is at once real and fictitious, virtual and true. A national theatre is not an imagined community but a community of imagination and imagining therein is a creative cultural activity that maps out its territories by means of a process of interactivity and interrelationality. Ideally, a national theatre would involve its audience in a perpetual reconsideration and recreation of the national certainties that make up its understanding and perception of itself and others. Clearly, we do not live in an ideal world, either in reality or in play and I will have to assess to what extent this ideal is relevant to the various national theatres that I will study later.

~ 1 ~
The French national theatre: courting the crowd

The history of the national theatre of France begins in 1680, with Louis XIV's establishment of the famous Comédie-Française. This momentous event formed part of the process whereby the *Roi-Soleil* brought 'the publicity of representation at the court [to] its high point of refinement'.[1] As Jean-Marie Apostolidès suggests, his amalgamation of the troupes of the Hôtel de Bourgogne and the Théâtre Guénégaud was motivated by a desire to 'take over the entire dramatic performances of the seventeenth century, in order that they might participate in the *mise en scène* of the image of the king'[2] [my translation]. Thus the creation of the Comédie-Française can be seen as an attempt to assimilate bourgeois humanism into a noble, courtly culture. In order to secure this feat, the French national theatre had to be at the king's service. Ultimately, it also had to be a means of sustaining the publicity of representation that was focused on the person of the monarch himself.

Louis XIV, and later Louis XV, were in agreement that 'in France the nation is not a separate body, it dwells entirely within the person of the King'.[3] It was this vision that made 'the period of ancien régime monarchy one of the most brilliant in [French] history'.[4] The founding of the Comédie-Française formed part of a grandiose programme of national centralization designed to control and administer the arts in the service of the French monarchy.[5] Cardinal Richelieu's efforts to link the aesthetic rules of the ancients with the rules of state government can be understood as part of this campaign to secure consolidation by means of centralization. With l'Abbé François d'Aubignac's cooperation, Richelieu forcefully encouraged acceptance of a set of artistic criteria constructed according to the rational thinking of the classical mind. David Jory argues that Richelieu's aim was to establish a correspondence between the laws governing art and those governing human life and conduct. By authorizing a set of classical rules that could be 'grafted onto the French theatrical tradition',[6] a turbulent society would be made to accept the principle of reason or, more specifically, *raison d'état*. It was thus that Richelieu spearheaded Louis XIV's administration of a prestigious national culture that articulated its nationhood by means of its identity with and allegiance to the *Roi-Soleil* himself.

If we evaluate this dazzling era within the larger, developmental context outlined by Habermas, whereby the early capitalist economy of the sixteenth century gradually undermined the feudal foundations of power until, in the eighteenth century, the establishment of national and territorial power states finally marked the emergence of distinct private and public spheres, it assumes quite a different and much more problematical guise. The autocratic manner of Louis XIV's foundation of the Comédie-Française makes the vision of the gradual emergence of a new, liberal public sphere seem irrelevant to a discussion of the development of the national theatre in France. In actual fact, it was the king's understanding of the threat posed by such a development to the modus operandi of his autocratic regime that motivated his attempt to exclude both the nation and its national theatre from this general process of change. According to Jan Clarke's account of the history of the Théâtre Guénégaud the first rumours of a pending merger had begun to circulate in 1673 at the moment of Molière's death.[7] There can be little doubt that Jean Baptiste Molière was a pioneering influence on French theatre, not only for his brilliance as a comic dramatist but for the spectacular manner in which he combined the varied roles of dramatist, actor, director and company manager at the Théâtre Guénégaud. Indeed, it seems particularly telling that Louis XIV sought the closure of a theatrical era in which Molière, the most successful actor/manager of all time, had soared to success in a manner that held the mirror up to the monarch's own relationship with his subjects rather too faithfully.

Louis XIV's decision to take control of the nation's theatrical space in 1680 indicated his awareness that, sooner or later, France would partake in the general movement to establish a new public sphere and that this movement was a threat to his authority. The king's awareness of the need for political acumen in the presentation of his role to the public implies that whilst he was aware of the first stirrings of a critical, public body, he was confident of his ability to control it. The accuracy of his judgement was proven by early indications of an awakening interest in debate and discussion amongst the French public. One such indication was the appearance of a gazette written in the form of a series of letters from Jean Loret to one of his benefactors, Mlle de Longueville. Loret's letters had no great literary merit but were significant in the context of the press and its role in the perpetuation and publicizing of the discussion that was, by the eighteenth century, to become the trademark of Habermas's public sphere. Although they took shelter under the cover of private correspondence, the letters were, in fact, a journalistic account of matters of topical interest such as fêtes, fashions, new books, theatrical productions and plays.

Loret's subterfuge is justified by the fact that later more overt attempts to set up newspapers, such as Colletet's *Journal de la Ville de Paris,* were directly controlled by means of official sanction. Nonetheless, when in 1672 Jean Donneau established the *Mercure Galant,* he no longer deemed any pretence of privacy necessary. However frivolous it may have appeared to some sections of the French populace, the *Mercure Galant* was to become a permanent influence in French public life. According to Pierre Mélèse's assessment, 'addressing itself to everyone and dealing with everything, this publication was destined to succeed, and so it did'[8] [my translation]. It was a confident and successful publication but its popularity brought new difficulties to the fore. As Mélèse points out, the *Mercure Galant* linked politics with literature 'without really penetrating either the one or the other, and focusing on entertainment rather than instruction'[9] [my translation]. As a result, it revealed the paradoxical relationship between the press and the emerging public sphere that it was instrumental in bodying forth. On the one hand, the press brought the tools and the opportunity for debate to the masses. On the other hand, it threatened to set an alarmingly low level for that debate by popularizing the frivolous and the insignificant.

Louis XIV was quick to recognize both the representative potential of the press and that of the national theatre, and to capitalize on his own position of power in order to control them. Whilst other sections of the French public were not as alert to the potential contribution of theatre to the debate that would eventually secure France's entry into the new liberal public sphere, there was a growing awareness of drama as a medium by which constructive criticism of society could be presented to the nation at large. It was, in fact, Edmé Boursault's play, *Mercure Galant*, that alerted the public to some of the dangers of the press and its produce, products such as the popular journal itself. As Elizabeth Goldsmith points out, the play casts doubt on the authenticity of information in the press and highlights the fact that everyone's true identities, that of the publisher and of the people written to and written about, are hidden somewhere behind their social masks. At bottom, she argues, the discourse people use to create their social selves is revealed as suspect.[10] What is ironic about Boursault's attitude towards the theatre is that although he uses his play to ridicule a national ailment, he clearly sees the theatre as a sterile place that has not yet been infiltrated by the 'popular' or the 'public'. In his play, the king is still the centre of social interaction and it is his approval that motivates the actions of those characters struggling for ascendancy in the social forum. It was from this hierarchical perspective that Boursault used the drama to reveal the folly of the people to the nation.

The role afforded to the king in Boursault's play provides a fictitious replica of the monarch's actual superiority in the 'real' context of contemporary French society. However, in his discussion of the king's understanding of this role at this point in the history of France, Jean-Marie Apostolidès queries traditional assumptions about the nature of the royal image fashioned and promoted by the monarch via the artistic institutions at his service, in particular, the theatre itself. He argues that, during the early period of his reign, Louis XIV conceived of his sovereignty as a sacred calling, reminiscent of medieval ideas of kingship. Accordingly, he saw the theatre as an interior space in which the mystery of his kingship could be bodied forth. It was in this space, Apostolidès maintains, that, just as 'the king lends his body to the nation that has no existence beyond him, the actor embodies images that the prince can, and should ... no longer'[11] [my translation] represent, due to the shift in his status from the sacred to the managerial. This account suggests that Louis XIV was aware, at least at some level, that he was crossing the threshold from the religious to the secular and that his understanding of the political risks implicit in this transformation informed the role that he assigned to the theatre of his time. However, whilst Apostolidès's presentation of the theatre of Louis XIV's early reign as 'an interior space'[12] that allowed collective mourning for the redundant values of medieval society may be valid on a thematic level, on a formal level it is less so [my translation]. His argument that the subject matter presented in the theatre during this period shows varying aspects of the monarch's personality may well hold true. What seems untrue is his suggestion that the theatre itself was structured as an internalized and interior artistic space. In fact, I think the opposite was true and that it was so as a result of a deliberate decision on the monarch's part to institutionalize this vibrant and alarmingly flexible medium.

When he authorized the 1680 merger that was to bring forth the Comédie-Française, Louis XIV seized the opportunity to establish an official statute for the company. The national company would comprise twenty-seven members, eighteen of whom would be whole shareholders; six, half shareholders; three, quarter shareholders and the remainder would be coerced into either retirement or unemployment. The company was placed under the control of the first gentlemen of the chamber, who reported directly to the king on matters of importance. The king also instigated a pension system worth 12,000 livres per annum, thereby providing the actors with economic security in return for their constitutional freedom. These initial changes were followed by other, more overtly restrictive actions, such as the royal order in 1672 that limited the company's musical capacity to two singers and six violins and the tax for the benefit of the poor that claimed a sixth of the company's receipts in 1699. This national theatre, then, was deliberately constructed as a declaration of its allegiance to and dependence on the figure of the monarch in the full public glory of his (and its) constitutional role. It is interesting to note that Louis XIV's actions seem to have gone against the tendencies of the players themselves in that, according to Clarke, during the last quarter of the seventeenth century, the internal organizational structures of Parisian theatre companies were characterized by 'a new egalitarianism'.[13] The players themselves shrunk from recognizing a leader from their midst. Indeed, Chappuzeau claims that,

> there are no people in the world who love monarchy more than the actors, who profit more by it, and who display more passion for its glory; and yet they cannot bear it for themselves. They do not want a

specific master, and the very suggestion of one frightens them ... They all want to be equals and call each other comrade.[14]

The acting profession's preference for the condition of equality is particularly interesting when considered in the context of the impending development of an egalitarian public sphere, membership of which was to be open to all, independent of heritage, material wealth or social ascendancy. Were the actors then at the forefront of this development in the sense that they already organized themselves according to the principles of the emerging public sphere, or was there another explanation for their public avowal of the principle of equality? It may be that the actors organized themselves in this way for a very specific reason – the fact that their profession as a whole was denied the right to citizenship by the ecclesiastical and monarchical authorities of the era. Pierre Mélèse's description of the ferocity with which the Church adhered to its excommunication of the actor compounds this principle of exclusion. He describes how 'not only were the actors excommunicated, but the Church extended this reprobation to all those who came into contact with their profession, from near or afar ... This severity was not revoked in the face of death'[15] [my translation]. Clearly this situation was a persistent affront to actors but their appeals against the edict, such as that made to the Pope in 1696, met with uniform rejection. Even after the 1789 revolution, the civic rights of actors and actresses remained a bone of contention.

In her study of revolution, Hannah Arendt refers to the fact that in the Greek city states of the ancient world, men sought a space in which they could become equal not by virtue of a God-given birthright but by means of citizenship.[16] Equality, she explains, was not understood in terms of condition but based on membership of a body of peers who met one another as citizens and not as private persons. The equality of the Greek world was achieved by means of social and political, in other words, man-made institutions. This kind of equality safeguarded freedom because if an individual assumed rule then he was immediately deprived of the peers in whose company he could be free. This freedom, Arendt suggests, became manifest in certain human activities that were only valid when others witnessed them. The life of a free man required the presence of others and 'freedom itself needed therefore a place where people could come together – the agora, the marketplace, or the polis, the political space proper'.[17] The terms of Arendt's discussion provide a possible rationale both for the importance of theatre in Greek society and for its festival nature in the sense that it could well be argued that the Greek theatre itself was a place where large sections of the Greek populace came together to co-witness a communal, creative activity. Might it be that the actors of seventeenth-century France were organizing themselves according to similar criteria and that Louis XIV's decision to intervene in that process was vital to his own survival as monarch? After all, if we apply Arendt's criteria to the theatrical world, we see Greek theatre presenting an illusion of freedom that was much more inclusive than the reality represented by the polis and its membership. Whilst a national theatre set up and governed by the actors alone might be as unrepresentative of the reality of social and political life as its Greek counterpart, its artificiality would render it no less alarming to an individual in a position of power or control, such as Louis XIV himself.

Whether Louis XIV deliberately turned his back on the theatre he had created, or whether, as Henry Carrington Lancaster suggests, he became uneasy about his soul as he grew older,[18] there can be little doubt that his actions subsequent to 1680 were damaging to the Comédie-Française. Having previously transferred occupancy of the Palais Royal – home of the remaining members of Molière's troupe subsequent to his death – to Jean Baptiste Lully and his operas, the king required the Comédie-Française players to vacate the Rue Guénégaud in order to facilitate the development of a medical school, Collège des Quatre-Nations, on the site. This order to move brought about a crisis for the national theatre company because it threatened their sense of identity within the context of the nation itself. From the middle of the seventeenth century onwards, a waning interest in tennis had allowed French theatre to claim possession of the many *jeux de paume* or tennis courts that were dotted around French cities. Whilst there were limitations to the spatial opportunities provided by these spaces, they were invaluable in that they established residential rights for theatre at the heart of so many French cities and towns. Louis XIV's ousting of the national company from their home challenged this right in a fundamental sense. Efforts to find a new place of residence were thwarted time and time again by the Church, which seized the opportunity for assault now that 'attacking the theatre no longer meant going against the King's pleasure'.[19] After many vain attempts at purchases and leases, the company finally gained the royal seal of approval to acquire a suitable property in the Rue des Fossés-Saint-Germain-des-Prés. This move to the extreme west of Paris was hardly ideal in comparison to their previous location in the Rue Mazarine – one of the city's main areas of development – where a suitable mix of bourgeois and noble homeowners made for a ready audience. Nonetheless, the Comédie-Française actor, La Grange, considered the purchase of this property to be fundamental to the battle for the 'salvation of the national theatre'[20] [my translation]. Clearly delighted to have designated its own space once again, the company did not shrink from shouldering the considerable financial burden of erecting a theatre on this site.

In the context of the national company's search for a designated place or space, Apostolidès's comment on another, concurrent development affecting our understanding of space as a whole, assumes a particular interest. He argues that circa 1640 perspective gradually began to influence literary and theatrical environments. This novel influence is evident in the work of the seventeenth-century stage designers, Mahelot and Laurent, who serviced both the Hôtel de Bourgogne and the Comédie-Française.[21] Apostolidès describes how the painter, familiar with abstract optical laws, dominates the world he wishes to represent because geometrical lines seem to begin from his eye before finding their centre in a unique point that exists somewhere beyond the universe. According to Apostolidès, the Italian theatre architects of the Renaissance named this central somewhere the 'king's place'[22] [my translation]. The attribution of this vantage-point to the king, he argues, highlights the monarch's position as the regulator of civil society from a central focal point with the application of perspective. It is this that makes him, 'the nation's creator, the people's father, an image of God and the sun whose infinite rays define social conventions'[23] [my translation]. In France, the discrepancy between the monarch's location at the centre of the visual and spatial theatrical experience and his deliberate destabilization of the national company's ownership of an independent, geographical space is ironic.

The national company clearly saw the naming and claiming of a designated, theatrical space as a vital step in the process of defining their identity, both on a personal and on a public level but the growing success of another theatrical medium, the Théâtre de la Foire, was possibly the first indication that the term national might not be a 'given' value and that the process of negotiating the identity of a national theatre company might need to be extended beyond both the royal sphere and the confines of the Comédie-Française itself. Despite the fact that the Théâtre de la Foire had its roots in the Middle Ages, it continued to be a popular form of entertainment in seventeenth-century France. Far from claiming an established space, 'it was content to camp, wherever it could, for as long as was possible'[24] [my translation] and then to up camp when it struck on bad times. It made no claims to represent a national standard of any sort but a description of its audience suggests that it did appeal to a large and varied portion of the French population. Fortunat Strowski, an enthusiastic eye witness, recalls how:

> Jostling, crowding, insistent, people of all classes mingle, some trying to edge forward, treading on each other's feet, stopping and shaking with the general laughter prompted by a 'barker' or a clown, unaware of the tiredness of their legs or the pungency of the dust. A shack comes into view where you can, at last, sit down? Everyone goes in, gets impatient; they desire action, exciting and relaxing things, and that everything should happen quickly, very quickly.[25] [my translation]

According to Strowski, the typical Théâtre de la Foire artiste had no formal actor training and the repertoire was varied and included acrobatics and circus-orientated entertainment. What held the crowds spellbound was the sight of 'the graceful little girl, decked out in roses, who danced on the tightrope, the hero who sat down between heaven and earth in order to set up the stove, light the fire and beat the omelette'[26] [my translation]. Strowski's description of a circus-style entertainment might suggest that this was spectacle rather than theatre, however, he goes on to argue that the appearance of discussion and dialogue amidst the Théâtre de la Foire performance material, circa 1679, revealed its true identity. It was, he claims, dominated by words – and words are theatre.[27]

The battle between the Comédie-Française and the Théâtre de la Foire that came to a height in 1698 places discourse at the centre of the French theatrical experience. Strowski's account of the Comédie-Française's terror at the popularity of its second-class rivals reveals how the national company focused their legislative onslaught on the principle of their monopoly of dialogue and debate,[28] turning to the law to prevent the use of dialogue by its new rivals. Initially, the national company established a monopoly over the performance of plays in general, but the Théâtre de la Foire retaliated with the practice of presenting a number of non-sequential sketch-like scenes that did not amount to a coherent play, yet contained all the elements thereof. The national company's response was to turn to the law once again and secure an extension of their monopoly so that it now covered any performance that included dialogue of any kind. However, whilst the national company instinctively bowed to the voice of monarchical authority, even to their detriment, its intrepid competitors did not. Their creative response to the ban imposed on them by the authorities highlighted the inevitability of the changes encountered by French society at this point in its history. In order to avoid extinction, the Théâtre de la Foire invented ingenious ways of activating debate and dialogue that masqueraded as something else. The most famous of these inventions was the telephone scene[29] where one protagonist interpreted the mimed gestures of any number of other silent characters with whom he or she shared the stage space, thus creating a kind of mono-dialogue. Just as Jean Loret's news bulletins had sought protection in the intimacy and privacy of the letter-form, the Théâtre de la Foire invented 'conversation in isolation'. In so doing, it captured a particular moment in a process of social development that would eventually come to maturity in the eighteenth century.

Despite the threat embodied by the Théâtre de la Foire, the years between 1660–1722 and 1757–89 were periods of prosperity for the national company due to their popularity with the nobility and the upper strata of French society.[30] The economic importance of this elite manifested itself in the gradual encroachment of boxes or *petits loges* on the theatre's internal spatial arrangements. The dominance of the boxes over the parterre and even the stage itself was made even more pronounced by Louis XV's decision in 1753 to allow the company to rent out the boxes annually or for life. The custom of decorating and furnishing these boxes according to the dictates of personal taste was a travesty of the tradition of theatrical decor in that it created exclusive, private areas nestling within the larger, demonstratively open space of the theatre. It was evident that the nobility did not see their national theatre as a place of interaction where communal values could be discussed and formulated but as a place in which one staked a claim in both spatial and social terms. Theatre was, like an early Greek city state described by Arendt, a place in which one confirmed one's own identity and independence, not by seeing but by being seen. Louis Sébastien Mercier's description of the Parisian noblewoman, who sits behind her fan in which a discreet little pane of glass has been inserted in order to allow her to see without being seen, seems at face value, to be quite a different pattern of behaviour in that it facilitates discretion rather than exhibitionism.[31] In fact, it is a different response to the same principle of self-preservation and assertion via detachment that must have rendered the national theatre of the early eighteenth century such a sterile environment, in artistic terms at least.

The eighteenth century has been described as a time when the sycophantic relations between the nobility, the court and the theatre came to a height. Guibert and Razgonnikoff's description of the way in which theatre and city exchanged mutually misleading reflections of cultivation and brilliance suggests that the lines between artifice and reality, fact and fiction had become irrevocably blurred.[32] The dalliance between courtiers and players, many of whom were linked by social ties, despite the stigma still attached to the acting profession, was facilitated by the national company's temporary residence in the Tuileries on the invitation of Louis XV. Despite the economic importance of the nobility at the Comédie-Française in the late seventeenth and early eighteenth centuries, some critics claim that the eighteenth century was a period when 'everything conjures up the bourgeoisie'[33] [my translation] and when the more bourgeois section of the audience outnumbered the aristocrats. Whether or not this was the case, the theatre had evidently become more important as a locus for the performance of 'real' social rituals than a vehicle for the artificial and artistic representations of reality. In 1691, La Grange documented the great display mounted by a drunken gentleman who forced entry to the parterre without paying, abused the actors and even wounded an innocent bystander.[34] By the latter half of the eighteenth century, it was the members of the national company themselves who were blurring the lines between performance and actuality. An example of such an incursion is provided by Claude Alasseur's account of the actress Mlle Clairon's refusal to appear on stage with her fellow actor, Dubois, who had been expelled from the company for non-payment of debts but then reinstated due to his daughter's influence with Cardinal Richelieu's son.[35] The actress's rebellion led to her imprisonment but she was supported in it by the whole of Paris, including some key members of the nobility. This dramatization of an internal feud for the benefit of society at large and the alarming way in which it spilt out of the theatre itself into other public institutions such as the Paris gaol, might well make Louis XIV's promotion of classicism as an instrument of imperial policy seem prudent.

In his study of some of the plays staged by the Comédie-Française during the *ancien régime*, Stoyan Tzonev claims that Louis XIV's demise sounded the death knell of the aristocracy.[36] Their influence in the theatre in the decades immediately following his death may well have resulted from the fact that Louis XV's peaceful reign had consigned them to leisure. Whatever the explanation, there is no doubt that their allure became tarnished as the century progressed. The bourgeoisie, on the other hand, steadily gained in strength and social status until they were, 'the most prosperous class … thanks to the expansion of industry and external commerce during a seventy-seven-year period without invasion, without pillage, without civil war'[37] [my translation]. Mercier was one of the foremost in staking the claim of the bourgeoisie to theatrical rights and representation. He formally identified the theatre's cultural and social significance within a national context, signalling its dual role as both a subject for and a means of public debate. By the middle of the eighteenth century, the discursive pamphlet had also matured to become a common vehicle for contribution to national debates, such as the argument concerning the right of the author to ownership of his dramatic works that came to a head with Beaumarchais's foundation of the Society for the Rights of Authors in 1777. The method by which Beaumarchais set about founding and organizing this society reveals a curious combination of approaches. Initially, he issued a private invitation to a select group of like-minded people to dine with him at his home. The next meeting, however, saw the same group assemble, on 3 July, little more than a week later, in the guise of an official, administrative body. The swiftness of this mutation from private to public, coupled with the typically middle-class character of the administrative body that resulted from this consultative process, provides a clear indication of the social shift that brought about the rise of the bourgeoisie. Alasseur may well be right to suggest that it was at this point that the bourgeoisie was 'beginning to realise her importance to the nation ... beginning to think that it is she who, in reality, energises the country; that she alone works ... and that this should give her the right to participate in political life'[38] [my translation].

It was to be another creative act on Beaumarchais's part – the writing of *Le Mariage de Figaro* – that would signify the bourgeoisie's growing mastery of the media available to it for expression of its central concerns. According to Frederick Hemmings, *Le Mariage de Figaro* amounted to a 'kind of declaration of class war'[39] because it manifested contempt for the privileged classes. Earlier in this chapter, we noted Apostolidès's argument that the full spectrum of Louis XIV's person and personality were apparent on a thematic level in the plays written for performance during the early part of his reign. The king's authoritarian control over the theatre meant that as an artistic institution it could only represent his 'official' self. As a result, there was a dichotomy between the statement being made on the level of theme and that being made on the level of form. In the case of Beaumarchais's *Le Mariage de Figaro* both these statements came together to voice the concerns prevalent in the new, liberal sphere that had been struggling towards definition since the latter half of the preceding century. Louis XVI was aware of the controversial nature of the play and although it was scheduled for private performance at the palace by the national company, he banned its public production. The royal tradition of commissioning artworks for the purpose of manipulating national values explains the rationale behind this prohibition. The king was well versed in the practice of manipulating public opinion. The success of Louis David's royally commissioned picture *Le Serment des Horaces* was a prime example of the power of art to function as 'a clarion call to civic virtue and patriotism'[40] and state commissions had been actively encouraging the manufacture of 'serious historical paintings to stimulate patriotic pride'[41] for some time. Just as the king chose to inflict certain works on the public, he also chose to protect them from others. It was the depth of his understanding of the influence and power of artistic products that made his concession to popular pressure, when he eventually released *Le Mariage de Figaro* for public performance in April 1784, quite so important. His capitulation signalled the weakening of his authority in relation to both the public at large and the artistic and administrative institutions over which he had traditionally maintained control and there were many who were disgusted by the 'laxness of a government which allowed itself to be reviled in this manner'.[42]

Le Serment des Horaces was reputedly inspired by a Comédie-Française production of Corneille's *Horace* towards the end of 1782. In the event, the picture was based not on Horace himself but on an image of youth pledging an oath of national allegiance that makes a mockery of death. The finished work caused a stir in Rome where it immediately became the talk of the coffee-houses. It was displayed in Paris in 1785 and was followed up by *Brutus* in 1789. At this point, something fascinating happened: the actors of the Comédie-Française, who had first inspired the artist to ponder on Corneille's *Horace,* copied his rendition of *Brutus* in a *tableau vivant* at the close of a performance of Voltaire's play of the same name. Hemmings describes this event as a:

> memorable illustration of the tendency during the revolutionary period for the different arts to coalesce in the heat of political passions. In this particular instance it was the theatre that provided an opportunity for a public manifestation of enthusiasm for a masterpiece of graphic art.[43]

I think there was more than this at stake. It was not that the national theatre had signalled its approval of a piece of graphic art but that it had modelled its own artistic activity on a medium other than, and arguably alien to, itself. Historical tableau was not the traditional business of theatre, but in this case the Comédie-Française surrendered its own artistic identity, albeit momentarily, in order to play a real part in a public debate with a political edge. The audience was being manipulated in the sense that it was being drawn, under false pretences, to participate in an activity that merely postured as an artistic event. Suddenly, the national theatre had become the location for a very different kind of drama. Granted, it was still a place in which the public performance of identities was being undertaken, but the nature of those practices of social interaction had been radically and deceptively changed. This change was not entirely spontaneous in that 1789 was the year in which the political and social landscape of France underwent its most radical transformation for centuries. Considering the thematic of both Voltaire's play and David's picture, appreciation of either might well have been construed as public manifestation of enthusiasm for republicanism itself.

Despite the national company's momentary abandonment of the practice of live theatre, Sylvie Chevalley cites Marie-Joseph Chénier's *Charles IX* as evidence of the fact that, in eighteenth-century France, the persuasive effect of theatre equalled that of contemporary broadcasting media.[44] The case of *Charles IX* was clearly a vital part in the process that established the ascendancy of theatre as a medium of public management and manipulation. When Chénier threw caution to the wind by choosing to dramatize the explosive subject of Charles IX, he immediately came up against the resistance of the Comédie-Française. The company refused to perform the play, but, just as Voltaire had manipulated the parterre in order to secure the success of his play, *Sémiramis*, Chénier launched leaflets into the parterre from the gallery and made a speech in favour of his play in the auditorium. Effectively, he hijacked the company's theatrical space and transformed it into an arena for public, political debate. He followed up this assault with an appeal to the Commune of Paris to whom the national company had been answerable since 1789. The Commune subdued the Comédie-Française's resistance and the play was performed in November 1789. As anticipated, it instigated a great disturbance amongst the audience and became a political weapon in the sense identified by Danton when he commented 'if Figaro sounded the death-knell of the aristocracy, *Charles IX* will kill off the monarchy'[45] [my translation]. It is significant to note that Chénier proclaimed himself the renovator of the tragic genre – a medium that the monarchy had traditionally controlled by authoritarian rule since the days of Richelieu's neo-classicism. Chénier claimed that theatre should mobilize the crowds and that he would modernize tragedy in order to appeal to his audience as a citizen as opposed to as a writer. What

Chénier achieved (if achievement is a meaningful term in this context) with *Charles IX* went beyond the revitalization of an 'outmoded' dramatic genre. It repeated the process accomplished by the Comédie-Française's *tableau vivant* – the transformation of an artistic medium that occasionally served as a vehicle for the expression of political or social truths into an aspect of political and social life itself.

It was François Talma who, having entered the Comédie-Française in 1787, took on the role of Charles IX, dressed in a 'sober black velvet coat with white ruff and white silk stockings – a costume copied from Clouet's portrait of the king'.[46] Whilst Hemmings's attribution of the play's success to the actor's physical appearance may well jar on the sensibility of modern theatregoers, even if it accords well with the values advocated by modern mass media and image merchants, he is rightly identifying a new stage in the developmental history of the national company and the nature of its interaction with the nation. There can be no doubt that Talma cut a dashing figure as Charles IX and it is known from the evidence of La Grange's *Registre* that an actor or actresses's wardrobe was both costly and highly valued. La Grange valued the eighteen outfits that made up his own wardrobe at the point of his marriage, in 1672, at 5.235 livres.[47] He described them as fit for royalty and their opulence is indicative of the national theatre's role as a reflection of the king's public image.[48] Talma, however, broke with this tradition and is well-known as the 'harbinger of change'[49] at the Comédie-Française due to his insistence on the accurate historical representation of the characters he portrayed. The clash between the Comédie's respectable and respected standards in matters of dress and his daring policy of truth to nature is an amusing indication of the changes that were sweeping over both the theatre and society of France at this point in its history. What Talma was doing by basing his own costume on that of the historical figure whom he was embodying on stage, as opposed to that of the king himself, was revolutionary. His costumes delivered a fatal blow to the hierarchy of representation that had prevailed in the national company hitherto. He was no longer lending his person to the king's service, but marketing his own persona. The image that he embodied on stage no longer referred to a central, monarchical authority but to his own presence as actor in the current theatrical space. Granted, there was a reference to the particular, historical personage being portrayed but there was no argument regarding the order of ascendancy in that representative relationship. In the context of the claim that in eighteenth-century theatre the actor's physical presence afforded weight to philosophical ideas, Talma's transformation of the actor's representative role reveals itself to be much more than a simple matter of fashion.[50] I will return to this subject later because it is a recurrent theme in the developmental history of the Comédie-Française but one that can be more fully explored in relation to the rise of Boulevard theatre in the nineteenth century.

The November 1789 production of *Charles IX* was brought to a close in the name of civil peace after a run of thirty-two performances, but this was not the end of the road for the play. The following year calls for the play to be put on again were met, once more, with refusal. This time, Chénier turned to le Comte de Mirabeau for assistance. When he rose to his feet at the theatre and called publicly for the play, he was merely following in Chénier's footsteps. This time, however, the consequences of his actions were more comprehensive. In reaction to Mirabeau's demands, two conflicting responses were made from within the Comédie-Française itself. On the one hand, the actor Naudet flatly refused Mirabeau's request, on the other, Talma promised compliance. In true dramatic style a duel was announced, not between Mirabeau or Chénier and their adversaries, but between Naudet and Talma. Guibert and Razgonnikoff are right to suggest that at a time when the national company recognized no true authority, 'felt abandoned by the court and refused to submit itself to the Municipality ... the smallest knock to the ego appeared like an affair of state'[51] [my translation]. The Comédie-Française members had set about playing out notions of nationhood, conspiracy and betrayal of the fatherland, not on the stage but at its periphery. Amongst themselves, they fixated in a quasi-fictitious way on the roles they sought either to fulfil or to evade at all costs. The conflict between the two actors Naudet and Talma escalated 'from threats to exchanging of oaths, from blows to a duel, from a duel by arms to battle by press'[52] [my translation]. These roles were no longer fictitious ones, embodied within a specific playing space, but semi-real ones that had spilled out of the designated playing area yet still had a performative feel to them. Perhaps this playing out of conflict, in no-man's-land, just outside the territory officially earmarked for art and artifice, was a prelude to the real experience of revolution. If so, whatever its drawback in terms of the integrity of theatre as an art form, it may well have been preferable, at least in terms of human suffering.

Against this unsettling background of metamorphosis, the call for a second national theatre was inevitable. A national theatre that could slip its artistic leash at will, surrendering its identity as an art form in the service of political propaganda, was as dangerous to the nation as it was to the monarch himself. When the call came for change, it was made as part of a general attempt to redefine the relationship between the theatre and its public. French dramatists were at the forefront of the drive to establish a second national theatre as a result of their continuing professional frustration with the Comédie-Française. By 1790, the Commune of Paris had seconded their call in a report on the city's spectacles. It was increasingly felt that the national company's insistence on their monopoly of France's theatrical repertoire in the name of notional, national standards of truth and beauty meant that it actually served as a barrier to the spread and development of culture. The company did make an effort to adjust to the demands of the time, and in February 1790 their programme revealed a concerted effort to put a different sort of patriotism in the repertory. Yet when Talma proposed an opening address for the new season that struck conservative members of the company as too radical, the true cost of this exercise in acclimatization was revealed; the company split into two warring factions. Once more, drama left the confines of the theatre as the public voiced their discontent at the Comédie's expulsion of Talma and the Commune of Paris was forced to insist on a truce in a matter that, under any other circumstances, would have been a private dispute to be resolved internally.

The national company's failure to adapt to the social changes taking place around it resulted, in part at least, from its adherence to the vestiges of monarchical authority. If we accept the definition of the company as a '[p]roduct of monarchical power, created by Louis XIV, at the height of centralization, for his pleasure and for the diversion of the hierarchical society that he had succeeded in assembling around himself'[53] [my translation],

The French national theatre

it is difficult to conceive of any place for it in a democracy. Nonetheless, there had been another, fundamental change brought about by the 1789 revolution that may well have unsettled the company as much as any challenge to its royal roots: the question surrounding the legitimacy of granting rights of citizenship to members of the acting profession as a result of the Declaration of the Rights of Man. The initial pronouncement, issued on 26 August 1789, had left members of the acting profession in limbo. The declaration awarded citizenship to all active Catholic taxpaying citizens employed in a reputable profession. Where did this leave actors? The hasty amendment made regarding non-Catholics, and the debate that followed in order to secure the awarding of citizenship to actors so as to secure one national unit, highlighted the rather unsettling fact that the great equalizing force of democracy was no less an acquired skill than was monarchy. Whilst Maximilien de Robespierre's declaration that a new law was unnecessary to cover the case of actors because '[t]hose who are not excluded are called'[54] resolved the practical difficulties, it could only paper over the cracks inherent in this particular manifestation of democracy [my translation].

The acting profession was jubilant in receipt of its long-coveted citizenship, but there was a contradiction between the passive acquisition of their newly acquired status as citizens of France and the fundamentally active and creative character of their professional lives. They, 'like most of their contemporaries took part as 'spectators in the tennis court oath, in the storming of the Bastille, in the night of the 4th August, swept along by the speed of events and without participating in them directly'[55] [my translation]. This description highlights the passivity of their participation in the events that led up to the revolution and recalls both Alexis de Tocqueville's impression of the nation as a force that sweeps its citizens with it and his reservations regarding the egalitarian quality of democracy. Ironically, the revolution redeemed actor's and actresses's rights to full and equal participation in French society at the very point at which the positive action characteristic of their professional lives was placed in jeopardy by the ousting of theatre from its central place in the nation's artistic life. Just as the Comédie-Française's response to David's *Brutus* captured the moment at which theatre was in danger of surrendering its artistic identity, the actors had, by becoming citizens, surrendered their representative roles and rendered themselves redundant. After all, who needed theatre when life was itself so dramatic?

The revolution made a gift of citizenship to all members of the acting profession; it introduced other regulations that were less appealing to members of the national company. The introduction of a law allowing all citizens to set up a theatre that might present any available dramatic genre left the Comédie-Française struggling to accommodate itself to its new republican environment. From the point of view of its survival, it was imperative that the national company should set about winning over a petite bourgeoisie quite different to its previous aristocratic clientele. As an initial step in this re-orientation and in response to the attempted flight of Louis XVI in June 1791, the company relinquished the royal part of their title. This gesture was to be the first in a series of placatory measures by which it sought to regulate its relations with the new authorities but the process was not to be an easy one. Upon consideration of the stringent policy of theatrical censorship set in place under republican rule, Adam Burgess's argument that the age that followed 1789 was one correctly labelled 'the Age of Nationalism'[56] as opposed to the age of ascendant civil society, rings true.

Burgess's claim that civil society began as one way of opposing absolute monarchy but soon evolved into an emergency measure to limit the effects of non-democratic statehood of any kind is supported by evidence of the revolutionary regime's theatrical censorship. Ironically, in the revolutionary and post-revolutionary era, the emergence of civil society was hampered by the nationalist programme set in motion by the revolutionaries. The phenomenon of the forty-eight sections of the Parisian Commune was a positive spatial re-organization of the city according to democratic principles. Arendt described this municipal council, along with the various popular societies that appeared in its wake, as places that facilitated the manifestation of the public spirit, 'the ambition to equality, the claim to be able to sign all addresses and petitions ... with the proud words "Your Equal"'.[57] These societies set out to deal with every aspect of the equality, the unity and the indivisibility of the republic. As such, they seemed particularly important both in terms of the aims of the 1789 revolution and in relation to the rise of both the new public sphere outlined by Habermas and the civil society that formed the basis of Burgess's ideal. Nonetheless, or perhaps precisely on this account, on his rise to power Robespierre tried to quash them on the grounds that the revolutionary government was coming under unbearable pressure from their constant petitioning. Robespierre evidently saw the Comédie-Française as a comparable threat and in 1793 he issued an order for the arrest of many of the company's actors on charges of being found lacking in their civic duties. The company's monarchical affiliation may have perturbed Robespierre, but the idea of a national theatre that operated on a principle similar to that of the other Parisian societies – as a forum for the articulation of a rational, egalitarian debate on the level of both form and content – was equally antithetical to his ideal of theatre as a 'public school of principles, of good manners and of patriotism'[58] [my translation]. At this point in time in France, it seems that despite the superficial links between the principles of democracy and the egalitarian character of this sphere, in reality any demos or rule of the majority could not but see such an artistic institution as a threat to its own survival.

In the context of the 1789 revolution, Hemmings argued that once absolute monarchy had been replaced by popular consent there was an urgent need to discover 'ways and means of moulding public opinion and persuading the masses of the rightness of national policies'.[59] This was an open admission of the fact that the democratic process that had done away with autocracy was as dependent on the manipulation of public opinion as was its royal predecessor. During the revolutionary period, the chosen method for the achievement of this aim was the launching of a series of national fêtes, designed as deliberate and elaborate attempts to 'proclaim the new order and to establish it by means of public and communal acts'[60] [my translation]. This raises the question of why the revolutionary government invested time and energy in the construction of a new national artistic medium for communal celebration when they had one to hand in the form of the national theatre itself. Hannah Arendt offers a possible answer when she argues that 'revolutions are the only political events which confront us directly and inevitably with the problem of beginning'.[61] The modern concept of revolution, she insists, is bound up with the notion that the course of history suddenly starts anew. On the eve of revolution, it is felt that 'an entirely new story, a story never known or told before, is about to unfold'.[62] Arendt uses a theatrical analogy when she claims that, in the case of the 1789 revolution in France, 'none of the actors had the slightest premonition of what the plot of the new drama was going to be'.[63] Her choice of terminology highlights the sense of immediacy identified with theatre and Peter Szondi's definition of theatre, as a medium that not only seizes the present moment but is unable to function effectively in a more extended timescale that includes either a past or a future, supports this interpretation.[64] Arendt also highlights another characteristic of revolutionary thought that might be applied to a discussion of theatre when she argues that in a post-colonial era revolutionary man had realized that it was action, as opposed to rest, that constituted human pleasure and that action was not a condition of poverty but of wealth. Theatre is an artistic medium that is constructed on a principle of action. On the level of content, it articulates itself by means of dramatic action; on the level of form, it constitutes a participatory community in which action is the focus of the communal coming together. Why then was national theatre cast aside by the revolutionary?

It is easy to understand revolutionary concerns regarding the manner in which the Comédie-Française reflected the vestigial power of the monarch and furthered an idea of art as representative of monarchical authority. After all, it cannot be denied that in the not so distant past the national theatre had serviced a closed social sphere focused on the court, in which membership was based on privilege and favour rather than on citizenship. This society and its theatre had deliberately rejected the principle of equality inherent in both the idea of citizenship and its artistic correlative – the theatre audience. Nonetheless, Robespierre had secured the demise of this national company by his incarceration of the actors and there seems no rationale to explain why the revolutionaries could not benefit from the natural affinity between national theatre and their desire for highly visible public celebration of a new socio-political order. The most convincing explanation is the fact that the revolution could not accommodate the idea of mimesis or artifice. At an earlier point in this chapter I argued that the moment at which actors became fully assimilated into French society was also the point at which they traded in the active role characteristic of their professional life as *actors* in favour of a passive role as *spectators* in the drama of real life. The decision to turn to the fête, in preference to the theatre, was motivated by the need to celebrate the creation of an undeniably concrete and uniform new order that had no need of indirect representation and in which participants were actively involved in the one and only meaningful role of fully fledged French citizens. With this in mind, it is interesting to note that actors and actresses initially took part in the communal effort of preparing the site at the Champ de Mars for the 1790 Fête de la Fédération but were later banned because their frivolity hindered the serious business of construction. Clearly, there was no place for play acting here. The ultimate proof of the revolutionary disdain for, or even fear of, artifice and imitation is provided by the fact that during the period 1790-4 – the heyday of the national fête and the lowest ebb in the history of the Comédie-Française to date – theatrical representations of any aspect of the fêtes were banned on the principle that theatre could only present a microscopic impression of the scale and grandeur of the reality of the fête itself.

Cécile Fridé's description of the revolutionaries' desire to 'make a "table rase" of the previous régime'[65] confirms the importance of novelty to the revolutionary mindset. Hemmings goes so far as to attribute the particular importance of the national fêtes to the evidence they provided of a 'deeply felt need in the French at this time to dramatize their sense of having liberated themselves from the shackles of the past'.[66] Arendt is of a similar opinion and argues that the violence of liberation had destroyed attempts to create a secure space of freedom associated with founding and building up – it was the business of the national fêtes to re-assemble this kind of virgin space. Fridé describes the fêtes as the point at which the 'moment seeks to embody itself and to besiege space'[67] [my translation]. She argues that in gaining control of space, the fêtes could drive home their contra-linear understanding of history as a present moment free from the past and defiant of the concept of evolution. The fact that this sense of novelty was fundamental to revolutionary thought was manifest in the establishment of the revolutionary calendar that began with the king's execution and the declaration of the republic. The architects of the fêtes were aware that the city of Paris was historically and socially marked and that these historically bound signals would need to be erased in order to secure the bare territorial canvas upon which they might capture the moment of revolution. It was this mindset that motivated the holding of celebratory events as part of the programme of fête activities, such as the Champ de Mars ball, where the stamping of hoards of dancing feet was to purify the ruins of the Bastille. It is no coincidence that Louis David, the painter of *Le Serment des Horaces* and *Brutus,* was the main designer of two of the three national fêtes. David set about re-sculpting the city landscape in order to present a celebration that focused on the citizens themselves in occupation of a new clean space, in the open air, over which the eye might roam with total freedom. The contrast between the free, even visual spectacle provided by the fête and the earlier idea of perspective as a visual viewpoint that culminated in one point of ultimate authority – the king's gaze – is symptomatic of the change in the balance of power that had come about as a result of the 1789 revolution. David's understanding of space was a particularly inclusive one in the sense that he felt confident that the people themselves could not only claim occupancy of the space but determine its form by their own physical presence. Whereas in the initial Fête de la Fédération the masses had been represented by select civil and military groups, David afforded them a direct, active role in later celebrations.

In the opening chapter of this study, I discussed the affinity between Hitler's cultural campaign as embodied in the Nuremberg rallies and the methodology of theatre itself. Fridé points to a similar phenomenon in relation to the revolutionary fêtes in the sense that, despite the fact that they avowedly distanced themselves from theatre, their organizers employed theatrical terminology and methodology in the planning and construction of events. In the final Fête de l'Etre Suprême the erection of an amphitheatre betrayed the affinity between the two modes of cultural articulation and Robespierre's dramatic appearance on the balcony in the 1790 fête had a distinctly theatrical feel to it. Fridé points to the similarity between Robespierre's role here and that of Louis XVI before him '[l]ike Louis XVI, Robespierre appears on the balcony ... Like Louis XVI, Robespierre is late ... Like Louis XVI, Robespierre makes his appearance after the people are assembled'[68] [my translation]. Whether or not Robespierre was modelling his role on the historical reality of an authoritarian monarch, the theatrical manner in which he claimed centre-stage alerts us to the dangers of a performance that refuses to admit to its own performativity. It was by similar means that Hitler manufactured his image of an ideal and elite nation that justified his invasion of Europe over a century later. The fête's parade of local troupes who represented their unique customs as part of an over-arching national whole brings another contemporary political charade to mind: Emelda Marcos's cultural celebrations as minister for the arts in twentieth-century Philippines. The common denominator is that both techniques form part of an exercise in the fabrication of a nation, all the more dangerous in that it denies its own artificiality. In the final analysis, they did not prove a dangerous medium in the same way as the Nuremberg rallies had because their main impetus was a reaching out in a spirit of egalitarianism and in defiance of traditional geographical boundaries, not only towards the entire French people but towards a wider European community. Nonetheless, the suggestion that theatre might have provided a more appropriate medium for what was, at bottom, a cultural and artistic representation of the revolutionary vision rather than an example of that vision in practice, is corroborated by the fact that lives were lost during the fêtes, even if inadvertently.

The lifespan of the national fêtes was short and by 1800 the Comédie-Française had been reconstituted as a society of talents under the auspices of Napoleon, who sought to revive it to its former glory as a flagship of national excellence. In this period of rapid political change, the company seemed to have rediscovered its own impetus and powered itself forward in search of national status that was to be awarded from within, rather than by an outside agent. In response to the invasion of social life by artifice and the consequent breaking down of the traditional barriers between reality and representation, the nineteenth-century French national theatre both responded to and participated in social change by trading in its institutional identity in order to promote the individual image. I have already discussed the description of the seventeenth-century game of mirrors in which the nobility, theatre and court exchanged mutually misleading reflections of cultivation and brilliance. By the nineteenth century, the forces of revolution had delivered a fatal blow to both nobility and court. Nonetheless, this pattern of reciprocal misrepresentation was re-enacted in terms of the relations between the citizens of Paris and their national theatre. According to Alex Cain, nineteenth-century French social life 'was an endless intricate dance movement, wherein the performers were themselves the spectators'.[69] The affluence of the third republic led to leisure, decadence and ultimately to sanitized exhibitionism, so much so that social life in Paris became a matter of spectacle where the 'great entertainment consists in *looking* and in *being looked at*'.[70] In the theatre, Cain argues, 'the audience spent more time watching other members of the audience than they did in watching the stage'.[71] He makes these comments in a translation of Mallarmé's fashion magazine, *La Dernière Mode,* published between August and December 1874. The appearance of this magazine at a time when Mallarmé had come to an understanding of the affinity between beauty and nothingness and his resultant sense of the redundancy of the poet in favour of the ascendancy of the word, is particularly thought-provoking. In the magazine, Mallarmé captures the spirit of the times by classing theatre as a fashion auxiliary and referring to the manner in which the six hundred costumes of a production of *La Haine* by Sardou are brought to life by 'strange and very beautiful personages as well as voices charged with emotion; for there is a drama somewhere in all this, a stirring one'.[72] What is this but fashion personified?

The isolated example of François Talma's marketing of his own physical persona towards the close of the eighteenth century has already been noted. By the nineteenth century, the French stage had surrendered to the fatal charms of the Parisian vedette. By the post-Napoleonic era, the Boulevard theatres had gathered sufficient strength to boast 'talents as glorious as those illustrated at the Comédie-Française'[73] [my translation]. This battle for ascendancy changed the validatory terms that had previously applied to the national company's assertion of its rights. It was no longer a question of determining an image of the nation that corresponded either to the dictates of political will or to social realities but of establishing an image of national excellence and style, independent of institutional affiliation. The emergence of the Boulevard's flamboyant and emotive theatrical style evoked much antagonism amongst those who considered the Comédie-Française not only as the only true route towards mastery of the acting profession but as a quasi-sacred national institution: an 'old and dear theatre that was for the ancients a second homeland'[74] [my translation]. A comparison of the two contemporary actresses, Marie Dorval and Mademoiselle Mars offers an insight into the main differences between the dramatic styles adopted by the two competing institutions. The former, whose greatest role was Kitty Bell in Vigny's *Chatterton,* is praised for her ability to play in a bombastic style 'with an abandon, a shimmering passion'[75] [my translation]. The latter, who reached the height of her dramatic career as Elmire in Molière's *Misanthrope,* is eulogized for quite different qualities: 'simplicity of means [and] the total absence of emphasis and artificial solemnity'[76] [my translation]. However, Samson's description of a training session with Talma where, 'deprived of all means of theatrical illusion ... a chair between his legs ... he was as tragic as when on stage and made us shiver by reciting verses from *Andromaque* or *Phèdre*'[77] [my translation] suggests that the transmission of skills from teacher to pupil at the Conservatoire might well have had more in common with the instinctive feel for theatre commonly associated with the Boulevard than is generally admitted. Talma's style of acting set the scene for an alliance between tradition and innovation and as the century progressed the steady traffic between the Comédie-Française and the Boulevards suggests that both the real and the reputed distinctions between the two were becoming less pronounced. The rise of Romantic drama triggered a further readjustment of theatrical boundaries, by undermining the concept of distinct and autonomous categories of acting. This environment was an ideal breeding ground for the phenomenon of the vedette – a theatrical creation which was as alien to Habermas's new public sphere, in artistic terms, as was the figure of the monarch, in political terms.

If we take a look at the example of Sarah Bernhardt, one of the most successful stars of the Parisian stage, we come to an appreciation both of the allure of the star and of the dangers that she or he posed. In a review of Sarah's debut in Racine's *Iphigénie,* the critic Sarcey attributed her success to her feminine charm, concluding that her main attraction was the 'remarkable beauty' of the upper part of her face.[78] It was not physical beauty, however, that brought Sarah fame. In fact, her own advice to aspiring actresses reveals her conviction that 'perfect beauty [was] not essential to the theatre ... an actress [might] have an ordinary face and yet be perfectly charming on the stage'.[79] What made Sarah special was the ability, identified by Jules Lemaître, to exploit her femininity as a seductive, communicative tool, 'it is woman who is playing ... She hugs, she embraces, she swoons, she is convulsed, she pines'[80] [my translation]. Sarah herself was convinced that acting was ultimately a feminine art, containing 'all the artifices which belong to the province of woman: the desire to please, facility to express emotions and hide defects, and the faculty of assimilation which is the real essence of woman'.[81] The description of her as 'feminine in the extreme'[82] confirms the impression that her charm was inextricably tied to her femininity and that this femininity was an invaluable tool in her repertoire as an actress.

Nonetheless, the example provided by Talma's success in the role of Charles IX and by the immense popularity of actors such as Mounet-Sully is evidence of the fact that personal charisma was not solely the province of the feminine. After all, Sarah came to the height of her powers in male roles, such as her portrayal of Shakespeare's Hamlet. It is easy to see how such genius, ostensibly reliant on nothing but itself, gave the star, whether male or female, such sway that they would not flinch at compromising the integrity of the theatrical event by refusing to enter the stage discretely in order to make an entrance amidst applause, by a central, double door![83] What theatre could contain the actor or actress whose art was that of making you admire them and who preferred rather than to enter into the leading character, 'to substitute'[84] themselves for it? The power wielded by these ostentatious and charismatic figures, sometimes deservedly, sometimes without either merit or shame, inevitably made them an obstruction to both the integrity and the development of theatre in France. Gradually, the performer became the sole focus of the theatrical event and the inevitable devaluation of other aspects of the theatrical whole is highlighted by one contemporary critic's view that stars such as Bernhardt rendered first-class dramatic works redundant, since such genius was better served by second-rate plays that could be manipulated, and even mutilated, to better reflect her glory. Ironically, it could be argued that the national company itself had lost its identity as a coherent group by succumbing to the image of the actor, a figure no less authoritarian and autocratic than either the *ancien régime* monarch or the republican revolutionary. The hierarchy of representation first dislodged by Talma had been well and truly undermined so that the individual actor or actress marketed their physical image and personal charisma as a national product in its own right. Almost imperceptibly – under cover of a dazzling display of theatricality – representation of the popular had replaced representation of the populace.

The spectacle presented by the cult of individuality rife in nineteenth-century French theatre and embodied in all its monstrous magnificence on the national French stage might be understood as a theatrical embodiment of the dangers inherent in the republican emphasis on the primacy of the individual. From a republican viewpoint, it stands to reason that the common denominator bringing this aggregate of individuals together should be equality. On the evidence provided by the French theatre, it was clear that the driving force that invigorated this kind of society was the instinct for inequality – the individual's overwhelming desire for power, prominence and superiority. David Bell argues that the French revolution of 1789 was a paradox in the sense that it asserted the rights of a nation that did not yet exist. Bell offers this observation as part of a larger argument portraying modern nationalism as rooted in the idea of the nation as a political artefact. With reference to revolutionary France, he claims that the failure of the revolution must be discussed in terms of the enormity of the task of making Frenchmen 'not just ... turning a small population of sociable, elegant, pleasure-loving fops into grave, sober republican citizens'[85] but giving a civic education to a collection of communities that were culturally and linguistically disparate and that had not yet come into contact with any centralized education system. The 'non-existence' of the nation at this point in the history of France may well account for the dismal failure of the national theatre to reflect the concerns of a politically or culturally united national body or even to constitute itself according to the principles of a coherent artistic community.

By the turn of the twentieth century, an alternative mode of nationalism looked set to radically alter the relationship between politics and culture in France. According to Zeen Sternhell, twentieth-century cultural nationalism launched an attack on the democratic and liberal nationalism of the revolutionary tradition that had conceived of nation as a product of political will. This, he claims, was the turning point of modern politics in France, from which transpired the Dreyfus affair, Boulangism and the establishment of *Action Française*.[86] I would argue that the beginning of modern French politics coincided with the beginning of modern French theatre in the sense that twentieth-century theatre practitioners re-evaluated the central concept of a national theatre in terms of a plurality of national alternatives. It was no longer a question of whether the Comédie-Française accurately represented a national truth but of establishing a network of national, theatrical investigation that might, or then again might not, include the spectacle of a centralized, subsidized national centrepiece.

I have already discussed the curious phenomenon of the divorce of the cultural institution of theatre from political life during the 1789 revolutionary period. By the twentieth century, theatre practitioners were reflecting on this estrangement and taking action to address it. Romain Rolland's *Théâtre de la Révolution* (a work made up of eight plays written between 1898–1938) recognizes the potential of theatre to reflect and reinforce social change – an opportunity passed up by the revolutionaries as a result of their fear of mimesis and the value they placed on will as a direct and active agent in national life. According to Valérie Battaglia, Rolland sought to re-establish the link between theatrical representation and social reality by creating a theatrical experience that constituted an active memory of the revolution. In this, he was motivated by the idea that the success of a political revolution might be secured by means of a cultural revolution.[87] Rolland's ideal of establishing a theatre for and by the people, offering them ownership of their national heritage and reflecting their image in its content and architectural constitution, measures up to the idea of a national theatre in touch with its people – a public space par excellence. This ideal offers a permanent artistic alternative to the spectre of social freedom identified by de Tocqueville as the point at which people democratically elect an elite chosen from amongst the people as a governing body before returning to their previous position of inferiority.

If Sternhell's argument that cultural nationalism was gaining popularity during the early decades of the twentieth century is valid, then it would stand to reason that Rolland's theatrical mission stood a good chance of success. In actual fact, the project never actually came to fruition. In her essay on Rolland and his proposed theatre, Battaglia attributes the failure of the venture to lack of funding and the instability of the political climate of the first half of the twentieth century.[88] I think it may well have more to do with the fact that Rolland's attempt to realign theatre and society took place too early, at a stage when both twentieth-century French society and its theatre were entering an experimental phase – the main goal of which was to attain the sense of individual identity that was a necessary precondition of interaction of any kind. This search for a national identity did not take place within but rather around the Comédie-Française. Most of the theatrical enterprises that took place during this period in France sought to investigate and elevate one or another of the artistic priorities traditionally considered worthy of national theatre. André Antoine's famous Théâtre Libre promoted a faithful correspondence between theatrical methodology and 'lived' and 'living' reality, whilst the symbolist Théâtre de l'Oeuvre sought to equate inner and outer experience by means of correspondence and correlation, relegating the omni-present actor of the nineteenth century to the status of a necessary evil. Jacques Copeau's Théâtre du Vieux Colombier – an artistic endeavour that inspired the influential *Quartel des Quatres* – tapped into the energy of collective and communal activity. Jean Vilar's Avignon Festival launched itself as a place of reconciliation for the youth of Europe in a spirit of communal venture that recalled the national fêtes of revolutionary times.

David Bradby argues that all twentieth-century theatrical reformers, from Copeau to Vilar, have been able to appeal to the republican belief that to bring a number of citizens together for a performance based on some matter of mutual concern was an activity of unquestionable value to society at large.[89] What characterizes the modern era in France is its preparedness to do this by the investigation and application of nationally valid principles to distinct and diverse theatrical enterprises rather than via one cultural channel such as the national fête or, indeed, the national theatre itself. It is true that the Comédie-Française operates today and that it is still an embodiment of national excellence in much the same way as the Royal National Opera or the English National Theatre is in England. Nonetheless, according to

Bradby, by 1996 France had five officially sanctioned national theatres, receiving 317.5 million francs of subsidy and playing to audiences of 883,000: the Théâtre National de Chaillot, Strasbourg Theatre, Théâtre de la Colline, the Odéon and the Comédie-Française.[90] In eighteenth-century France, Habermas's new public sphere established a common right of debate that capitalised on the artistic media available to it in order to extend its boundaries and explore its limitations. In contemporary France, the rejection of a central artistic truth embodied in a specific national theatre fosters a new theatrical sphere in which both national and theatrical truths are played out and played with.

~ 2 ~
The stage of the German nation: twin developments

From the moment of its foundation under the aegis of Louis XIV, the Comédie-Française was confident of its own identity. The national company's relation to its constituent members – its immediate public in Paris, the nation at large and the world beyond – was a matter of declaration rather than investigation or exploration. This clarity of definition was to be called into question in later years, but in 1680 the Comédie-Française was sure both of its own nature and of the nature of the world in which it assumed its rightful place. In Germany, matters were different. It might be argued that Germany's first national theatre saw the light of day in Hamburg in 1767 as a result of a drive by J. F. Löwen to establish a 'theatrical Shrine'[1] [my translation]. that would elevate German theatre to a new height. However, the pinpointing of this particular historical moment as the beginning of the nation's corporate theatrical life implies that the process of creating a national, theatrical experience was much simpler and more clearly defined than was the case. In Germany the artistic drive to establish a national theatre was in no way clearly related to a particular place, a particular professional company, a particular system of state sponsorship or subsidy or even, for the first century or so, to a clearly defined nation-state. In the process of constructing a German national theatre there were very few given criteria, only a general aspiration towards theatrical discovery and definition, originating in what Yeats would describe as 'the foul rag-and-bone shop of the heart'.[2]

What immediately strikes the reader of the history of the German national theatre is the glaring absence of any place for theatre in the geographical landscape of the country. A glance at the nation's political and geographical history provides a useful framework from which to analyse this deficiency because it reveals the link between the enormity of the struggle to carve out a place for a German national theatre and the fact that Germany did not constitute a nation-state, in the modern sense of the word, until as late as 1871. The Holy Roman Empire, a political conglomeration of lands under the control of the Emperor Charlemagne, was in existence from the eighth century to the nineteenth century and is sometimes referred to as the First German Reich or Empire. During this period, Germany formed part of an extensive territorial unit that, by the eighteenth century, included Austria, the former Czech Republic, Lichtenstein, Switzerland, eastern France, Slovenia, Belgium and some parts of the Netherlands. Despite the abolition of the Holy Roman Empire in 1806, Germany did not become independent but remained part of a German confederation that amalgamated as many as three dozen, fully sovereign member states. Subsequent to the Austro-Prussian War in 1866, this union was succeeded by a north German confederation, headed by Wilhelm I of Prussia with Bismarck as its president. It was this arrangement that finally led to the declaration of the Second German Reich in 1871, the point at which a modern nation-state can be said to have emerged, with the reservation that even this development had only partially resolved the questions raised by the 1848 revolution and the arguments over whether Austria should be excluded from a *KleinDeutschland* or 'small-German state' or included in a *GrossDeutschland* or 'large-German state'. It is this political history that made it so difficult to anchor the aspiration towards a German national theatre firmly in German national territory.

According to W. H. Bruford, during the early decades of the eighteenth century – a point immediately prior to the genesis of the idea of a German national theatre – not only was there no national, cultural centre that might host a national theatre, there were no theatres anywhere at all.[3] His comments do not refer to the lack of one, central playing space, such as that demarcated in both ideological and material terms by a national theatre, but to the existence of any place or space in which theatrical play of any kind might develop. Bruford describes how companies such as those of Schönemann, the Neubers and Ackermann erected temporary stages in halls or large attics or put up wooden booths in vacant spaces outside city walls.[4] His evidence is corroborated by Gertrud Rudloff-Hille's account of the staging of Gottfried Ephraim Lessing's plays. Rudloff-Hille describes how, towards the middle of the eighteenth century, wandering troupes performed

Lessing's dramatic works in 'the halls of public houses, yards or in other purpose built wooden booths in unoccupied spaces in the area'[5] [my translation]. Both these accounts highlight the fact that theatre companies had to discover and define their own playing spaces. They achieved this either by putting existing buildings – designed for social interaction but not specifically for theatre production – to their own use, or by laying claim to temporary spaces on the outskirts of the cities being visited. In other words, their spatial identity was dictated not by the company's inherent artistic aims or aspirations but by the constraints of an authoritarian civic structure.[6] They had either to squat in pre-existing communal spaces over which they had no inherent rights of occupancy or to take up residence in a social no-man's-land in which they escaped the city's architectural constraints but forfeited any status as part of the resident community.

The only other way in which a German theatre company might associate itself with a specific locale or place was by affiliating itself to one of the myriad, small German capitals that were in fact little more than 'extensions of the palace of some absolute prince, great or small'.[7] Travelling German theatre companies were quick to recognize the benefits of identifying themselves with such local rulers and actively sought their support. Princely patronage offered financial benefits and, more importantly, provided companies with a concrete identity by means of their affiliation with a particular, geographical locale and its inhabitants. This kind of piecemeal support contributed significantly to the survival of many theatre companies but it cannot be claimed that eighteenth-century German princes ever acquired the habit of serious patronage of the arts, either in their own interests or in the interest of the development of the arts in general.

This situation changed with the emergence of city-states that became a microcosm of the state and laid down a blueprint for state-sponsorship of artistic institutions. This sponsorship was to present its own difficulties, particularly in terms of the independent and free development of theatrical space. I will return to a discussion of this problem later but my immediate aim is to argue that the fact that the spatial definition of German cities had developed without reference to the existence of cultural activity was a serious handicap to the nation's theatre companies. A comparison of the situations in France and Germany at this point in time reveals the prime importance of a successful negotiation of theatrical space in terms of the development of a national, theatrical art. I have already noted that at a vital point in the history of theatre in France, a space became vacant for possession by the theatre within the pre-existing structure of French cities. Although they were not designed for theatre and their limitations may well have held French theatre back to some extent, the *jeux de paume* or tennis courts did provide a distinct territory for the theatre within the cityscape. Not only did they provide a physical space, but they also allowed theatre to capitalize on the pre-established principle of the importance of leisure activity and entertainment in France at this time. It might even be argued that occupation of these spaces provided theatre with the opportunity to brand itself as a step up from tennis – a superior means of self-cultivation that appealed not only to the body but to the mind and spirit.

German theatre companies were not fortunate enough to discover a place of leisure in which they might take up residence, but had to forage for spaces that were more readily associated with commerce and economic transaction than with the cultivation of mind, body or spirit. In Leipzig, Caroline Neuber's company played above a meat-market before making a theatre out of an old riding school in Zoten's Hof, where there were no seats except in the gallery.[8] Even Konrad Ackermann's first purpose-built theatre – according to one view, this building was the foundation stone of Germany's first national theatre that was to emerge a few years later in the same city – erected in Hamburg in 1765, was connected to the market-place by two shop-lined courts.[9] J. G. Robertson's description of the location does not make it clear whether Ackermann actively sought the close connection to business premises for economic reasons or whether it was a necessary evil dictated by the scarcity of space in the city in general. Either way, it is evident that German theatre companies had to carve out spaces for themselves within the context of an urban lifestyle and structure that may not have been consciously antagonistic towards artistic endeavours but certainly did not conceive of theatre, in terms of either a spatial or a social imperative. Not only did this early theatre have no physical home in Germany's cities, it had no point of contact with its audiences and had to advertise performances by posting playbills and making public announcements often delivered vocally to the accompaniment of drums. The fact that the advertisement of performances was a quasi-theatrical event in itself made it all the more difficult both to define the place of theatre in the social fabric of the nation and to outline a particular place in which it might reveal that significance. The blurring of the distinction between publicizing performance and performance itself was indicative of a general fluidity and flux in the constitution of the theatrical event per se that made the establishment of both a definitive forum and a form for German theatre an artistic imperative.

Another fundamental difference between the situations in France and Germany at this point was the existence in France of an official, formally sanctioned, theatrical standard, endorsed by the Comédie-Française. This text-based, literary theatre upheld standards of presentation at all levels and, whilst the popularity of the improvised work of its amateur rivals alarmed it, it never really lost faith in its own superiority. In Germany on the other hand there was no alternative to the travelling companies' spontaneous style. The fact that the main item on the theatrical programme was often peppered with impromptu dialogue might be explained by the precarious process of public negotiation fundamental to the company's economic survival. However, the common custom of playing an entirely improvised afterpiece, or *nachspiel,* was a more overt avowal of the fact that German theatre had not found a concrete, artistic form that would secure its existence beyond the immediate present. The fact that it could lay claim neither to a physical territory nor to a concrete, artistic form inevitably led to the absence of a benchmark of quality to which individual companies and German theatre as a whole might aspire. Nevertheless, there were several theatre practitioners and company leaders who sought to move the medium forward towards the definition of clear artistic aims and standards. As early as 1734, Caroline Neuber claimed that her aim had 'always been to observe the strictest morality in her performances'.[10] In response to the Church's antagonism, she and her husband struggled to establish standards of decency within their troupe. Minor rules and regulations such as the stipulation that single members of the company took their meals with Frau Neuber herself may seem trivial;[11] they were, however, indicative of a desire to establish a standard of internal interaction within the company that might influence the manner in which it was perceived by the outside world, and by means of which its relations with the larger social supra-structure in which it functioned might eventually be transformed.

A more outwardly striking symbol of this aspiration became manifest when the Neuber company was prevented from returning to Leipzig in 1737 by their rival, J. F. Müller, a specialist in *commedia dell'arte*. In response to Müller's antagonism, Frau Neuber staged a demonstration against the harlequin and his devotees, in a wooden booth, outside the Grimma gate. During this performance, the harlequin and his *commedia dell'arte* entourage were symbolically banished from the German stage. Bruford notes that this rite of expulsion is generally regarded as a turning point in the history of German theatre.[12] What is particularly interesting about the event, in my view, is its indication of the fact that there was no available forum for the discussion of national theatrical standards at this point in the history of German theatre and society. The fact that a discussion regarding national, theatrical standards was instigated by a private quarrel that centred on rights of occupancy indicates the immaturity of any liberal public sphere at this stage in the country's history. Not only was there no over-arching framework that designated the spatial dominion of German theatre, but matters of style and form were also decided on the basis of personality clashes, rather than artistic principles. It is difficult to pronounce on the extent to which Frau Neuber's actions were driven by personal or public concerns, but the fact that she staged her theatrical demonstration outside the city gates and, more importantly, outside the context of any wider, more objective, ideological and rational discussion or debate reflects the peripheral place of theatre in contemporary German society. Ironically, the event that saw the German national theatre taking its first shaky steps towards self-discovery and self-definition was sorely lacking in definition itself.

Earlier, I pinpointed 1767 as the year in which the German national theatre was first established. I did so with the reservation that to present one date as a crucial moment in this process belied the complex way in which a national theatre came into being in Germany. It also suggests that it is possible to label the theatre that emerged in Hamburg in that year as a self-evidently national institution when this is, in fact, far from the truth.

By contrast, Bruford refers to Koch's theatre that was built in Leipzig in 1766 and provided a home for comic opera as the first step towards later national theatres. He also argues that it was the first theatre to generate a national publication devoted to theatre criticism.[13] Koch's residence in the Leipzig theatre was short-lived due to accusations from the university that he was luring its students away from their studies with the superficial pleasures of light entertainment. In this context, it is interesting to note Lessing's comments regarding the propriety of subjecting the arts to municipal laws as was the custom amongst the ancients, because '[t]he aim of art ... is pleasure, which is not indispensable; and it may therefore depend on the lawgiver to decide what kind of pleasure, and what degree of every kind, he will allow'.[14] In the light of Lessing's perception of pleasure as a matter for legislative regulation, the university's objections to Koch's comic opera appear reasonable. Conversely, Bruford's attribution of the adjective 'national' to a theatre that confined itself to the pursuit of pleasure rather than dedicating itself to the satisfaction of man's essential need for knowledge and truth – the criteria that Lessing felt would place it beyond the bounds of legislation and law – seems rather unreasonable.

Subsequent to his departure from Leipzig, Koch was invited to Weimar,[15] where his company was subsidised by Duchess Anna Amalia for a three-year period from 1768 onwards. This connection with Weimar – a duchy that was to play a vital role at the heart of the debate concerning the nature of the German people and their national theatre, under the influence of both Johann Wolfgang von Goethe and Friedrich Schiller – provides some justification for Bruford's view of this as Germany's first truly, national theatrical venture. There were, however, other endeavours that could lay equal claim to national prestige, such as Ackermann's pioneering establishment of a purpose built theatre in Hamburg that he later turned over to the officially designated national theatre, or the establishment of a German-speaking national theatre at Vienna in 1766. The latter venture was instigated by Emperor Joseph II as a means of terminating the tradition of leasing out court entertainments to aristocratic managers. Its particular importance stemmed from its establishment of a democratic system of control by committee. This egalitarian, organizational mechanism might well be considered one of the fundamental characteristics of a national theatre – an artistic institution run by its own members for the people at large. On the other hand, the Vienna theatre's status as a German-speaking national theatre, as distinct from a German national theatre, was a potential weakness in its credibility as a national institution. Whatever its strengths and weaknesses, it too had other, rival claimants such as the somewhat later, but significantly successful, 'Court-National Theatre'[16] set up in Mannheim in 1777, comprising the best members of Seyler's troupe and some of the members of the recently closed Gotha court theatre. The fact that Bruford talks of this theatre as a device intended to compensate the town for losses it incurred due to the transfer of the capital of Karl Theodor to Munich in 1777,[17] suggests that the creation of a new centre for theatrical life was recognized as a means of endowing the city with kudos, character and vibrancy, even if the appellation 'national' was as yet, an unawarded honour.

Despite the plurality of the claims made on the national theatrical title, I think it can be argued convincingly that the Hamburg theatre, set up in 1767, qualifies for the epithet 'national' because it was the first theatrical institution to couple the instigation and advancement of a debate about theatre, located in the emerging public sphere, with the establishment of a national standard of theatrical interaction, within a consciously defined theatrical forum – the Hamburg theatre itself. The process of constructive discovery that gave life to a German national theatre is characterized by its symbiotic relationship with the emergence of the new, rational public sphere as described by Habermas. It was neither a precursor to, nor a product of, that sphere but developed in tandem with it. It is the remarkable synchronization of development in these two distinct circles, the one artistic, the other social, which justifies the identification of the Hamburg effort of 1767 as a decisive point in the history of the German national theatre.

The theatre building in which the Hamburg National Theatre was to be housed was originally built for Konrad Ackermann in 1765, with no specifically national brief in mind. In fact, Robertson's description of it highlights structural inadequacies, architectural evidence of economic constraints and a decor inspired by aristocratic aspirations, all of which belie its national status. It is described as a simple theatre, erected at a cost of 20,000 talers, 55 x 103 foot long with a 51 x 51 foot stage so 'faultily constructed that the crossbeams at the top were visible from the auditorium'.[18] Little could be seen from the back seats of the auditorium and compliance with fire regulations was unsatisfactory. The 34 x 25 foot high proscenium was ennobled with two pairs of imitation Corinthian pillars, painted to resemble marble. A gilded vase on a pedestal stood between each pair of pillars. In keeping with these aristocratic vestiges, the parterre was designed so that it could be covered for masked balls. According to Robertson, when the Hamburg consortium took over, there was no significant change either in the building's outward appearance or its repertoire.[19] He argues that the fact that it was described as national and was nominally controlled by a consortium involved no essential break with the past.[20]

Whilst this is true, the distinguishing feature of the national Hamburg theatre, as it appeared in 1767, was the fact that its internal organization and administration were modelled according to democratic principles, characteristic of popular rule and gave the theatre, at the very least, the appearance of popular appeal. In my discussion hitherto, the complexity of German state politics has emerged as a prohibitive factor in the history of the German national theatre. In the case of the Hamburg national theatre, the liberalism or, perhaps, the expansiveness of German notions of nationhood actually had a positive impact in the sense that the democratic tendencies of the Hamburg national theatre may well have resulted from the city's non-feudal traditions. Hamburg was a free city from the Middle Ages to the nineteenth century and played a significant role in the development of the democratically driven, Hanseatic League: a trading network that facilitated trade across eastern and western boundaries from the thirteenth to the sixteenth century. To date, it is known as a city built for citizens by citizens and its continuing pride in its independence was reflected in its recent reassertion of its title as the Free and Hanse City of Hamburg. In twentieth-century England, William Archer and Harley Granville Barker invested considerable time and energy in the invention of a democratic constitution and organizational structure that could be grafted on to the national theatre of their dreams. This was the aim and achievement of their joint publication, *A National Theatre: Schemes and Estimates,* in which they constructed an ideal model for any future English national theatre. In the case of the eighteenth-century Hamburg national theatre, the pre-existing conditions of civic life in Hamburg accomplished this feat without artifice or effort.

It is probably fair to claim that the Hamburg National Theatre came into being as a direct result of the efforts of one Johann Friedrich Löwen. Löwen had originally been employed in Ackermann's theatre as a kind of literary adviser but was later replaced by Ast, who was afforded the preferred title, house-poet. Subsequently, driven by the desire to remedy the defects of German theatre and establish a centre of national theatrical excellence, Löwen criticized his previous employer's style of management and launched a general attack on the figure of the actor-manager. The personal history shared by the two men renders his objectivity in this respect somewhat suspect. It also confirms the continuing importance of the individual's subjective experience in matters of artistic form – a phenomenon that had initially manifested itself in the context of Frau Neuber's artistic indictment of harlequin in response to competition from her contemporary rival Müller. In the first instance, Löwen disguised his attack on Ackermann by his decision to publish it in the guise of a letter to a friend. Gradually, he dropped the pretence of privacy or intimacy and followed this initial publication with a letter to a puppet-player, no longer an unidentified friend, but to all intents and purposes a professional colleague. Later, the publication of his *Geschichte des deutschen Theaters* revealed the fact that he was actively engaged in a deliberate attempt to initiate a public debate about the German theatre. Löwen's criticism seems to have struck a chord with the members of Ackermann's company in as far as Robertson feels that it was his criticism, coupled with dissent from amongst his own ranks, that led Ackermann to relinquish his theatre in return for an economic settlement that included the payment of an annual rent, the receipt of one-third of the profits from any masked balls and the purchase of the stage properties and wardrobe.[21] Robertson's impression of internal dissent is important if considered from the point of view of the development of the public sphere because, whilst it may not provide evidence of growing public opinion or awareness in relation to theatre, it is a sign that the theatre was becoming accountable to a public, even if that public only consisted of company members themselves at this stage.

Having ensured Ackermann's capitulation, Löwen set about securing the financial backing of twelve Hamburg businessmen who pledged to support the national theatre for a stipulated period of ten years. This consortium-style financial backing, coupled with Löwen's rejection of a self-elected actor-manager in favour of a manager chosen by the players themselves, established a democratic ethos particularly suited to a national artistic endeavour. However, even at this early stage in the history of the venture, one is reminded of Alexis de Tocqueville's indictment of a democracy that facilitates the articulation of a public voice only for the brief moment required for the nomination of a leader from amongst a people who subsequently return to their previous state of subordination. This seems to have been the case in terms of the management of Löwen's theatre. Löwen entrusted the national theatre's internal management to Konrad Ekhof and it was not long before he became as autocratic as Ackermann in his distribution of roles and choice of repertoire. Ironically, Ekhof had already attempted a democratic experiment in the area of theatre management when he established an actor's academy in 1753. According to Bruford, the academy encouraged actors to meet weekly, in council, to discuss the principles of their art and the challenges of their current projects.[22] Nonetheless, these values do not seem to have played a decisive role in determining Ekhof's managerial style at Hamburg. What is more, the two leading spirits amongst the Hamburg citizens who had pledged their support to the venture, Herr Seyler and Herr Bubbers, both had a personal interest in one of the female stars of Löwen's theatre, Madame Hensel. Whilst Löwen had many commendable ideas concerning the establishment of national play-writing competitions, a national training centre for actors and a national schedule of lectures on and about the theatre, none of these schemes actually materialized. As a result, it is difficult to evade the suggestion that German theatre had not really moved from the confused situation where subjectivity and personal interest appeared to be the primary, determining factors in the matter of negotiating artistic style and form.

Despite these reservations, Habermas himself highlights the importance of Löwen's Hamburg venture when he describes how, 'in 1766, as a consequence of the critical efforts of Gottsched and Lessing, Germany finally acquired a permanent theater, i.e., the

"German National Theater"'.²³ In describing the national theatre as the product of the critical efforts of Lessing and Gottsched, he reveals the fundamental connection between the vigour of the critical debate about theatre and the standing and significance of the artistic institution itself. I wish to take this argument one step further by proposing that it was Lessing's connection with and contribution to the Hamburg national venture that was the one factor that justified its claim to national status and significance. Lessing's contract of employment marked a vital stage in the development of both the German public sphere and the role of theatre within that sphere. He was not employed by the Hamburg theatre as a resident dramatist but as a critic. His critical input in the form of the *Hamburgische Dramaturgie* generated a forum for discussion that extended beyond the temporary period of a particular performance and emphasized the life and liveliness of theatre by contrast with other literary forms. There were precedents to Lessing's critical efforts. Löwen himself had written commentaries on the performances of Schönemann's company at Hamburg and since 1740 Gottsched had published his plays and translations in a new periodical, entitled *Die Deutsche Schaubühne*. In more recent times, the popular publication *Hamburgische Unterhaltungen* had devoted much space to the discussion of Hamburg's theatrical entertainments and the publicity benefits of this approach were becoming clear.²⁴ Nonetheless, it was Lessing's *Hamburgische Dramaturgie* that brought to a head the interest in the aesthetic foundations of dramatic art, instigated by Friedrich Schlegel and Gottsched. Lessing's chronicling of one particular theatre's repertory – the Hamburg National Theatre itself – realized a general desire to extend the remit and influence of theatre in the life of the German nation.

Lessing evidently felt that the development of a distinctive and mature social character was vital to the affluence of any nation. As a result, the importance of character in matters of national identity and creativity is not confined to his analysis of things German but is a general principle of his critical analysis. In a discussion of the French drama, he argues that it is not the narrow miserable French theatre that accounts for the chilliness of plays such as Voltaire's *Semiramis* but the immaturity of the French spirit at work thereon.²⁵ Lessing characterized Voltaire's dramatic art as chilly but he was also aware of the coldness of the German people towards their own theatre. The Germans, he argued, had no theatre because they neither actively desired nor engaged with one. In fact, he goes as far as to suggest that they only frequented the theatre 'from idle curiosity, from fashion, from ennui, to see people, from a desire to see and be seen'.[26] In identifying himself with the Löwen venture, Lessing took a significant step towards bringing about change. In a letter to Lessing in which his connection with the Hamburg venture is discussed Nicolai, Lessing's brother, admits that he does not yet fully understand the meaning of the term 'national theatre' but that he recognizes the accessibility of Hamburg as a potential site for such an artistic institution. He writes:

> I don't know what the term National Theatre means, that was first used with reference to the theatre in Vienna for a time, that was hardly representative, and that the Gentleman Players since then have used for very shallow entertainment; but Hamburg is a very exquisite theatre to visit, certainly the foremost place in Germany[27] [my translation].

Earlier, the importance to the theatre of the allocation of a designated playing space, both within the physical and social framework of a city and, by extension, of a nation, was discussed. Lessing's contract and contact with the Hamburg theatre facilitated the process of branding it as one such national theatrical space.

Lessing's own plays also played a significant role in the process of providing German theatre with a specific, spatial definition because they sketched out an innovative delineation of the stage space itself. Rudloff-Hille describes the stage setting typical of the eighteenth-century German theatre as a complex system of interchangeable, decorated wings or panels that could be assembled horizontal to, or at a tangent from, the proscenium frame in order to create either the illusion of perspective or of a flat stage.[28] These decorated panels could be manually or mechanically interchanged and presented various domestic and outdoor scenes with the aid of several curtains that could be lowered in between the panels to create yet more optical illusions of place and space. This complex and cumbersome system was rationalized under the influence of Enlightenment thinking and Rudloff-Hille demonstrates how Lessing's plays reflected the simplification of the stage setting and the adoption of either a deep or a shallow stage that involved far fewer scenery changes.[29] Lessing's contribution to the process of clarifying and de-cluttering the stage space itself can usefully be considered in the same light as his decision to pledge his allegiance to the development of a national theatrical space or place at Hamburg.

Any discussion of the definition of theatrical space is to some extent an anomaly, not only because the playing space has two distinct identities – the one defined by its geographical and physical location, the other by the shape of the activity occurring within that space – but also because both these identities are fluid. The former is the more concrete of the two because it is often, although not always, embodied in a building of sorts. The latter is determined by the spatial dynamics of the theatrical activity itself and is in a constant state of flux, both within individual performances and from one performance to another. Lessing recognized the need to regulate these spatial formulations by the application of a national standard, based on sound, aesthetic values and vision. By now Gottsched's early efforts to establish indicators of aesthetic quality were considered mediocre. Lessing's own assessment of Gottsched's failure to 'keep pace with his century'[30] demonstrates his awareness of the immaturity of the enquiry into and debate surrounding the aesthetic principles of dramatic art. As a result, he set about addressing fundamental questions concerning the aim and nature of drama and its relation to the community that gave it life and whose life it in turn represented. In asking these questions, he highlighted one of the basic functions of theatre – that of 'coming together'. Lessing put the question 'why build a theatre, disguise men and women, torture their memories, invite the whole town to assemble at one place?'[31] In so doing, he registered and reinforced the importance of theatre as an interactive activity that strengthens communal identities. Lessing himself immediately provided an answer to his own enquiry by stating that dramatic art is the 'only one by which pity and fear can be excited'.[32] Whilst he freely admitted that at that time German theatre preferred to excite all other emotions, he was confident of the superiority of pity and fear as means of arriving at beauty and truth: that truth that he describes as 'necessary to the soul'[33] and against which it is tyranny to do the smallest violence.

T. J. Reed claims that Lessing's impulse to relocate tragedy amongst the bourgeoisie was due to his belief that tragedy was felt most strongly amongst equals. If so, this conviction reveals his understanding of theatre as a coherent artistic structure in which a process is activated and then completed via the cooperation of separate entities, working toward a common goal. The specific advice he offered, in his *Hamburgische Dramaturgie,* to distinct groups within this whole was informed by this general understanding. Although he soon met with sufficient objection to silence any commentary on the national theatre's actors and actresses, he did accomplish some constructive criticism of acting styles. In so doing, he established his admiration for Eckhof as someone who could convey feeling to the audience in the most authentic and natural manner. Eckhof's skill as a performer led him to reflect,

> how far is the actor, who only understands a passage, removed from him who also feels it. Words whose sense we have once grasped, that are once impressed upon our memories, can be very correctly repeated even when the soul is occupied with quite other matters; but then no feeling is possible. The soul must be quite present ... [34]

In a recent paper entitled *The Art of Acting and the Non-Act of Being in the Eighteenth Century,*[35] Wendy Arons claims that there was a shift in the representation of the human being on the stage in the eighteenth century when naturalness came to be equated with truth. She argues that the bourgeois project of sincerity rendered acting suspect because it legitimized a discomforting artificiality that threatened the transition from an ostentatious court society to a more authentic mode of being. Lessing's emphasis on Eckhof's manifestation of sincerity, coupled with other comments he made urging a natural style of acting, indicates his commitment to a representative style that encouraged a common commitment – on the part of both members of the acting profession and members of the audience – to immersion in an inclusive dramatic present. This seems an impressive blueprint for the dramatic activity of a national theatre, in that it inevitably implies a principle of egalitarian, creative participation on the part of actor and audience member and a fundamental interest in investigating the general significance of the specific quality of human experience. Nowhere does

Lessing use the word 'national' in his discussion, but it seems to me that the kind of theatrical activity he had in mind was national, both in terms of the egalitarian and communal nature of the dramatic process and in its ultimate aim.

It is true to say that Lessing's pioneering criticism established a place for theatre and theatre critics within the context of the rational and informed debate developing in the public sphere. Nevertheless, it also highlighted some of the difficulties involved in this process. Despite the short lifespan of both Lessing's experiment in theatrical criticism and the Hamburg theatrical venture itself, the combined influence of both projects did much to stimulate interest in and discussion of German national theatre and German nationhood. By 1777 periodicals devoted to the stage, such as H. A. O. Reichard's *Theaterkalender*,[36] were reflecting and stimulating critical interest in the activity of some fourteen German theatre companies. More importantly, after the experiment of the Hamburg theatre, the words 'national' and 'national theatre' gained clear definition. According to Bruford, the former was understood as representative of the entire nation, the latter as a non-commercial, permanent theatre, subsidized for educational purposes.[37] Bruford also underlines the importance of such an artistic institution to the German nation as a whole, by pointing out that there was no other available forum for public discussion in the 'national language, almost the only cultural possession that was common to the whole people'.[38] The lack of any common ground other than that of a shared language was particularly acute in the case of Germany due to the fact that it was not yet a nation-state and would not become one until as late as 1871. The emergence of a new public sphere that demanded both knowledge and information also gave rise to the unscrupulous publication practices of companies like Dodsley and Company, who set about clandestinely printing and distributing parts of the *Hamburgische Dramaturgie*. This kind of opportunistic activity was the result of the uncoordinated expansion of economic and social spheres in contemporary German society. It testified to an awareness of the emergence of a new, liberal public sphere but was also detrimental to the healthy development of that sphere.

Fortunately, in response to his particular difficulties in this respect, Lessing took a positive step towards the establishment of regulatory criteria, designed to rectify the destructive effect of the practice as a whole. In the absence of protective copyright laws, Lessing set about thwarting Dodsley and Company by issuing a series of notices in a Hamburg newspaper. Bruford tells us how in the *Kaiserlich-privilegirte Hamburgische Neue Zeitung*, Lessing informed his readers that henceforth his criticism would appear in volumes rather than as serial numbers.[39] It is particularly interesting to note here how the newspaper has become a forum for advertising the protection of other, distinct modes of written publication and a means of counteracting the degeneration of the public sphere itself. In the face of a mass demand for cheap commodities that not only demeans the material available in that sphere but the nature of the sphere itself, the newspaper came to the service of theatrical scholars such as Lessing. This phenomenon is markedly different from the case of the *Mercure Galant* when it was published and popularized by Jean Donneau in seventeenth-century France. However slow its development in other respects, Germany's adeptness in activating separate sections of the same press industry against each other provided evidence of considerable progress and ingenuity in the context of its manipulation of the development of the liberal, public sphere.

Subsequent to the close of the Hamburg venture, the campaign to establish a German national theatre took a different direction, but one that had been presaged by the early involvement of Ernest Augustus II and, later, that of his wife, Duchess Anna Amalia, in patronage of theatre in the Duchy of Weimar. Before his death, in 1758, the duke had set up a court theatre that consisted of a troupe of six married couples, based at the ducal palace at Wilhelmsburg.[40] Subsequently, Duchess Amalia's connection with the troupes of both Starcke and Koch continued this tradition.[41] In 1775, Duke Charles Augustus invited the young Goethe to take up a ministerial position at Weimar; Goethe's acceptance of this offer inaugurated an unforgettable era in the history of the theatre at Weimar that justifies its designation as the next national theatre of serious significance, after the Hamburg venture. Tellingly, the intellectual discussion, instigated by Lessing's theatre criticism and fuelled by both Goethe and Schiller's writings on theatre during their association with Weimar, continued the connection between the establishment of a national theatre and the flourishing of a liberal, public sphere, dominated by rational argument about nationhood and national theatre. I will return to this point in some detail later, but firstly will take a look at the city-state to which Goethe had been so cordially invited.

According to T. J. Reed, in 1775 Weimar was the size of a small English county and had a population of 100,000.[42] As such, it provided a typical example of the German penchant for a political framework of dominance on a small, local scale. Nevertheless, the cultural clout accumulated by Weimar, during the last quarter of the eighteenth century, bore no relation either to its significance as a power base or to its territorial size and scope. Weimar became a cultural microcosm of the German-speaking nation and it did so under the direction of two of Germany's most prominent critical and creative thinkers, Goethe and Schiller. Reed notes that in the 1770s and 1780s it was a commonplace of critical discussion that a national theatre 'might ... be the means to shape society and create a nation'.[43] Whilst it may not be feasible to argue that at this stage this expectation was shared by a large, nationally representative body or force, it is safe to assume that somewhere from amongst the energies, desires and demands of Duke Charles Augustus on the one hand and Goethe and Schiller on the other a theatrical mission emerged that could be defined in these terms. Reed refers to Goethe and Schiller as the two great arbiters of 'Weimar Classicism',[44] but the process of negotiating and articulating the imperatives of their national undertaking at Weimar is complex and difficult. It is true to say that both Schiller and Goethe dedicated themselves to the promotion of classical, artistic values at a national level. Their correspondence is famed for its documentation of their search for a standard for classical tragedy during which they designated Sophocles's *Oedipus Rex* as the perfect exponent of tragic drama. Nonetheless, it is also true that their drama and their theatre both show experimentation with anti-enlightenment methodology. Goethe's initial production at Weimar was, in fact, a 'festival play with songs and dances'[45] in celebration of the duchess's birthday. In another exotic production that had Faustian overtones with its procession of devils, each representing a different vice, Goethe's embodiment of pride appeared 'on stilts and wearing wings of peacock tails'.[46] Perhaps a more significant, if less spectacular, indication of the complexity of the definitive task undertaken at Weimar was provided by Schiller's early attempt to build on Lessing's endeavour to relocate tragedy among the bourgeoisie because he too felt that 'tragic sympathy is evoked most strongly by social equals'.[47]

Despite his admiration for *Oedipus Rex* as the ultimate blueprint for tragedy, Schiller did not always apply a similar format to his own dramatic creations. In *Mimesis*, Eric Auerbach takes a look at *Luise Millerin*, a play written by Schiller in 1784, prior to his contact with both Weimar and Goethe. Auerbach describes the play as one that 'undertakes to apprehend the practical contemporary present directly and to base the particular case on the general conditions'.[48] He goes on to argue that the final connection of sentimental, middle-class realism with idealistic politics and concern for human rights was established in the *Sturm und Drang* period.[49] *Luise Millerin*, he says, 'represents an extreme case of the literary rendering of reality in terms of principles and problems'.[50] Because the miller's family is portrayed tragically, realistically and in terms of contemporary history, the play becomes one of the first attempts to 'make an individual destiny echo the fullness of contemporary reality'.[51] This new type of drama can usefully be considered as a particular manifestation of modern drama as it is characterized by Peter Szondi.[52] Szondi argues that a new dramatic medium came into being in the Renaissance as a result of the bold intellectual effort made by a newly self-conscious being who, after the collapse of the medieval world-view, sought to create an artistic reality within which he could fix and mirror himself on the basis of interpersonal relationships alone. Szondi's theory of the genesis of a new dramatic genre is broadly in line with Habermas's concept of the emergence of a new public sphere. According to Szondi, the subject of a modern drama was first and foremost a rational being and, as a result, the emotional relationships that would drive the dramatic action of a modern play forwards would lead to social readjustment or at least a reaffirmation of the values of society and reason. Habermas's discussion outlines a comparative process taking place in the realms of society and social life. The correlation suggests that this modern drama, as distinct from any classical dramatic format, would make the perfect artistic medium for the discussion emerging in the new public sphere. Schiller's early dramatic works suggest that he was bent on exploiting this correspondence to the full and our analysis hitherto confirms that this seems an appropriate way forward for German national drama and theatre.

Auerbach's inspiring critique points out that despite a certain lack of realism in the motivation of some characters, such as Luise herself, *Luise Millerin* made a breakthrough into things political. He attributes this progress to the fact that the central love obstacle motivating the dramatic action was no longer the result of private difficulties but instead derived from a public problem such as that of class structure.[53] In this context, it is possible to read Shakespeare's *Romeo and Juliet* in terms of a love obstacle, created by clan-like competition amongst feuding families. This conflict is used as a means of creating the illusion of political opposition, but it is, in fact, nothing more than private feuding. The resultant incongruity may well be responsible for the difficulties encountered by an audience who attempt to understand Romeo's nature and behaviour as a manifestation of the spirit of his times rather than an individual response to a particular set of domestic difficulties. Whatever our evaluation of the artistic status of love is in this Shakespearean tragedy, Auerbach argues that the *Sturm und Drang* movement redignified love by presenting it as 'a condition of natural virtue',[54] and therefore the most noble of all human sentiments. *Luise Millerin* is true to this vision in that the love interest becomes the focal point for a politically founded realism. Auerbach has reservations about the extent of Schiller's success in this play and in the final analysis he describes it as melodrama rather than tragedy.[55] Nevertheless, it outlined an exciting way forward for a German theatre that might engage meaningfully and actively with contemporary national concerns and interests.

Despite the apparent advantages of this mode of dramatic creativity, Auerbach notes that,

> in the age of Goethe, no further attempts were made toward the tragic treatment of an average contemporary bourgeois milieu on the basis of its actual social situation ... the trend of German literature in general, turned away from realism in the sense of a concrete portrayal of contemporary, political and economic conditions, with its forceful mixing of styles ... The combination of a forceful realism with a tragic conception of the problems of the age simply does not occur.[56]

He argues that this change of direction is particularly ironic because it was in the latter half of the eighteenth century in Germany that the aesthetic foundation of modern realism –

historicism – was laid. He contends that it is only when people come to understand historical dynamics that they realize that the meaning of human events can only be understood when what is unique, and therefore universally valid, is sought and discovered not only in the upper class stratum of society, but in art, economy, material and intellectual culture and in the everyday world of working men and women.[57] Furthermore, he claims that in Germany the development of historicism provided a means of overcoming the separation of artistic styles so that reality was no longer excluded from high tragedy. Auerbach conceives of this assimilation of different styles into a coherent and inclusive, artistic whole as a basic prerequisite of contemporary realism. Yet, he argues, in Germany contemporary realism did not achieve complete development.[58] This may well be due, in part at least, to the fact that Schiller turned away from modern realism and opted to emulate classical patterns of dramatic construction and practice. In an unpublished doctoral thesis on the presentation of irrationality in German drama, Myfanwy Jones argues that Lessing was prepared to make aesthetically damaging compromises in order to comply with the constraints of the contemporary social and moral order.[59] I suspect that this tendency may be indicative of a desire to use his drama as a means of bolstering the unity of the Holy Roman Empire that was eventually to come to an end in 1805. Whether or not this is the case, Jones's argument that Lessing tailored his dramatic action in order to sustain the national status quo can be extended to include the observation that Schiller was, in fact, prepared to change his artistic course completely in order to achieve a national drama that would assert Germany's cultural, territorial and socio-political unity. His decision to break with a bourgeois style of tragedy, rooted in the representation of contemporary, political and social realities, provides a particularly striking indication of a national preference regarding the methodology of constructing and expressing national identity in the theatre.

In his discussion of *Luise Millerin,* Auerbach is dealing with an aspect of Schiller's work that predates his friendship with Goethe and his association with Weimar, but he extends his argument to a consideration of the motivation for and nature of Goethe's acceptance of the offer made him by Duke Charles Augustus in 1775 – the starting point for Weimar's spectacular development of cultural activity and status. Auerbach rationalizes Goethe's acceptance of his new post in terms of an attempt to escape the conditions of bourgeois life. He says that Goethe never really conceived of the reality of contemporary social life as the germ of future development. Rather, he resisted the trends of modern life because he felt that they necessitated an uncompensated, impoverishment of intellectual life. For the same reason he remained aloof from the political patriotism that might have led to social integration in Germany.[60] It is true that Goethe regretted the absence of a 'center of social *savoir vivre*'[61] where writers might congregate and develop in their separate ways but in a common direction. Nevertheless, his terror of the political upheaval necessary if the cultural environment was to be transformed in this way outweighed both the artistic and the socio-political rewards that might result from such a coming together. He was adamant that 'we shall not wish for upheavals which might prepare classical works in Germany' – works that he realized can only materialize when an author discovers in the history of his nation 'great events and their consequences in a felicitous and significant union'.[62]

Auerbach's comments on Goethe's *Wilhelm Meisters Lehrjahre* and the way in which the young man justifies his desire to become an actor casts light on Goethe's own predilection for the theatre. Wilhelm explains,

> here in Germany only the nobleman has the possibility of a certain generalized personal culture ... A bourgeois can achieve great merit; at a pinch he can even cultivate his mind; but his personality will be lost, try as he may ... While the nobleman gives everything by presenting his person, the bourgeois gives nothing through his personality and is not supposed to. The former may and should 'appear to be'; the latter must only 'be' and what he attempts to 'appear to be' is ridiculous or insipid. The former is expected to act a part, perform a function, the latter ... must develop specific skills to make himself useful ... his nature ... should not possess harmony, because, in order to make himself useful in one way, he must neglect everything else.[63]

Wilhelm, like Goethe, has no desire to change the social order that makes him what he is but he is intent on achieving release from the confines of his everyday life, by means of artistic illusion. He declares his intention of becoming an actor in order to satisfy 'an irresistible propensity for the very kind of harmonious development of my nature which is denied me by my birth'.[64] This presentation of the acting profession as a means of acquiring the nobleman's freedom to develop his personality outside a mechanistic context throws interesting light on the previous chapter's discussions of the affinity between the actor and the ruler and shows why a ruler would both fear and desire to use actors and their theatres. It also suggests to me that Goethe's early propensity for theatre, and spectacular theatre at that, might well be an indication of his desire to escape the confines placed on his personal development by the social order of his contemporary society, without disturbing that social order more than was absolutely necessary. In this he was true to his friend Schiller who, despite holding different political views to those of Goethe, also allowed his artistic aspirations to be determined by his desire not to threaten or undermine the contemporary social order.

Whilst the process of establishing a link between national and classical drama and theatre was not as straightforward as some critical accounts suggest, there can be no doubt that Goethe and Schiller reached a consensus that this was the best way forward. Their collaboration at Weimar aimed at revolutionizing both the quality and the character of German theatre and contributed towards the development of the liberal, public sphere that was struggling to take shape in the Germany of their times. One of the first steps taken in pursuit of this goal was the founding of a literary journal entitled *Die Horen*. According to Bruford, this effort was presaged by Wieland's attempt to designate his *Der deutsche Merkur* as a national journal in emulation of the *Mercure de France*.[65] In a similar way, Schiller's publication was an exercise in extinction publishing in as far as it aimed at promoting itself as a national hallmark that would result in the publication of fewer journals of a higher standard. The ironical fact that Goethe and Schiller often had to supply most of the material for this journal themselves indicated that the aims and aspirations that they struggled to achieve in the name of the nation were often not instigated by a direct expression of national will. Schiller admits to this when talking of how to seduce the reading public into engaging with *Die Horen*. He suggests a rather unscrupulous course of action, involving making the German public ashamed to admit that they cannot think and making them praise the publication against their will. Interestingly, he describes his aim as making them 'appear to be what they are not'.[66] The success of this foray into the world of the populist masses is called into question in view of J. T. Reed's recording of the fact that between 1789 and 1813 the Dresden theatre gave one evening in three to a play of Kotzebue, one in twenty-five to Goethe, Schiller and Lessing, and hardly any to Shakespeare.[67] In correspondence with Goethe, Schiller offers a realistic appraisal of its influence when he notes that he has read a review of *Hermann und Dorothea* in the *Nürnberg Gazette* and that despite the fact that it shows little awareness of 'an insight into the poetic economy of the whole',[68] its proof of the German appreciation of the general, the rational and the moral provided hope of future development. It seems possible that their mutual critical efforts were slowly taking effect or, at the very least, that they were right in their perception of the German *geist* as a native of the new liberal public sphere by virtue of its natural propensity towards rational objectivity.

In his analysis of Goethe's Germany, Reed highlights the irony of the fact that the period when Goethe and Schiller invented classicism coincided with the era of the French Revolution.[69] He goes on to argue that Goethe and Schiller put their trust in ethically inspired individual action in a situation of stability and manageable dimensions. Revolution, he observes, by contrast, meant mass action, ideologically inspired, in a situation of disorder and of unmanageable dimensions.[70] Goethe and Schiller's artistic project at Weimar counteracted the turbulence of revolution. In their view, national theatre had the potential to provide an artistic situation of stability and of manageable dimensions in which ethically inspired communal action might transpire if they, as individuals, could provide it with suitable inspiration. They set about this task by publicizing the value and significance of a national theatre on the basis of the unifying effect of its thematic content and aesthetic effect. Schiller argued that he could not,

> possibly overlook the great influence that a good permanent theater would exercise on the spirit of a nation. By national spirit I mean opinions and tendencies which are common to the people of one nation and differ from those of other nationalities. Only the stage can produce this accord to so great a degree because it takes all human knowledge as its province, exhausts all situations of life, and sheds light into every corner of the human heart; because it unites all sorts and conditions of people and commands the most popular road to the heart and understanding.[71]

Schiller argued for an understanding of the theatre as a moral force, capable of exercising an influence on the thoughts and manners of a whole people. He set forth his understanding of the German *geist* as a reflection of the ruling spirit of the age and then argued that theatre was the most efficacious method of anchoring this spirit at a national level:

> Humanity and tolerance are becoming the ruling principles of our age ... How great a share in this divine work belongs to our theaters? Is it not the theater that makes man known to man and discloses the secret mechanism that controls his conduct? ... It is only here that the great of the world hear what they rarely if ever hear elsewhere: the truth. Here they see what they scarcely ever see: man ... The stage is the common channel in which from the thinking, better part of the people the light of wisdom flows down, diffusing from there in milder rays through the entire state. More correct ideas, purified principles and feelings flow from thence through all the vein of all the people ... Night leads to victorious light.[72]

Interestingly, he argued that the jurisdiction of the stage begins where the domain of secular law comes to an end. If one recalls Lessing's feeling that municipal law has a right to regulate an art that aims purely and simply at pleasure but forfeits this right when it aspires to the revelation of truth and the attainment of knowledge, it is clear that Schiller took for granted that a national theatre would aspire to, and hopefully achieve, the latter. Peter Jelavich argues that Schiller was convinced that there was only one means of realizing the 'process of democratization'[73] whereby public discourse might generate the principles of correct government. The only way forward was to address the problem of aesthetics through the agency of a national theatre. If Germany had a national theatre, he argued, 'we would also become a *Nation*'.[74]

Schiller argued that education was of vital importance to the state, and it was here that he revealed the conservative nature of his understanding of a national theatre, as a state aid so to speak. In the context of this conservativeness, it is worth noting that whilst Goethe's Weimar theatre offered free entry to anyone three times a week, anyone meant only courtiers.[75] In keeping with Schiller's manifesto for a national theatre, the drama he wrote for Weimar was classical in character and is indicative of the ultimate hold of a classical set of national standards there that Goethe, even in the very early days when he was still staging festivals in honour of the duchess's birthday, was also writing fine monodramas like *Proserpina*. These lyrical monologues, modelled on themes from Greek mythology, were written to show off the talents of the actress Corona Schröter.[76] Her influence on the creative process, as opposed to that of Goethe's material sponsor, the duchess, is fascinating in that it suggests that the figure of the classical actress (or at least a reproduction of that figure) was both the inspiration and the figurehead of Goethe's idea of a national theatre, notwithstanding his sponsor's propensity for theatre as social celebration and festivity.

According to Martell Gordon, the first half of the nineteenth century was a period when intellectual thought and educational development in Germany were governed by *Bildungsbürgertum* and *Bildungsliberalismus* – a vision that focused on the free development of the individual personality and considered the formation of character to be the ultimate goal of cultural activity.[77] Gordon discusses the way in which this kind of society used culture as a mechanism for the refining of passion and the sublimation of instinctive human energies, through the agency of a central, patriarchal figure around which the family unit took shape.[78] This is particularly interesting when linked with Habermas's discussion of the slide of the 'patriarchal, conjugal family'[79] of the bourgeois type into a pseudo-private sphere, as it gradually lost its practical function as a mechanism for economic survival and security and a mode of socialization. When extended to include analyses of the behavioural pattern of the nation as a whole, rather than the smaller social groupings therein, this discursive framework often leads to the conclusion that Germany followed a *Sonderweg* or alternative route that set it apart from its contemporary European counterparts. In this context, Goethe and Schiller's pursuit of a national theatre that might present ethically inspired, individual action in a situation of stability and manageable dimensions may be seen as an attempt to stem the downward slide identified by Habermas. In this sense, their attempt to establish a national theatre might be understood, ironically enough, in terms of a general reaction on the part of the nation against popular revolution and liberal democracy.

There is little doubt that Germany clung to its feudal elites in the face of economic development much more stubbornly than its

European counterparts, but the testimony of writers such as Karl Marx makes it clear that by the 1840s the forces of social and political change were astir. The 1830s had already witnessed the rise of a German national movement and the institution of the *Zollverein*, a customs union aimed at facilitating trade and commerce amongst thirty-eight German states, excluding Austria. Goethe identified an even earlier point, 1805 (the close of his correspondence with Schiller) as the moment at which a new mode of self-cultivation became necessary.[80] His impression that the subsequent search for this new mode of being led to much miscultivation rings true but, by 1840, Marx was confident that the birth of the 'political movement of the middle class or bourgeoisie, in Germany' [81] indicated a new way forward. Tellingly, Marx linked this development with the appearance of the *Rheinische Gazette* of Cologne in 1842 – a date he pinpoints as the birth of the newspaper press in Germany.[82]

Marx's account of the requirements made of, and the resistance mounted to, the state by the Committee of Provincial Diets plots the gradual rise of a modern, anti-feudal representative constitution in Germany.[83] The demands made by this body on Frederick William IV of Prussia included a call for a parliament, a constitution and support for German unification but the contrasting claims of those faithful to the imperial crown of Prussia versus those who stood by the Habsburg crown of Vienna could not be resolved and in 1850 the Prussian ruler declared his own constitution. This move eventually led to Bismarck's instigation of a 'revolution from above'[84] that culminated in the establishment of the new German Empire in 1871. This union, initially under the leadership of the German Emperor, Wilhelm I of Prussia, (Bismarck and Wilhelm's interpretation of the emperor's function and status as head of this confederacy were fundamentally different) was always an uneasy marriage and one that according to Nicolaus Sombart 'never succeeded in overcoming the intrinsic difficulties of its geopolitical position'.[85] In *The Invention of Tradition*, Eric Hobsbawm argues that one of the main political challenges facing the Second German Reich was the need to provide it with historical legitimacy.[86] In this context, it may well strike the reader that Bismarck, or indeed Wilhelm I himself, might have used theatre, and specifically national theatre, to the achievement of this end. However, Sombart's claim that this loosely linked league of princes fashioned into a nation by Bismarck was culturally impoverished, suggests that this was not the case. It may well be no coincidence that the theatre's propensity for egalitarian interaction between audience and spectacle made it a particularly unpopular artistic medium in a period characterized by a Bismarckian antipathy towards democratic institutions of all kinds.

Some consideration of Georg Büchner's *Woyzeck* – one of the most widely known dramatic products of this period – manifests the difficulties of the relationship between art and politics in this period in the history of German national life. In his history of Germany, W. H. Carr refers to the unsettling influence of the Frankfurt incident of May 1833, when a small group of men stormed the guardhouse at Frankfurt with the intention of arming the public and declaring a republic.[87] This incident had no long-standing political repercussions but it is significant in that it describes one of Büchner's early forays into the world of revolutionary politics – an adventure separated by a short period from his writing of *Woyzeck*. In an earlier chapter, I discussed the problematic phenomenon of the divorce of the cultural institution of theatre from political life in France during the 1789 revolutionary period. This divorce was rationalized in terms of the revolutionaries' fear of mimesis and the value they placed on will as a direct and active agent in national life. Whilst *Woyzeck* was also inspired by revolutionary zeal, it does constitute an artistic response to the socio-political realities of German life. In fact, its particular significance lies in the unsettling manner in which it forges this link. *Woyzeck* depicts an irrational anti-hero whose subconscious plays havoc with his conscious self to the extent that his experiences make no recognizable dramatic or theatrical sense. The play is clearly far from typical, according to any criteria, national or other. In fact, its depiction of the dissolution of the rational mind, along with the reasonable, ordered society that might have sustained it, is particularly problematic in terms of the idea of a national, theatrical endeavour because it asserts the primacy of the unconscious in the constitution of both individual and collective experience – a factor that neither society nor theatre had been forced to reckon with hitherto. The play's disturbing vision of the human consciousness in chaos might well justify the cultural poverty of Bismarck's era, not only to

Bismarck himself, but to many others, irrespective of their social and political orientation.

In the previous chapter, Romain Rolland's Théâtre de la Révolution project was discussed in terms of an attempt to re-establish the link between theatrical representation and social reality. Rolland's aim was to create a theatrical experience that constituted an active memory of the revolution and promoted the success of the political revolution by means of a cultural one. In the second half of the nineteenth century in Germany, a similar challenge arose but a different solution was found: that solution came in the hugely successful and challenging form of Richard Wagner. Wagner, like Büchner, was convinced that only political revolution could clear the way for the art of the future and, by 1848, 'the revolutionary situation ... was to ... absorb his entire energy and commitment'.[88] Whilst Wagner might well be accused of shaping his political and philosophical views according to the dictates of his art, this can be justified by his conviction of the indestructible link between the two. He combined faith in the purity of the German soul, with a vision of social and political revolution as a prerequisite for artistic and spiritual regeneration. Whereas, some decades later, Rolland would regret the fact that France's political revolution was not followed up by a cultural revolution, Wagner sought to achieve this very synthesis in his contemporary Germany. Wagner's totalitarian vision of German art as derived from an organic theatrical unity to which all the separate elements 'should ... happily find their way back',[89] enabled him to evade the explicit and overt chaos of Büchner's artistic vision. This vision might also be understood as an artistic correlative for the geopolitical reality of the new German Reich of 1871.

Wagner was not a dramatist and his greatest artistic venture, the Bayreuth Festival,[90] did not constitute a national theatre per se. However, I think it is fair to argue that Wagner's overwhelming influence on Germany's cultural scene in the latter half of the nineteenth century can be meaningfully discussed in both theatrical and national terms. Ironically enough, Wagner found no support for his Bayreuth venture from either Bismarck or Wilhelm I, despite his intention that it should be a showcase for the national German spirit and a celebration of the German pursuit of truth and beauty in its own indigenous cultural heritage. In fact, Wagner's nationalist agenda came in for considerable criticism from figures such as Thomas Mann and Friedrich Engels who argued that his desire to make himself a central German voice was in itself un-German and that his artistic feats represented only an exuberant struggle towards unrestrained subjectivity.[91] Eduard Hanslick shared similar concerns because he felt that Wagner's was an art of superlatives and that a superlative has no future because it is not a beginning but an end.[92] The fact that Wagner's greatest support came from Ludwig II, King of Bavaria, who resolutely resisted Bismarck's attempts at national integration, might have posed a moral dilemma to a more conventionally conscientious artist. It does not appear to have been a problematic issue for Wagner, but it did perturb the Bavarian public. Early in 1867, an article appeared in the *Augsburger Allgemeine Zeitung* in which the king was urged to give up his costly alliance with the composer in the interests of the Bavarian public.[93] In a similar vein, the Munich paper *Der Volksbote*'s accusation that Wagner was trying to oust Pfistermeister, a government minister, confirms the fact that the public was as convinced as Wagner himself of the link between the artistic and political domains.[94]

Despite this resistance, Wagner pursued his aim with single-minded determination. He chose Bayreuth as the ideal location for the forthcoming festival, both in order to avoid the fashionable, spa-loving audiences he detested and because of its complete lack of a musical or literary tradition. By May 1871, he had announced that *Der Ring des Nibelungen* would materialize two years later.[95] His artistic mission had the appearance of an egalitarian and democratic affair in that it aimed to raise the necessary revenue of 30,000 by the issue of 1000 patronage certificates, at a cost of 300 thalers each, entitling attendance at the festival to their holders. Moreover, a chain of Wagner societies was established throughout the country, making it possible to buy a certificate in the name of the society via the subscription of its members.[96] Ludwig's private purse was called upon many a time to shore up the festival's finances and it was not until 22 May 1872, on Wagner's fifty-ninth birthday, that the foundation stone of his purpose-built festival theatre was finally laid.[97] However, whilst the festival – branded by Wagner as a monument to the German spirit – was a success on many fronts, the attendance of King Wilhelm I at the grand opening in 1876 was probably more in recognition of the power of Wagner's individual will and spirit as opposed to in celebration of a national, collective identity, either cultural or political. In fact, I would go so far as to propose that Wagner's musical drama hijacked the dramatic form and, in so doing, denied some of its most fundamental characteristics and prevented its development elsewhere in Germany at this time. Claude Debussy claimed that Wagner's superimposition of the symphonic form onto dramatic action killed opera.[98] Arguably, it did the same to drama, both within and without the Wagnerian opera house. Nietzsche felt that Wagner did for music what Victor Hugo did for language: he argued that the great composer recognized all the qualities of music, extracted them and developed them. However, he also admitted that this process inevitably destroyed the individual integrity of each distinct element. In an attack on the decadence of European culture, he proposes that 'poets in France have become sculptors, musicians in Germany have become actors and culturemongers – are these not signs of decadence?'[99] It is difficult to answer in the negative.

It was not until the turn of the twentieth century that an answer was made to the various calls for a German republic that had surfaced from time to time since Wagner's rallying cry of 1848. On November 9 1919 the socialist, Philip Scheidemann, declared a republic in a somewhat rushed attempt to scupper Karl Liebknecht's intention of establishing Germany as a soviet republic. Thus the republic came to Germany almost by default. This new political mission seemed to have been spawned by chaos and the antagonism with which it was received by a large part of the German public was scarcely tempered by the half-hearted welcome it received from others. In fact, the rational republicans – the so-called *Vernunftrepublikaner* – who accepted the principles upon which the republic was based, despite a lack of enthusiasm for its character and methods, populated a deactivated public sphere. In their experience, rational debate had led to a passive mode of reluctant acceptance, as opposed to a lively and enlivening means of self-discovery and definition. As far as the opponents of the republic were concerned, the idea of political parties was seen as divisive in comparison to the more unified, political tradition of the Bismarckian era. Even more significant, perhaps, was their innate resistance to and mistrust of the concept of the popular will. Ironically, a republican form of government based on the legitimization of the idea of a common will was faced with the monumental task of persuading the people of their need for democratic representation.

The political paradox at the heart of the Weimar Republic may well account for its vital importance as a centre of cultural expression and experimentation and, in particular, for the prominence of theatre in that process of cultural evolution. What the Weimar Republic failed to achieve on a political level it managed, to a greater extent, on an artistic level. Franz Neumann described the Weimar Republic in terms of an ideal based on the aspiration that antagonistic interests were to be harmonized by means of the device of a pluralistic, political structure, hidden behind the form of a parliamentary democracy.[100] However, he also noted a fundamental flaw in the Weimar vision: the fact that the reality of Weimar society was not harmonious and 'was a long way removed from the ideals of pluralism'.[101] The 1789 French Revolution was a political effort to overthrow a monarchical regime and establish a new democratic, political structure. In Weimar, culture itself was enlisted in the struggle over the political future of the German people. This phenomenon established the possibility that a national theatre might have provided a cultural forum for the correction of Weimar's central political fault because it might have provided another place in which the act of agreeing could have been undertaken.

In his study of Weimar culture, Larry Eugene Jones argues that the decision to launch the new republic from Weimar, the location of Germany's late eighteenth-century neo-classical revival, indicated its leaders' hopes of legitimizing their political endeavour through its association with the humanistic legacy of Goethe and Schiller.[102] The republic's constitution had been drafted according to the basic principle of compromise amongst all social and political groups. As soon as the republic had been officially declared, the Weimar theatre was suddenly baptised a national theatre. Operating from the premise of the nation members' equal rights to active participation in the democratic form of theatrical play, this new national theatre might well have appeared to be the ideal mechanism for the realization of the newly created republic's egalitarian aims. By virtue of its provision of meaningful aesthetic experience, it might even have provided a release for those who did not actively support the republic and were averse to the realities of life within Weimar's political structure. However, the fact that the proponents of the republic did not establish one central national theatre at Weimar, but rather declared that all the nation's theatres were national indicated one of the republic's main weaknesses: the fact that the act of agreeing was often substituted by the agreement itself.

In a discussion of the modern concept of citizenship, the historian Max Weber argues that the truly modern bourgeoisie or national citizen class came into being as a result of the development of capitalism within the closed nation state.[103] According to this line of thought, the desire for a national theatre in closed nation states can be explained by the need for mass representation or representation of the masses, in the context of western capitalism. If capitalism is understood as a system that caters for the material needs of the masses and, in so doing, implies that those needs are all identical, then it follows that national theatre could cater for the artistic needs of the masses on the same premise. Moreover, Weber claims that the political construction of capitalism and the artistic institution of theatre are particularly compatible because the dialectic form of theatre reflects the way in which the bourgeoisie came into being, as a result of dealings between state and capital in the context of economic survival. For Weber, freedom, creativity and personal responsibility did not lie outside the scope of this society. On the contrary, 'interpersonal relations, organizations, institutional structures, and the macrosocietal setting constituted the arena in which freedom, creativity, and responsibility could become manifest'.[104] Nonetheless, they also imposed severe limitations and constrictions on such creativity, thus creating the possibility of alienation, not only in the economic sphere but in all spheres of human relations. Despite the nominal national title afforded to all theatrical enterprises at Weimar, theatre there was often characterized by a sense of isolation and alienation, both from its own traditional methodologies and from the society in which it came to life. In my view, this phenomenon suggests that the internal tensions at the heart of the Weimar Republic were a manifestation of the difficulties arising from the rise of capitalism in modern society as a whole.

Despite Weimar's reputation as a centre of cultural vibrancy, it stood accused of lacking charisma and of possessing no symbols that might aid the consolidation of German identity in relation to the new republic. Walter Laqueur records the fact that Thomas Mann saw the potential in Weimar for the coexistence of politics and culture.[105] Even as he does so, he points to the absence of a Goethe/Schiller type interchange between its intellectuals. According to Lacqueur's assessment, no new channels of inter-personal communication had been discovered and no great, representative journal had emerged at Weimar. The most comprehensive, such as Efraim Frisch's *Neuer Merkur,* only had a circulation of 1,400 copies.[106] In this sense, the development of the liberal public sphere seemed to have come to a halt at the very point at which it might have been expected to discover its full strength. In a study of the way in which national monuments bolstered the sense of a German national identity during the Wilhelmine period, Rudy Koshar questions the idea of a nation as an imagined community by arguing that national imagination is often bolstered by material monuments. 'In the age of the modern national state', he argues, 'every part of the memory landscape, every moment of the social heritage, could be a national idea.'[107] In this context, he interprets Kaiser Wilhelm II's building of the Siegesallee in Berlin as a manifestation of his activist-political-cultural strategy. The nineteenth century, he says, was the age of the monument and the monuments were the products of a bourgeois public in that whilst they may well have served to glorify the national state, they also relied heavily on popular action both for their construction and for their subsequent appreciation.[108] Despite this claim, Koshar admits that the *Reichstag,* the seat of the German parliament, built between 1884 and 1894, did not manifest a typically national style. He argues that its status as a building that took the architecture of privilege and transformed it into a symbol of parliamentary government was severely tainted by Wilhelm II's refusal to allow the architect to put the words 'To the German People' on its gable.[109] If these were the symbols of Wilhelmine Germany, then the Weimar Republic might well be better off without any. Nonetheless, the expressive and manipulative power of national symbols in fixing and securing political allegiances was, and remains, inescapable. If the Weimar Republic was to be sure of success, it needed to establish itself as that kind of enduring *Heimat* symbol, identified by Alon Confino in his study of Württemburg's re-evaluation of the role of locality in the construction of national identity.[110]

The short lifespan of the Weimar republic made it particularly difficult for it to shed its feudal imagery in favour of a new, democratic image. However, there was a point in its history when it seemed that one of the creative minds of the Bauhaus school might provide a theatrical answer to the need for a charismatic symbol to play a creative role in the construction or evocation of national identity. Oscar Schlemmer – one of the Bauhaus's great designers – became obsessed with the idea that the German nation no longer had any symbols and, even worse, was incapable of creating any. In the face of this crisis, he proposed a theatre that would function as a national symbol by virtue of its structural ability to transform the mind. Schlemmer argued that the emblems of his time were mechanization, abstraction, technology and invention, and that theatre must take account of these.[111] It should, he was convinced, be an image of our time and was the one art form most peculiarly conditioned by those times. He perceived of the stage as the union of the most heterogeneous assortment of creative elements and thought that one of its main functions was to serve man's metaphysical needs by constructing a world of illusion that aspired to the transcendental on the basis of the rational.[112] This vision of theatre casts new light on the traditional importance of the rational in German political ideology in that it identifies unjustified theatrical play as a means of discovering comprehensive meaning. Whilst Schlemmer's work placed him outside mainstream theatre, he did talk of the national and native quality of his and his students' work. On the other hand, his dedication to that 'which is universally valid for the creative theater'[113] took his theatrical mission beyond the usual confines of national theatre. Whilst this may actually constitute its national significance, it also curtailed the scope of its appeal and the extent to which had Schlemmer wished to make such an assertion, it could claim to be representative of a national spirit.

In his analysis of Weimar culture, Lacqueur talks of a great break in the German cultural tradition as the country was introduced to a futurist, avant-garde manifesto, at the turn of the twentieth century. He sees the German public's relationship to futurist art as one of distrust and disbelief and suspects that the German public thought modernist art might well be a 'huge joke'.[114] Evidently, the coherence of the German, liberal public sphere had been undermined to such an extent, by this particular point in time, that it was as much a forum for opposition as it was for rational discussion. In this sense, the declamatory and oppositional nature of the public sphere in early twentieth-century Germany mirrored the party system that structured the republic's political environment. Clearly, the modernist movement in German theatre was not the exclusive locus of idiosyncratic and irrational modes of theatrical play such as expressionism and Dadaism. There were the naturalist plays of Hauptmann that were a direct representation of social realities, although they did not always centre on contemporary social issues, and Brecht's experimental 'total' theatre that asked the audience to adopt a critical and constructive attitude towards the realities and challenges of their economic and social environs. Neverthless, Lacqueur argues that even Hauptmann was characterized by an 'olympian detachment'[115] characteristic of Weimar society.

This detachment is clearly identifiable in German expressionist theatre's reliance on the self as the source of both its thematic material and its formal methodology and in its irreverence for external social norms and values. This type of theatre, championed by the likes of Leopold Jessner in the Staatliche Schauspielhaus in Berlin is defined by George Lukács as a movement hesitating between proletarian revolution and bourgeois reformism.[116] This description throws interesting light on Kaiser's presentation of the disaster that follows bourgeois revolt in *From Morn to Midnight*. It is also insightful when applied to an analysis of expressionist theatre in general, in that it suggests reasons for both its failures and its successes. The life and energy of German expressionist theatre fails to conceal an underlying experience of isolation and forlornness. This phenomenon, typical of German society in the 1920s, is described by Nietzsche as 'the perplexity of the multitude of persons who remain unfulfilled'.[117] Clearly, the artistic impulse driving this particular manifestation of German theatre forward is not one that lends itself to ideas of coherent national units, artistic or otherwise. National theatre was unlikely in a situation where communal action was neither a fictional nor a real possibility.

The voice of expressionism was not the only one heard in Weimar Germany. There were other prominent theatrical enterprises that promoted different values and sought to generate an experience of communal identity and shared experience. Max Reinhardt was dedicated to a communal theatre much more akin to ideas of national theatre. He broke with the traditions of court theatre, staged mass scenes, brought more of everything to the stage and dismantled the barrier between stage and audience that 'had been as sacrosanct as the frontiers between nation states'.[118] According to Yvonne Schafer, Reinhardt first put the vacant market that was home to the Großes Schauspielhaus to use as a theatre in 1919, in order to realize his vision of 'a great theatre without loges and balconies ... no court theatre, no peep-hole theatre, rather a theatre for the masses'.[119] A place of free trade and commerce was thus transformed into a forum for the exchange of artistic ideas and experiences, aimed at the nation as a whole, the masses themselves. Reinhardt's efforts, however, were ended by the advent of the Second World War and the rise of Nazism. His surrender of his theatres to the German nation in 1933 provided a final indication of his vision of his theatrical art in terms of an endeavour towards the common and the communal.

Erwin Piscator was another theatrical entrepreneur who sought to activate the proletariat and bring the people to the theatre. But despite having the backing of the Communist party, he never really succeeded in his aim of getting the workers into the theatre. It may well have been Ernst Toller who came closest, if not to the establishment of a national theatre, then at least to the expression of nationally felt concerns and truths. Stephen Lamb reads *Hoppla, wir leben!* as evidence of Toller's conviction that the establishment of a political supra-structure of parliamentary democracy could never provide a guarantee of personal freedom unless it was accompanied by a 'planned organisation of production and consumption according to the needs of the community'.[120] All Toller's characters, he continues, 'seem deprived of the feeling of an active and autonomous membership of a community'.[121] Whilst a national theatre might well have had the potential to fill this lacuna, at least on an artistic level, in the absence of any such central, artistic institution what is reflected in Toller's drama in particular, and in Weimar theatre in general, is the republic's failure to achieve a democratic process of debate, decision and representation that might have driven the nation onwards towards a definitive sense of belonging and a confidence in its own national identity.

It may be fair to argue that the nominal nationalization of theatre at Weimar was an example of the invasion of the theatrical space by political forces and amounted to much the same thing as Hitler's hijacking of theatrical form for more overtly political purposes later on. Clearly, the results were spectacularly different when Hitler commanded the theatrical space. In the introduction to this book, I discussed Hitler's terrifyingly effective manipulation of the theatrical space and the theatrical event itself, placing his own image and his political ideology centre-stage in a communal experience that both elated and anaesthetized its participants. In this context, it is of interest to note Louis Snyder's comments regarding the Lustiania medal in his discussion of the roots of German nationalism. He tells of how these medals were collected and exchanged by Germans much like football or cigarette cards. Their aim was a light-hearted kind of political critique and Snyder describes one that commented on Hitler's putsch of 8 November 1923. On the reverse of the medal, the Feldherrnhalle was represented as a 'stage setting across the top of which was the inscription *Münchner Theater*'.[122] Snyder does not comment on this theatrical interpretation of political events, but it might well have been an early indication of the theatricality of the Nazi vision and the manner in which theatre would lose its own inherent nature by becoming a forum for political rather than artistic articulation and experiment.

In the foreword, I discussed both the effectiveness and the perverseness of the national theatrical forum of Nuremberg. Rather than covering this ground again, I will take a look at the effect of Nazism on the traditional theatrical scene in Germany at this time. When Goebbels launched the first National Theatre Festival at Dresden in 1934, the Nazi administration had already set up a central bureaucracy for the regulation of national arts with Goebbels as head of 'Ministry for Popular Enlightenment and Propaganda'.[123] Ten days before the first national social festival at Dresden, he introduced the Unified Theatre Law, designed to assure his control over the 20 per cent of independent theatres that were not subsidized by the state.[124] Henceforth all performance spaces were German and therefore national. The control of Germany's theatre was considered a factor of vital importance by the Nazi administration. Both Goebbels and Göring were fully aware of the manipulative potential of theatrical spectacle and they vied for supremacy in their control of both the former Großes Schauschpielhaus and the Staatstheater.[125] In January 1934, the Staatstheater was renamed the Theater des Volkes – a national theatre, home to a national company, the Theater der Nation. The Theater des Volkes opened on January 18 1934 with a production of Schiller's famous national classic, *Die Räuber*.[126] According to Thomas Mann, the German attitude toward theatre, and national theatre in particular, had been characterized since the time of Schiller by an innate respect for its educative and enlightening powers. Now it was being put to its most unscrupulous use yet.

Hitler's aim of nationalizing the masses achieved stunning embodiment, not only in Nuremberg but in the nation's other theatres. However, Hitler was not intent on discovering the German nation's inherent identity, but rather on moulding the people into a nation, or rather a nationalized group. The German people were to come to an awareness of themselves, not as a collection of individuals, united by a common cause or spirit, but as 'unified "Volk" tied together by traditions sanctified by blood'.[127] The emphasis was not on revolution, but on opting into a community, informed by eternal German values. Hitler characterized the masses as lacking in intellect, but possessing 'faith ... persistence ... stability'.[128] Nazi ideas of the *Volk* were derived in the main from the work of thinkers such as de Lagarde, Langbehn and Moeller. George Mosse argues that de Lagarde and Langbehn developed an ideological system in which concepts of religion, national creativity and education fostered a positive identification of the individual with a collective enterprise in which the *Volk* took centre stage.[129] Ernst Wachler, he claims, was instrumental in introducing a theatrical form that had close links with this ideology – the open air theatre in the forest. Wachler's goal was to construct a modernized version of the meeting place where the ancient Germans had worshipped at their religious shrines and from whence they had administered their laws. According to his vision, *Volk* plays would be performed in natural surroundings that evoked an aura of the past. He embodied this idea in 1907, when he founded the mountain theatre in the Harz, described by Mosse as one of the first serious attempts to 'objectify the ideological by means of the visual arts'.[130] National Socialism, he argues, adopted Wachler's ideas on a grander scale.

Goebbels had inherited two of Reinhardt's theatres and it is ironic to note the similarities between his ideal for the theatre and that of his Jewish predecessor. Reinhardt rejoiced when he felt that the 'masses began to participate ... theatre was reality for them, and soon it no longer was stage against auditorium, rather a *single* great auditorium, a *single* battleground, a *single* great demonstration ... evidence of the power of agitation of political theatre'.[131] Goebbels shared the same elation for different reasons: his overall aim was to use the theatre to control the leisure time of workers. Robert Ley, who headed the Strength through Joy organization that was part of the German Labour Front (GLF), declared that concern for 'the care of the German people at the workplace, after hours, in their free time, at home, and in the family is the highest goal of the GLF'.[132] In other words, the Nazi regime aimed to infiltrate all spheres of human activity and interaction in order to condition the kind of public sphere that might emerge were matters left to follow their natural course. The GLF aspired to the connection of all spheres of human activity so that people recognized the link between work, income and leisure. This might well be a step backward in Habermasian terms (historically anyway), but it was one that led to a greater coherence of experience, both individual and social. As a result, the establishment of artistic fora did not become a means of generating rational, independent debate amongst equals, but of reinforcing mass beliefs that permeated all aspects of German life. The opening night of the Theater des Volkes was free to all and it soon became the people's theatrical home. In a review of a performance of Goethe's *Götz von Berlichingen,* a reporter exclaimed, 'here is the storm of revolution, here wave the flags of awakened peoples, and here a Germany is dreamed of, which will be great and free'.[133] The divergence between Goethe's benign expression of national pride in this historical play, a product of the *Sturm und Drang* period, and the national vision that it was called upon to advocate in twentieth-century Germany provides a prime example of the manipulation of an artistic product in the service of alien and, in this case, alarming ideals.

According to R. A. Pois, the 'nationalisation of aesthetics'[134] was a Nazi motto. Art, he argued, at least in as far as it was defined by the vital human characteristic of creativity, disappeared into politics and 'conventional, political life had been transformed into aesthetics, theatre in particular'.[135] I would agree with this assessment but go on to argue that theatre lost out in this transition and became other than theatre. Nazi theatre did not employ artistic articulation as a means of discovering, corroborating and empowering a specific national identity, but rather dedicated its attention to the task of inventing a nation by means of an artistic process that, ultimately, lost its artifice because it was no longer representing, but being.

It might have been expected that Hitler's defeat by the Allies in 1945 would bring theatrical activity in Germany to an abrupt halt. It is easy to understand why a country that had brought shame upon itself by its adherence to a programme of extreme ethnic cleansing in the name of National Socialism would subsequently shy away from the very idea of national identity and would not pursue the theatrical correlative to nationhood provided by the phenomenon of national theatre. Furthermore the action taken by the Allies in response to the German defeat deliberately destroyed the country's physical and ideological unity. Defeated Germany lost its core and its future history was characterized by division rather than unity. Berlin, the country's pre-war capital, was carved into four sectors divided between the European allies and America in the west and Soviet Union in the east. As Michael Patterson points out, post-war Germany had no 'theatre capital'.[136] This decentralization and division was compounded in spectacular fashion when on May 24 1949, the Federal German Republic was founded and on October 7 1949, its east German counterpart, the German Democratic Republic, was declared. German national unity had reverted to its pre-1871 state of diversity and division and the stringent restrictions governing east/west German traffic that culminated in the closing of the Brandenburg gate in August 1961, in response to the flight of more than two million Germans from the east to the west, symbolized the ultimate fragmentation of the mid-twentieth-century German nation. Both the nation's own legacy of guilt and the conquering forces' paranoid attitude to the German past and future conspired to make a unified German nation and a central German national theatre that might represent that nation a thing of the past.

However, German theatre in general was not in decline. Peter Fischer notes that the war seemed to have whetted the German appetite for theatre of any kind and calibre, so much so that outside observers were 'struck by the phenomenon of a totally ruined nation flocking to see shows within months of the collapse of 1945'.[137] Critics agree that this theatre had little intrinsic worth and made no real attempt to deal meaningfully with the post-war German experience, either in the east or the west.[138] Despite the fact that east and west German theatre was heavily subsidized – by 1968, 165 German theatres were subsidised by the different German authorities to the tune of £35 million per annum – it was felt that the new civic theatre buildings built in this period served only to underpin the 'theatre-makers' terrible harmlessness, immutability and lack of imagination'.[139]

This situation gradually changed under influential German directors such as Bertolt Brecht, who founded the east Berlin Deutsche Schaubühne in 1962, and Peter Stein, who made an equal success of the West Berlin Schaubühne founded in 1970. In fact, despite the geographical straightjacket that separated east and west Germany, making it physically impossible for any one German theatre to serve the populace as a whole, the nature of the theatrical mission aspired to and indeed achieved by Brecht's Deutsche Schaubühne gave it some national significance or, at the very least, the potential for national significance, under a different set of national conditions. Brecht, one of the most influential of all European theatre directors, strove to ensure that his theatre might 'uncover the elements of crisis, of that which is problematical, rich in conflicts within this new life, else how can we ever show what is creative in it?'[140] This mission was continued by his successor Manfred Wekwerth who declared that 'the working class and their allies are building a new society. It is one of the purposes of our performances, one defined by Brecht, to enable the people of this German state to master the new, complicated reality with the aid of artistic means.'[141] The responsive and responsible relationship between this theatre and its public gave it a social significance, akin to that of national theatre, despite the fact that its physical environment confined its influence to a sector of German society and therefore precluded the application of the term national, in its usual sense, to the theatre.

In 1990 the democratic revolution that led to the reunification of Germany brought down the Berlin wall – the most prominent symbol of the ideological divide between east and west Germany

– and restored Germany as a nation. The German national theatre has not, to date, been given an equivalent new impetus and lease of life. It would be difficult to contest the 'undoubted splendour'[142] of modern German theatre but the 'complex double past of newly reunified Germany'[143] has not led to the emergence of a central national theatre representative of the artistic aspirations and activity of the nation as a whole. Siobhan Kattago argues that all the places of reunified German memory, the nation's *lieux de mémoire,* such as the Neue Wache, are problematized because they underline the diverse and different histories of a nation, divided by several distinct yet interrelated pasts. She asks which past is the more primary for reunified German national identity, 1945 or 1989 – 'National Socialism or the democratic/national moment of reunification?'[144] A German national theatre has yet to answer this question and the terms of debate in papers such as *Die Zeit* that ask whether the selection policy of Berlin's cultural senator Thomas, with regard to directorships of Berlin theatres, is driven by a desire to implicate an East/Western split in German theatre or, conversely, by the desire to bring together that which belongs together,[145] suggests that a new journey of national theatrical discovery may have only just begun.

~ 3 ~

The English national theatre: O brave new world, That has such people in't[1]

In France, a national theatre was set up as an agent of monarchical power. Subsequently, it underwent a transformation that reflected the development of the new liberal public sphere, itself a product of the transition from a medieval to a modern western European society. The campaign to establish a German national theatre began later than in France, at the point at which the new liberal sphere first began to emerge. Its ensuing history ran parallel to the development and the eventual deterioration of that sphere under increasing pressure from the 'weakening of the forces of social bonding, privatization, and diremption'[2] that have, according to Habermas, characterized the discourse of modernity since the close of the eighteenth century. What sets England apart in terms of the pattern established in France and Germany is the fact that the national theatre campaign did not see the light of day until the turn of the twentieth century. Ironically, England set about establishing its national theatre – a potential locus for the creative interaction of the nation as a whole – as the liberal, public sphere was giving way under rising pressure from capitalism, commercialism and individualism.

The lateness of the campaign to establish an English national theatre should not be taken as evidence of the nation's inability or unwillingness to participate in the development of the liberal public sphere. Eric Evans argues persuasively that the 'extensive politicisation of urban Britain',[3] once deemed to have taken place at the very end of the eighteenth century and only within a narrow social context, actually occurred from the 1730s onwards and embraced a wide proportion of the population. His impression that urban and provincial coffee-houses did for the well-off what 'public houses increasingly did for the craftsmen, small master manufacturers, skilled workers and even apprentices'[4] corresponds to Habermas's account of private individuals coming together as a body to debate, exchange and, most importantly, validate common values and concepts. Nonetheless, the overwhelming sense of belatedness that characterized the English national theatre campaign does point up some of the specific difficulties with which the country was faced in its efforts to establish and maintain this sphere – difficulties that arose not from the nature of English national life and experience in particular, but rather from the challenging nature of the idea of a new liberal public sphere in itself.

Postmodernist critics of Habermas, such as Jean François Lyotard, have argued that the concept of a potential consensus, shared by a 'self-corrective critical community of enquirers'[5] is outdated, rooted in a tradition of social philosophy that stretches back to the Enlightenment. Whereas Habermas's work might be thought of, in very general terms, as an effort to create a science of society, Lyotard rejects both the truth of scientific knowledge and the possibility, or indeed the desirability, of the idea that society might function according to a Habermasian formula of egalitarian collectivism. Habermas's work constructs a useful ideological framework from which social progress can be analysed, but there can be little doubt that the concept of a new liberal public sphere was, in fact, so idealistic that it was never fully realized in practical terms. In the context of the present discussion, this element of idealism is not problematical. On the contrary, it enriches analysis of a cultural medium that celebrates its own virtuality and the virtuality of the life it presents and represents. That is not to say that the difficulties with which the construction of the new liberal public sphere was fraught do not emerge in the course of this discussion. Invariably, they do.

In France, the challenges of ensuring democratic and egalitarian social participation were faced in spectacular and alarming fashion in the 1789 revolution. The aspiration towards social change that inspired republican France and propelled the revolution forward was mirrored in the transformation of the Comédie-Française from an agent of monarchical power to a theatre of the people. The shortcomings of both the revolution and the new or revised national theatre have been discussed elsewhere but the point here is that the 1789 revolution brought about sudden and widespread social change that, however short-lived, permeated many different levels and aspects of society. In England, by contrast, the mechanisms of political power that facilitated the nation's effort to fashion a coherent, political identity militated against the drive towards democratic and egalitarian participation in the new liberal public sphere. As a result, whilst some sections of the English populace developed distinct identities, claimed equal rights and entered into dialogue with each other, others fell by the wayside.

In eighteenth-century England, the middle classes had no direct input into or involvement with the power structures of English society. G. E. Aylmer argues that one of the most striking characteristics of the state in eighteenth-century England was the lack of a local bureaucracy to support the English crown. He maintains that most of the general administration at the local level was undertaken by landowners under loose central direction, giving rise to the curious phrase 'self-government by the king's command.'[6] The opportunity to address this imbalance presented itself when the so-called self-government by the king's command eventually broke down under pressure from growing urbanization and changes in economic and social life. The dawn of the era of ministerial government provided hope for a more equitable representation of the nation in and through the structures of political power. In the event, this hope was largely a false one. In his *Constitutional History of (Medieval) England* (3 vols, 1874–1878), William Stubbs voiced his conviction that the English parliament had always functioned, since its inception in 1295, as a political instrument designed to establish and maintain parliamentary democracy. The anti-Stubbsian school contested this view, claiming that parliament was, initially at least, a judicial instrument, 'a body destined by the monarchy to facilitate the exercise of royal justice'.[7] This debate broadened out to consider related issues such as the question of the power and influence of the Commons: considerable according to Stubbs' evaluation, but negligible according to later assessments.

In the light of this discussion, it is interesting to note Aylmer's impression that the composition of parliament and in particular its House of Commons at the turn of the eighteenth century, the point at which it eventually established continuous session and became a central force in British life, was visibly problematic. Aylmer argues that, despite the fact that the House of Commons was clearly intended to provide a forum of expression and articulation for the constituents of the new public sphere, it was actually made up of landowners and their representatives, as opposed to common citizens. It was this factor, he claims, that occasioned a reversion to old patterns of landowner superiority both in social and political terms.[8] This curious situation may well account for George Orwell's impression that most generalizations made about England 'base themselves on the property-owning class and ignore the other forty-five million.'[9]

In France, the close link between the nation's political and cultural experiences and aspirations tied art and artistic institutions, such as the Comédie-Française, to the ebb and flow of political events in the country. As we have seen France's national theatre began its history as an agent of monarchical power; later, in the revolutionary period, its nature and status mirrored republican social and political aspirations. In turn, its demise (albeit temporary) coincided with the fall of the republic itself. This alliance of culture and politics gave the Comédie-Française formidable status and influence at several points in its history. At the same time, it also denied the national theatre an opportunity to carve out an independent existence that would enable it to formulate its own relations with the nation by artistic means and solely in artistic terms. The German national theatre avoided the spectre of centralization to a much greater extent than its French counterpart. However, this freedom came at a price – the fact that the establishment and development of a German national theatre took place outside any coherent social, political and cultural framework relegated it to a peripheral position in the life of the German nation. In Germany social change was not powered from the centre, either autocratically or democratically, until Bismarck's establishment of a nation state in 1871, a point at which Bismarck's own priorities and policy subdued democratic institutions of all kinds, including Germany's national theatre itself. Despite these drawbacks, there can be no doubt that the campaigns to establish and sustain national theatres in France and Germany were driven and shaped by both countries' responses to the stimuli provided by the development of a new liberal public sphere that was gaining ground throughout Europe from the close of the seventeenth century onwards. By contrast, eighteenth-century England was far behind both its French and German counterparts in theatrical terms because it did not even begin to address the issue of the importance of a national theatre to the English nation until the turn of the twentieth century. Thereafter, the painful slowness of the campaign continued a tradition of tardiness that reached embarrassing proportions. Lord Esher's pronouncement in 1955, shortly before the long-awaited realization of the English National Theatre project, summed up the sense of frustration and excitement that would finally end the theatre's long pre-history: 'at long last, after years of gestation, enough to put an elephant to shame, the National Theatre is about to be born'.[10]

By the twentieth century, the English middle-class had finally found its voice and sought to exercise it in an exploration of the dynamics of its national culture. The national theatre campaign in England marked the point at which the English middle classes adopted a point of view and deliberately sought a way of opening up an arena in which egalitarian and democratic public participation could be both fostered and exhibited. The deterioration of the liberal public sphere meant that there was no longer any designated place in which they might articulate their common fears, concerns and aspirations. As a result, and with considerable ingenuity, the English middle classes reactivated the rational, egalitarian debate from which they had been excluded in the real world in the fictitious arena of the national theatre. The very fact that the difficulties with which the construction and maintenance of the new liberal sphere were fraught manifest themselves most spectacularly in negative artistic terms – in the conspicuous absence of an English national theatre – actually meant that the positive resolution of that deficiency had a more conclusive effect than that produced by similar achievements in both France and Germany.

There can be little doubt that the call for a national theatre in England did not come from the property-owning classes, but from another section of English society – the middle classes: educated people who had discovered new roles and voices for themselves in economic and social terms, people like William Archer, George Bernard Shaw, Henry Arthur Jones and Harley Granville Barker. The phrase 'the middle classes' was first introduced as the principal descriptor for social position in Britain in the mid eighteenth century and had become firmly entrenched in this role by the mid nineteenth century. However, as the century progressed, the term came under review as the move from economic to cultural determinism changed received ideas about modes of understanding and representing class. As Kidd and Nicholls argue, by the twentieth century the middle class was 'stratified, with enormous differentials in power and influence, income and status, between the *haute bourgeoisie* at one extreme and the *petite bourgeoisie* at the other'.[11] It may well be appropriate to describe those who issued the call for a national theatre as representatives of one of the many intermediate groups 'spawned by economic growth, attached to and dependent upon capitalism, but at some distance from real power beyond the capacity to trade in ideas, their greatest source of influence'.[12] As such, they could no more claim to represent the collective will of the nation any more than that of the middle classes themselves and Loren Kruger was right to claim that, from 'Effingham Wilson and Matthew Arnold in the nineteenth century to William Archer ... and others in the twentieth, we can see the tension between the idealist image of the reconciled nation and their sense that the people are simply not with them'.[13]

What then is the importance of this call in the context of the English middle classes and beyond that, the English nation at large? In his study *Imagining the Middle Class* (2003), Dror Wahrman argues for a degree of freedom in the space between social reality and its representation. On the basis of an acceptance of the principle of the existence of space between any given historical reality and its representation, he makes a plea for the acceptance of a multiplicity of interpretations in the ongoing debate about the nature and significance of class in Britain. I would argue that the supremacy of this principle in the theatre ensures that the tensions with which the history of the national theatre in England is peppered – the problematical notions of class and nation being two of the most obvious – render it more, rather than less, significant in terms of the cultural development of the nation as a whole. In the theatre, the space between any given reality and its representation can be realized in physical terms that are ideologically and physically fluid and expansive, yet nonetheless concretely experienced. Thus the theatrical space allows for the construction of knowledge that relies on the coexistence and interactivity of the subjective and the objective – a kind of intrepid but indeterminate knowledge that justifies the practice of national theatre as a creative and constructive mode of imagining the nation.

The paradoxical combination of apathy and enthusiasm that characterized the onset of the English national theatre campaign foreshadows the sense of tension that persisted throughout its subsequent history. On the one hand, there was despair and indignation at the perception of a national apathy towards the idea of a national theatre. Bernard Shaw's wry comment on the fact that the English people demonstrated quite a singular absence of will suggests that they lacked the active energy identified by Keith Springer as an essential component in the making of a 'national community'.[14] With his usual perspicacity and wit, Shaw asked:

> Do the English people want a national theatre? Of course they do not. They never want anything. They have got the British Museum, the National Gallery and Westminster Abbey, but they never wanted them. But once these things stood as mysterious phenomena that had come to them they were quite proud of them, and felt that the place would be incomplete without them.[15]

On the other hand, there was a core of committed and fervent workers in the cause of a national theatre who, like Henry Jones, were convinced that the indifference of the great English public would enable them to be gradually 'led out to take an interest in drama that can be worthily called a national art'[16] – the kind of drama that would merit a national theatre as its stage. The fact that this objective was eventually attained should not be taken as evidence of a national consensus at any point in the campaign's history, but it did introduce the possibility of a national coming together of theatre makers and theatre goers and, at the most basic level, the acceptance of an artistic addition to the English national institutional repertoire, countenanced in much the same spirit of quiet acceptance as that described by Shaw above.

The campaign, however, did have other attributes. First, there was the desire to commemorate past literary and theatrical achievements (primarily those of Shakespeare) on behalf of the English-speaking world and in so doing to use past achievement as an example and stimulus for new creative expression. Secondly, there was the desire to establish a new order in the administrative and practical workings of the theatre itself in order to escape the iron grasp of commercialism and the ghastly spectre of a theatre, 'without organisation, or purpose, or dignity'.[17] This vision, most ardently articulated by Matthew Arnold but shared by many others, also involved the more complex idea that a national theatre could order the relations between England and its new global environment by means of its positive orientation in the context of the world at large.

Alfred Emmet traces the movement for the establishment of England's National Theatre back as far as 1769, when the staging of David Garrick's Shakespeare Jubilee gave concrete form to a Shakespeare cult that was to inform much of the thinking regarding drama and the theatre in England and indeed ideas of Englishness for years to come.[18] The prominence of individual charisma and personality at the centre of an essentially national campaign suggests that the national community was expressing itself, at this early stage at least, through the medium of its theatrical celebrities. Whilst I would not suggest that Garrick launched his 1769 Shakespeare Jubilee as part of a deliberate effort to formulate ideas of English nationality and nationhood, his use of his own popularity in an attempt to widen Shakespeare's renown was clearly an effort to formulate a national standard, in both senses of the word. If we recall Otto Bauer's understanding of nationality as a mode of being based on a balanced relationship between the individual's inner self and the external world, it may seem rational that the movement towards national theatrical expression in England begins with one so successful at communicating his own way of being to his fellows. Indeed, whilst the flair, flamboyance and magnetism of characters such as Shakespeare and Garrick may not be typical of the English nation as a whole,[19] the susceptibility of the English spirit to the theatrical art, 'the passion for certain pieces and for certain actors',[20] manifest in their positive response both to Shakespeare and to Garrick himself may well be indicative of an underlying spirit of artistic adventure in the nation as a whole.

Henry Arthur Jones investigates the lure of flamboyant, fictitious characters on the imagination of the British public when he comments on the way in which the public imagination was captured by the Dickensian dissenting ministers, Chadband and Stiggins. He describes them as 'extravagant caricatures' capturing the essence of dissent 'in full and unchecked sway'.[21] George Eliot's portrayal of Reverend Rufus Lyon in *Felix Holt* is, he argues, a much more realistic portrait, yet Rufus Lyon has no great hold on the popular imagination. Jones asks whether the public instinct is wrong to seize on these outrageous caricatures and make them 'types and symbols of English dissent throughout the English race?'[22] He immediately follows up this question with a declaration that it is, in fact, a proper impulse.

Both Dickens's and Eliot's characters came to life in the narrative form of the novel, but Bernard Shaw claims that the stage is by far the most effective and efficient means of 'exhibiting examples of personal conduct made intelligible and moving to crowds of unobservant, unreflecting people to whom real life means nothing'.[23] Shaw's reference to an unobservant and unreflecting people lends credence to the impression held by some commentators that the English nation is characterized by a certain apathy or absence of will. J. H. Shennan claims that the nation defines itself negatively as opposed to positively when he argues that by the close of the eighteenth century Englishmen 'may not have known what they were for, but they were aware of what they were against',[24] namely the values of the French Revolution and the threat from radical elements within Britain itself. This viewpoint supports William Archer's assessment of the English national character as the main obstacle to the development of the English drama. He lays the blame squarely at the door of the English character:

> the main difficulty lies, not in any external conditions, but in the national character, with its instinctive shrinking from anything that savours of idealism ... The imagination of the average man – even of the average literary man – is very slow to take fire. His instinct is to suggest and exaggerate difficulties, instead of resolving to overcome them.[25]

Matthew Arnold's comment regarding the absence of any modern English drama highlights a similar deficiency – the lack of a common purpose typically associated with the concept of a public voice. He considers contemporary English society to be too diverse and fragmented to generate a body of representative dramatic literature. It lacks, in his view, a 'common view of life, a common ideal, capable of serving as basis for a modern English drama'.[26] However, Shaw is not focusing here on the inertia of the English public but rather highlighting the fact that the harsh realities of human life and endeavour tend to obstruct the process by which observation leads to reflection. The same point is made more explicitly by Henry Arthur Jones in his discussion of the positive potential of a national drama and theatre to 'create a daily beauty instead of a daily ugliness' [27] in the lives of the millions of ordinary English folk leading drab, monotonous existences in unhealthy and undignified working and living conditions.

The theatricality of dramatic presentation clearly substitutes recognition for reflection thereby facilitating the acknowledgement of types that then come to characterize national trends and tendencies. The ease with which the popular imagination seizes upon type – whether in the form of a Garrick, a Shakespeare or a Chadband – was exploited by Garrick himself at his Shakespeare Jubilee. Subsequent advocates for an English national theatre became aware of the temptation presented to the actor by this phenomenon. Apprehension concerning the possibility that an actor or actress hungry for public recognition might become and remain a type may have been grounds for a certain tendency towards elitism in the national theatre campaign. The awesome and authoritarian figure of the French *vedette* may well justify such fears. However, these factors were addressed squarely in the public discussion and debate surrounding the campaign and I will return to them later.

In 1848, a radical London bookseller, Effingham Wilson, published a pamphlet calling for the establishment of a house for Shakespeare 'in public ownership'.[28] This publication marks a distinctive point in the national theatre campaign because it is the first declaration of the existence of the English public as a concrete and entitled body, capable and desirous of entering the national property market. The circulation of a pamphlet assumes that there is at large a reading public who are both informed about and interested in the affairs of the day, at a national level. Moreover, the instigation of a rational and informed debate about national issues via the cultural media is clearly quite different from earlier attempts to call the popular imagination to the service of national aims. There had been press interest in matters of the theatre prior to this. The likes of Edmund Kean had graced the columns of *The Times* where he stood accused of representing that class of actor 'too beastly in their behaviour, when off the stage, to be tolerated and applauded on it'.[29] This attack on Kean in the press is interesting, not only because it makes for sensational reading, but because it provides evidence of an early attempt to invoke national standards of behaviour in the press. *The Times* reporter's public criticism of Kean's personal conduct in a private matter highlights the link between the real and the staged life of actors and actresses and is an implicit recognition of the extent of their influence on the public.

Wilson's pamphlet is more significant because it makes a formal, direct appeal to the reading public, not on the back of sensationalism but in the name of common, national interests. Wilson's call, however, was not the first move towards the establishment of a national theatre. In fact, a Shakespeare Committee had used the occasion of their purchase of Shakespeare's birthplace for the nation in 1847 as an opportunity to call for a national theatre.[30] I will return to a discussion of the idea and actuality of the committee in the history of the English national theatre at a later point and I think we will discover therein some of the most striking characteristics of English national life and spirit.

James Woodfield's argument that the campaign to abolish censorship of plays went hand in hand with the drive to establish a national theatre deepens the impression that the campaign was motivated by a desire to instigate rational, egalitarian participation in a communal enterprise. The struggle to free dramatists from the censorious grasp of the Lord Chamberlain and the endeavour to establish a national theatre that would not only find access to an eager public at home but negotiate between that public and other, foreign nationalities demonstrate a common desire to do away with authoritarian interference and carve out an autonomous space for identity articulation. The Licensing Act brought into official being by Walpole in 1737 was clearly contrary to the principle of democratic debate in that all authority was invested in the Lord Chamberlain, who was held to embody public opinion. This viewpoint was put very effectively by Lord Chesterfield's argument both for the expressive power of drama and for the impropriety of absolute authority in any sphere when the matter was debated in parliament. He argued:

> If Poets and Players are to be restrained, let them be restrained as other Subjects are, by the known Laws of their Country; if they offend, let them be tried as every Englishman ought to be, by God, and their

Country. Do not let us subject them to the arbitrary Will and Pleasure of any one Man. A Power lodged in the hands of one single Man, to judge and determine, without any Limitation, without any Controul or Appeal, is a sort of power unknown to our Laws, inconsistent with our Constitution. It is a higher, a more absolute Power than we trust even to the King himself; and therefore ... we ought not to vest any such Power in His Majesty's Lord Chamberlain.[31]

The lack of support for Lord Chesterfield and the ease with which the bill passed into law may well call to mind Orwell's comment on the Englishman's rather excessive respect for the law. When we consider that the censorship laws had been activated as a result of Walpole's desire to silence a satiric attack on his regime by Henry Fielding and furthermore when we note that Viscount Henry Bolingbroke's opposition campaign against the Whig prime minister focused on the claim that the monarch could no longer *ipso facto* symbolize the nation and therefore that one could argue the country was above the king, it is evident that the balance of power in England was coming under serious threat of readjustment. Both the censorship saga and Bolingbroke's political challenge to Walpole provide evidence of the falling away of the representative function of monarchy in its relation to the national power and people and the clearing of another new space for national articulation and representation. In 1889, W. H. Hudson called for the official censorship to be replaced by the 'truer Censorship of public opinion and a free Press'.[32] His question, if England was the country of free speech and of a free Press, 'why is it not the country of a free drama also?'[33] was still awaiting answer at the turn of the nineteenth century. Eventually, however, even censorship would succumb to the growing influence of the liberal public sphere.

The turn of the twentieth century saw the relaunching of the national theatre campaign with Richard Badger's appeal for a Shakespeare memorial in the country's capital. In *The Times*, 12 August 1904, Badger, an elderly and wealthy brewer from the north of England, pledged £2,500 towards the erection of a fitting memorial to Shakespeare in London. His call for an influential representative committee to carry out the process of raising funds is interesting on two counts: first, due to the stipulation that this committee must be representative, an implicit recognition of the fact that a national institution of this kind demands and deserves equitable representation; and, secondly, due to his request that the committee be influential – representative was clearly insufficient. One is reminded here of Tom Nairn's rebuke of Stuart Mill's condemnation of 'ethnic sulking' on the basis that 'there is no such thing as "equal terms" ... It is this inequality which has been the living marrow of actual development.'[34] Badger, I think, would go along with that view.

Richard Badger's letter was the initial stimulus for a fervent national debate; a debate that was not to be resolved until after his death. Gradually, the papers became the vehicle for earnest and heated discussion regarding a Shakespeare memorial. The burning issue was not the propriety of raising a memorial to Shakespeare. There was the occasional suggestion such as that made by Owen Hall of the Prince of Wales Theatre, that Shakespeare had not done as much as the authors of musical comedy to entertain the modern British public in recent years, but the main bone of contention was the appropriate form for the proposed memorial. Coincidental with Badger's letter was the private publication and circulation of William Archer and Harley Granville Barker's famous Blue Book, *A National Theatre: Schemes and Estimates*. The aim of this thorough study was to invent a national theatre by providing a blueprint for its organization and management. What the scheme actually proposes is a national theatre that reflects in its own constitution the democratic organization of the liberal public sphere that had first emerged in eighteenth-century Europe, went into decline thereafter, and was, by the turn of the twentieth century, in a condition of crisis.

Alfred Emmet's comment that the origins of the Archer/Barker scheme can be traced to 'some drawing room in the further West End of London'[35] immediately roots it in the civic sphere. The method of its circulation by privately published pamphlet is evidence of its furtherance of the rational debate instigated by Badger, developed via the media and accessed by a widening public. In a preface to the book, Harley Granville Barker discusses the book's import and aim in terms of the appeal it makes to a 'public mind' and, more specifically, 'the mind of the theatrical public'.[36] These terms of reference immediately prompt the question: what is a theatrical public and in what capacity does it exercise its so-called mind? Is Barker's thinking, theatrical public one that actually frequents the theatre or one that is aware of the theatre in some way or has attitudes towards the theatre? Archer throws some light on the implied connection between the emergence of an informed public, capable of engaging intellectually with its environs and the medium of national theatre, when he stipulates that a national theatre should be 'visibly and unmistakably a popular institution, making a large appeal to the whole community' with the aim of recruiting and fostering an 'intelligent, not necessarily an "advanced" public'.[37] Nonetheless, it is not entirely clear what he means by an advanced public nor whether this phenomenon is, in fact, distinct from an intelligent public. The difficulty encountered by both Barker and Archer in defining the nature of the public to whom they seek to appeal and whose attitudes and intellect they hope to cultivate recalls similar challenges faced, initially by Lessing and later by Goethe and Schiller, when they sought to enter into a constructive, cultural dialogue with the public at large by means of written publications such as *Die Hamburgische Unterhaltungen* and *Die Horen*. In both cases, it is clear that the effort of literary communication has as much, if not more, to do with creating a public mind as it does with freeing up channels by means of which that mindset can find adequate outlets of expression.

It seems alarming that twentieth-century England was grappling with impediments that had characterized the German theatrical situation over a century earlier but if we refer to the twentieth-century German equivalent – the period of the Weimar Republic – an era in which culture claimed centre stage but was found lacking, the English position seems more hopeful. The crisis at Weimar was due to the fact that the social devices designed to promote public interaction and interchange had broken down so that theatrical art and art in general were left to exist in a vacuum. In this context, it is clearly of vital importance that Archer and Barker struggle, however belatedly, to put a framework of communication in place before they attempt to locate a national theatre within that supporting structure. Archer's viewpoint becomes clearer when he talks of the exemplary role that a national theatre itself should fulfil in relation to the nation it represents. Whilst acknowledging the positive influence of pioneering theatres in Germany, he argues that 'it is the advance of the main body that gives the outpost work its national

... significance'.[38] A national theatre is clearly to become a validation point for all other theatrical endeavours in the country as a whole. It is interesting to note the sweeping scope with which Archer invests the national theatre of his imagination: its influence is not to be confined to England or to members of the English nation, but rather to reach out to all English speakers. He argues that 'the acted drama, ought to be, and indeed is, one of the great bonds of union between all the Anglo-Saxon peoples; but at present, unfortunately, it may be said to "draw the whole English-speaking world together in the bonds of a racial vulgarity"'.[39] His comment suggests that race is dependent on a community of language and that the acting out of the drama is a vital aspect of the exercise and articulation of that linguistic community. His most ardent desire is that:

> There were but one playhouse in each of the great cities of the English-speaking world where the poetry and humour of the past, the thought and aspiration of the present, were enabled to attract to them the better elements in the public – now scattered and unorganised for want of any artistic rallying point.[40]

In the declaration of trust put together in 1909 to launch the national theatre campaign in earnest, there are similar expressions of faith in the ability of a national theatre to embrace the English-speaking world as a whole. There is little doubt that the honourable and earnest members of that executive committee would have agreed with Archer that if this aim were ever realized then the theatre 'would be, what I have said it ought to be – a potent instrument of culture, and one of the intellectual glories of the race'.[41] Archer takes this line of thought further in a pamphlet tackling the need for a rational world order. Here, he points to the paradox between the limited capacity of the human mind and the sheer size of the modern world, advocating the expansion of the human intellect as the only means for us to assimilate the size and scope of our new global environment. He maintains that 'the human intellect, organizing, order-bringing must enlarge itself so as to embrace, in one great conspectus, the problems, not of a parish, or of a nation, but of the pendant globe'.[42] What Archer is in fact advocating is a brand of internationalism, on a conceptual if not a practical level. Tom Nairn alerts readers to the ambiguity surrounding this term when he comments on the way in which 'the logically prescribed common sense of internationalism' can become a device employed to negate or deny internationality: 'the non-logical, untidy, refractory, disintegrative, particularistic truth of nation-states'.[43] He does not accuse Archer of employing this device, but does characterize it as a particularly prevalent aspect of the effort to sustain the 'Western intellectual world-view'.[44]

Nairn reiterates Archer's sense of the vastness of the modern world when he refers to the fact that, 'For the first time in human history, the globe has been effectively unified into a single economic order under a common democratic-state model.'[45] However, he immediately recognizes that this has not led to internationalism but to a general folding up into 'a previously unimaginable and still escalating number of different ethno-political units'.[46] Geoffrey Barraclough offers some justification or at least a rationale for this phenomenon when he comments on the inappropriateness of the popular ideas that the 'enduring values and traditions of civilisation are linked, in some unique way, with western Europe'[47] and that it is from this European unity that our culture is derived as opposed to the national state – an illusion contrived by accepting the myth of a common medieval society. Perhaps it is possible to understand the terminology used at this point in the Blue Book in terms of an effort (not necessarily wholly or even partially successful) to arrive at a common view of life, a common ideal, organized well enough democratically enough, and on a sufficiently grand scale to reflect, represent and activate a contemporary English experience on the country's national stage. A kind of national experience that moved beyond the transition from medieval to modern society outlined by Habermas to arrive at a new kind of empirical internationalism in which cultural truth originated within the nation state but extended outwards to embrace or encompass a scattered linguistic community of far greater proportions.

In the very first few pages of Archer and Barker's scheme, the absence of any model in England according to which one might set up a national theatre is drawn to our attention. Archer labels this deficiency as an 'enormous obstacle' and comments on the anomaly that it is possible to 'buy a ... library or a picture-gallery ready-made, and present it as a "going concern" to whatever community you please'[48] and it will practically run itself. In actual fact, this obstacle points to one of the particular advantages of theatre as a national, representative artistic medium – the distinctively interactive nature of its engagement with its public. Archer demonstrates his awareness of this characteristic when he makes an indirect observation on the fact that theatre is a positive and participatory form of artistic enactment. He comments:

> It is true that we can read the great plays of the great dramatists; we can read them by ourselves at our own firesides; but how pale is a perusal compared with a performance, how inadequate, how unsatisfactory. Perhaps a mere reading will enable us to appreciate some of the purely literary beauties of the play; but it will hardly help us to apprehend its essential dramatic qualities – the very qualities which give the play its true value, and which stand revealed at once when the play is presented in the theatre.[49]

Archer does not go any further in the definition of this theatricality, but John Galsworthy's encouragement for the national theatre campaign provides more explicit comment on the organic nature of the theatrical form. When he offers his assessment of Shakespeare, he argues:

> If ever there was in this island a free, impersonal spirit, who, in essence, was at one with the changes and growth of life, it was the spirit of this same Shakespeare. He is the symbol of our dramatic art; only by doing service to this dramatic art can we fittingly commemorate his greatness.[50]

Galsworthy's words define drama as a representative medium that is true to the fluidity and inevitable forward movement of life and therefore suited to voice the vision and concerns of a society in flux and increasingly uneasy with the idea of indirect and inflexible representation of any kind. It may well be pertinent to recall de Tocqueville's comment on the popularity of the theatrical medium in a revolutionary age due to the physical presence of the audience and the active nature of their engagement in the event. George Orwell comments that in England 'even in extremist political parties, it is only the middle-class membership that think in revolutionary terms [whilst] the masses still more or less assume that "against the law" is a synonym for "wrong"'.[51] This observation casts interesting light on the prominent role played by the middle class in the national theatre campaign and suggests that there might have been some justification for the assumption that, at this stage in the history of the campaign at least, national drama was in danger of becoming a synonym for a particular brand of artistic elitism, fostered by the 'minority in favour of a National Theatre'.[52]

In Matthew Arnold's famous response to the visit of the Comédie-Française to London, he emphasizes the need for a national theatre not only to provide a true reflection of the life of a nation but to play an active part in the development of that national life. He commends French theatre for its ability to capture the quality of French national life as embodied in its charismatic capital. It is worth noting here that both France and England benefited from the fact that London and Paris provided ideal locations for national theatres whereas Germany suffered from the absence of any such official cultural centre in which to locate the country's national theatre. Although French theatre, Arnold argues, is:

> The theatre of the *homme sensuel moyen* ... whose country is France, and whose city is Paris, and whose ideal life is the free, gay, pleasurable life ... of the senses developing themselves all round without misgiving; a life confident, fair and free, with fireworks of fine emotions, grand passions, and devotedness ... lighting it up when necessary.[53]

French adaptations, however, he declares, are quite ill-suited to the English stage and popular taste for the very same reason. They are, he regrets, 'pages out of a life which the ideal of the *homme sensuel moyen* rules, transferred to a life where this ideal, notwithstanding the fervid adhesion to it of our young generation, does not reign'.[54] Arnold's insistence on the role of a national theatre as a mirror of the nation brings to mind similar observations made years later, in 1942, by the minister for labour, Mr Ernest Bevin, when he classified the theatre as an artistic form endowed with a refreshing permanence in a mechanical age of constant change:

> In this mechanical world, he said, we look to the theatre to preserve the characteristics of our people ... and I look forward, at the end of this great struggle, to the living theatre not only coming into its own as a means of livelihood, but to its becoming one of our great national institutions to convey to the people of the world the character of the ordinary British people.[55]

Arnold much regretted the estrangement of the middle class from the theatre during the Puritan period but felt confident that a change was afoot. He perceived the call for 'expansion, for intellect and knowledge, for beauty, for social life and manners'[56] that was driving the British public (how representative a public, I am not sure) back to the theatre. As a result, he came to the conclusion that since the theatre is one of the mightiest means of satisfying these needs, we must bring it to proper order: 'the theatre,' he declared, 'is irresistible; *organise the theatre*'.[57]

The Blue Book grapples with this organizational task and in so doing reveals the link between the liberal public sphere and the theatrical event itself. In it, Barker argues for a national theatre that would 'become a part of our civic institutions'[58] – a quasi-governmental institution that bridges between official public life and the private existence of individual citizens. He was convinced that in order to ascertain this aim, the theatre's 'working conditions must be organised as becomes a healthy and stable civil service'.[59] Ideally (with due respect for Archer's warnings against idealism), it appears a national theatre would be organized as a reflection of the new civic life of a nation that had secured the transition from a feudal society in which power was represented more or less directly by the monarch, to a democratic middleman's world. It is worth noting here the objections made by one Mr Lynch during the parliamentary debate on the question of the establishment of a state-assisted national theatre on 23 April 1913. Despite the general sense of agreement and accord prevalent at this debate, Mr Lynch put a provocative question. At home and abroad, he said, Shakespeare was generally accepted as the poet of the English people. Indeed, the speaker who had opened the debate, Mr H. J. MacKinder, had already commented that whilst he, along with every one else, had 'long been aware that the name of Shakespeare is great', he was flattered to discover that German youth were nurtured in his plays – a fact that testified to the 'depth and breadth of the influence of Shakespeare, and therefore of our country' in Europe.[60] Mr Lynch's question, however, put forward a contrasting view: he asked whether Shakespeare was not a bad model for a national theatre because he was not a man:

> greatly alert to the more modern influences even of his own time, and so far from being the great eponym and governor of English literature

to come, he was rather the closure and apotheosis of the feudal system, which he did so much to glorify.[61]

In terms of the relationship between the aspirations of a civil society and the constitution and practical workings of the national theatre proposed by Archer, this is a pertinent point.

In 1879, Arnold had called on the English nation to 'believe that the State, the nation in its collective and corporate character, does well to concern itself about an influence so important to national life ... as the theatre'.[62] Although Archer gallantly designated his proposed national theatre as a 'free gift to the nation',[63] the practical suggestions he makes regarding its finance suggest that the thorny subject of the state's relations to a national theatre were far from being resolved. Some comment is made on state funding, but it is deemed both unlikely and unnecessary at a national level. The idea that a national theatre might be set up on private finance but could then go on to provide an example to be emulated by the provinces with the use of public money is an indication of the link between national prestige and freedom from state support. This viewpoint might well be considered with reference to Henry Irving's comments in 1878 when he positively objected to state support for a national theatre on the basis that British institutions should maintain their tradition of freedom from the state[64] – the pitfall of this approach is made evident by the bankruptcy of Irving's own quasi-national theatrical venture at the Lyceum. Archer's conviction that legislation would follow the establishment of a national theatre in London and that this legislation would address current deficiencies at local government level, empowering 'municipalities to do what is required of them in this respect',[65] brings Aylmer's comments on the curious absence of a local bureaucracy in English political circles in the seventeenth and early eighteenth century to mind. Archer's recognition of the weakness of local government in contemporary England and his acknowledgement of the need to use legislation as a means of addressing this problem demonstrate the necessity of linking the periphery to the centre if national ideals are ever to become local currency, so to speak.

Due to his reservations regarding state subsidy, Archer concludes that the establishment of the national theatre 'ought to be, and probably will be, effected by the public spirit of individual citizens'.[66] This ties the private individual in with the public sphere by means of an economic deal. Archer's thorough and sensitive discussion of the relations between the donor and the theatre and its public demonstrate his understanding of the dangers inherent in any form of sponsorship or patronage in matters of national concern. He makes this understanding manifest very early on in the scheme when he regrets that 'there is no clear-cut channel, as it were, in which liberality and public spirit can easily flow in the direction of theatrical reform'.[67] It is also an interesting comment on the fact that the public body calling for the establishment of a national theatre was, as yet, asset-less and, to all practical purposes, penniless. It is small wonder that it should make so earnest a bid for cultural collateral. The series of suggestions made in the scheme to cater for the needs of any potential donor whilst maintaining the moral and social boundaries of the theatre make interesting and amusing reading. The idea that the theatre should not initially be ornate but donors, having perceived its value as an artistic and social institution, might wish to embellish it with 'a marble staircase ... [or] a mosaic floor',[68] betrays a disjunction between the instinctive feeling that opulence and beauty is somehow inappropriate, or at least unnecessary, for a site of national cultural significance and the opposite feeling, namely that it is also a particularly appropriate manifestation of national pride and prestige.

Archer is at pains to pay tribute in his modern national theatre to the tradition of civic pride which 'impelled the Romans to write their names in letters of bronze on the edifices with which they adorned the city'.[69] This civic pride, he feels, was no ignoble sentiment and might well be imitated by the inscription of the donor's name in a prominent place in the vestibule. There should, moreover, only be one donor to ensure a sense of individual pride and to ensure that the building should be the 'record and monument of one great effort of public spirit, rather than of many small'.[70] However, this desire to focus on a worthy individual (worthy in economical terms at least) militates against the very essence of public spirit. Archer's subsequent consideration of an alternative option with regard to a Guarantee Fund is proof of his own reservations on the subject. He follows up his initial suggestion with the proposal that an appeal might be made for more and smaller donations on the basis that the public (or at least a representative portion thereof) would then have an interest in the economic success of the venture. The proposal that a set of statutes be drawn up to maintain the equilibrium between the influence of donors and guarantors and that of normal members of the public provides further evidence of incongruity. This 'machinery of government'[71] would enable any parties who felt dissatisfied to instigate the changing of statutes through an act of reconstitution. The national theatre, then, was to do without government funding but not to exist outside the legislative powers of government.

Archer's stipulation that government of the national theatre should be kept distinct from its ownership is aimed at promoting fairness and democracy, but the constitution of the proposed board of trustees is alarmingly conservative. Its fifteen members were to be made up of representatives from the universities of Oxford, Cambridge and London and the Royal Academy. The London County Council was to provide two members and the remaining members were to be appointed by donors. Vacancies would be filled by co-opting, by royal nomination and on the advice of the prime minister – a curious combination of governmental and monarchical authority but one that was typical for the appointment of bishops and awards of honour reminiscent of Aylmer's 'government by the King's consent'.[72] Small wonder that Thomas Hardy feared that the lack of divergence between members of the board of trustees might lead to philistinism.

Despite its occasional eccentricity, Archer's attempt to structure his national theatre so that it reconstructed the democratic constitution of Habermas's liberal public sphere was strikingly thorough and extended beyond constitutional and administrative matters to include the organization of the actors themselves. The argument for an equitable distribution of roles and for the provision of variety and security at all levels of the acting profession echoes the aspiration towards equality at the heart of the transition from medieval to modern society. The democratization of the acting world was an important issue in its own right in that the existence of a star system was harmful both to the development of the stars themselves, to less fortunate and popular actors and actresses and to the dramatic art in general. This danger was manifest particularly strikingly by the phenomenon of the nineteenth-century French *vedette*. Matthew Arnold's admission of his fervent admiration for Rachel is proof of the irresistible magnetism of these stars. Arnold recalls how in his youth, 'after a first sight of the divine Rachel at the Edinburgh Theatre, in the part of Hermione, I followed her to Paris, and for two months never missed one of her representations'.[73] He goes on to make a comparison between Rachel and Sarah Bernhardt in which he argues for Rachel's superior intellectual quality:

> Temperament and quick intelligence, passion, nervous mobility, grace, smile, voice, charm, poetry, – Mdlle. Sarah Bernhardt has them all. One watches her with pleasure, with admiration, – and yet not without a secret disquietude. Something is wanting, or, at least, not present in sufficient force; something which alone can secure and fix her administration of all the charming gifts which she has, can alone keep them fresh, keep them sincere, save them from perils by caprice, perils by mannerism. That something is high intellectual power. It was here that Rachel was so great; she began, one says to oneself as one recalls her image and dwells upon it, – she began almost where Mdlle. Sarah Bernhardt ends. [74]

The fear he harbours of the insincerity identified with the intrusion of wilfulness and affectation into the craft of acting – it is this fear that brings about the 'disquietude' that accompanies his enjoyment of Sarah Bernhardt's playing – suggests that theatre can function, at its best, as an ennobling force, but also that there is an inherent danger in dramatic art that lacks this quality.

Despite his eloquent attempt at objectivity, Arnold's comments highlight the vulnerability of the spectator in a theatrical environment in which the relationship between audience and actor is immediate and deeply affecting. Winston Churchill attempted a similar rationalization of the passionate relationship between the public and its theatrical stars when he declared, in a banquet held in honour of Ellen Terry in 1906, that the nation's admiration for her was, in fact, proof that 'the British were sincere lovers of the drama'.[75] In view of this phenomenon, Archer's description of his proposed system of actor selection as 'the survival of the fittest' [76] is not as surprising as it initially seems. His temporary adoption of the linguistic terminology, not of an environment of rational debate but of a much more instinctive and natural world brings to mind our earlier discussion of the charisma of spectacular theatrical characters and the capacity of theatre to stimulate an instinctive response.

Barker's discussion of the circumstances necessary for the actor's healthy professional development is evidence of his desire to cultivate a much more balanced interplay between the national theatre and its audience. He has a very pragmatic approach to the figure of the actor and actress that draws a striking parallel between their working lives and the workings of life in general. His argument that actors and actresses are entitled to more leisure time and that this is vital to their physical and emotional wellbeing links their ability to fulfil their professional role within the company with the opportunities available to them to participate fully in society at large. Barker argues that the servants of the theatre:

> must be left opportunities to retain that social citizenship which formerly they altogether renounced, and which now the pressure of the prevailing system does not afford them. If they are to depict social life they must be encouraged to enjoy it, not considered and left to become mere emotional acrobats.[77]

His recognition of the negative effect of alienation from human society on the actor highlights the precariousness of social identity in a world in which the way in which people are seen affects what they subsequently become. Henry Irving's argument that the stage and the acting profession possess moral qualities makes it clear that the healthy actor can repay his society in kind because 'the best way to make the world a better community to be in, and not so bad a place to be of, is not to shun, but to bring public opinion to bear upon its pursuits and its relaxations'.[78] This early preoccupation with the necessity to provide an inclusive theatrical environment for theatre professionals remained a feature of later stages in the life of the national theatre campaign. A paper that investigates the pros and cons of a drum-revolve stage at the South Bank national theatre complex reveals the fact that this line of thought has been developed so as to arrive at the concept of the vital importance of sculpting a theatrical arena in which both actor and spectator might co-inhabit an expansive and inclusive space. The paper insists that the theatre should not throw away the key 'to the outside – physically, mentally and emotionally' but that a stage must be created that will allow the actor to perform 'within the audience's own "grasp", at the same time surrounding him [and by inference the audience] with space' so that an actor can both '"come into" the stage' and 'go out into the world'.[79]

This world has now come to encompass the performer and the spectator so that their productive interaction is facilitated by the sharing of an inclusive theatrical space.

Archer and Barker's Blue Book did much to formalize ideas regarding a national theatre, but at the point of its circulation, a stage space of any kind had yet to be imagined. In fact, developments were afoot to push forward with Mr Badger's plans – plans that did not involve a theatre at all. A public meeting was held at the Mansion House on 28 February 1905 under the chairmanship of the Lord Mayor, where the Provisional Committee adopted the proposal to erect a fitting memorial to Shakespeare in London. It was resolved to set up a general committee to determine the form of the memorial and a press release was issued outlining proposals for a monument to be erected at Portland Place, with particular thanks to His Majesty for his gracious assent to the transfer of the existing statue of the Duke of Kent elsewhere. The raging public debate that followed the meeting was proof of the fact that a previously unknown heavyweight had claimed his rightful place in the ring and was preparing to launch a championship bid – the Great British public itself.

The press release, issued in advance of a meeting scheduled for 5 March 1908, instigated a varied debate conducted in the main in the press itself. Once the call for a national theatre had been made in contra-distinction to Badger's appeal for a commemorative statue to Shakespeare, it was as if the public imagination had at last been fired. It is difficult not to recall J. Shennan's assessment of the reactionary nature of English self-definition at the close of the eighteenth century when Englishmen may not have known what they were for but they were well aware of what they were against. It seems that twentieth-century Englishmen suffered from much the same malady and had, in accordance with the British way of doing things, been stirred to act on behalf of a national theatre by the thought that they might be encumbered with an unwanted national statue. Perhaps a more positive view would be that the tradition of artistic anaesthesia highlighted by Orwell's comment on the English nation's affection for 'hideous statues' and planless building' [80] had finally come to an end. F. C. Burnand's warning, issued in *The Times* on Wednesday, 1 March 1905, supports this viewpoint and expresses the desire to take a step forward out of the nation's past commemorative traditions. Burnand comments, 'if you are proposing to give Shakespeare a statue in London, just look round at the specimens we already possess, and – beware'.[81]

Whatever the nature of its impetus, the national theatre debate offers a fascinating insight into the spirit and the social, economic and political science of the English nation. John Hankin's provocative assessment of the nature of the English theatregoer and English attitudes towards the arts in general are particularly informative in this context. He proposes an ingenious, if slightly unlikely, scheme based on a system of financial sponsorship that involves the various 'industrious branches of commerce' [82] in London – restaurateurs, cab drivers, dressmakers and even chocolate manufacturers – in a theatre subsidy scheme. This scheme is made necessary by a peculiarity of the English national character that inspires a millionaire or a peeress to 'sponge for a seat at a play with a relentless ardour that nothing can baffle. That is, if the play has any artistic pretensions.'[83] Hankin explains this phenomenon by claiming:

> Art, in fact, is a thing for which people will not and do not pay, and the English, as a business nation, are quite alive to the advantages of this arrangement. They will pay for food, and for drink, and for fine raiment, for the lust of the flesh and the lust of the fine eye and the pride of life. But for music or for literature, for fine art or fine drama, they will not pay.[84]

According to Hankin, the English man and woman will not pay for art because their business acumen tells them not to. His argument is supported by a similar comment in the report of the Mansion House meeting that claims that the 'city had not cared as it should have for the poets', largely because they were neither 'business' nor 'dinners'.[85] If we relate this argument to Habermas's discussion of the representative burden shouldered by art and culture in pre-eighteenth-century society and the point at which they were cut free from these ties, due to the weakening of powerful institutions such as the court, the monarchy and the Church, it becomes evident that a wealthy, reputedly cultured twentieth-century public has reinvested art with a slightly different representative role – the reflection of the economic prosperity and social status of some of its most prominent members.

Hankin's revelation of the creed of cultural entitlement amongst those wealthy gentlemen called upon by Archer to display their liberality in relation to the national theatre did not bode well for the development of English dramatic art or the national theatre itself. However, the manner in which the battle for and against a national theatre came to a conclusion provides a more positive impression of the English national character than that outlined by Hankin's observations. Subsequent to some adept political manoeuvering, spearheaded by Lords Plymouth and Lytton and facilitated by Beerbohm Tree, a compromise was reached. As a result, Mr Alfred Lyttleton could address the next public meeting at the Lyceum on 18 May 1908 in the confidence that his declaration of the resolution to establish a national theatre was truly representative of the wishes of the crowd and that he was indeed justified in declaring, 'me, I am the crowd'.[86] Geoffrey Whitworth's assessment that this agreement had been reached in a spirit of 'statesmanship and good sense that had prevailed over bitter rivalry'[87] rings true. If the journey had been somewhat circumspect, its conclusion had provided exemplary proof of the congeniality between gentlemanly British conduct and the attempt to establish rational public debate as the arbitrator between the power of the state and the power of its people.

In 1913, the campaign for a national theatre finally entered new territory in which it was able to push for concrete change – 'the sphere of practical politics'.[88] The unionist member for the Camlachie division of Glasgow, Mr John MacKinder, brought a proposal of support before the House of Commons for a London-based national theatre, 'to be vested in trustees and assisted by the State, for the performance of plays by Shakespeare and other dramas of recognized merit'.[89] It may well be relevant to note that the call for state aid had been presaged by a donation of £70,000 by Mr Carl Meyer who later received a baronetcy for his munificence. However, the change in the balance of power brought about as a result of a growth in the influence of the public made state aid a real possibility for the first time since the 1820s, when 'the state's responsibilities were held to begin and end with administering justice, collecting taxes, and defending the country'.[90] The usually cautious officialdom was evidently receptive to the new sound of public opinion. Despite the fact that this foray into the field of politics did not bring about immediate results – the House was divided 162 ayes to 32 noes and democracy had its way – the putting of the question did much to raise the profile of the national theatre campaign.

The most significant issue that emerged as a result of this vote was the definition of the national theatre as a 'place' – a designated space for the articulation and interrogation of matters of national interest and importance. In the context of England's effort to secure new territory via its national theatre, it is useful to recall Robert J. Kaiser and Walker Connor's discussion of the territorialization of national identity: the promotion of an idea of the nation as an unchanging entity rooted to a particular place. They argued that as actual places become more fluid and flexible, ideas of culturally and ethnically distinct places become more prominent. Their suspicion that the depiction of these places as neutral and eternal was misleading made them wary of the manufacturing of territorial attachments by political leaders or other representatives of power. Lenin's comment on the fact that the pressures of modern life and the irresistible tide of economic development that bears standardization and conformity with it made ever-increasing demands on available world space'[91] provides another perspective on the problem of space in modern society. In more recent years, Tom Nairn elaborated on this idea when he noted that 'for business purposes ... the boundaries that separate one nation from another are no more real than the equator'.[92] Both these comments on the predatory nature of economic imperialism direct us towards the motivation of a nation struggling to establish some sacred space to call its own. In the case of the English National Theatre the struggle to claim this theatrical space was fraught with difficulty.

The first indication of a growing national awareness of the expressive potential of theatrical place or space is given by the use of a specific theatre building as the location for public participation and protest. This event came about in March 1908 when the lessees of the Lyceum theatre, Mr H. W. Smith and Mr Edward Carpenter, kindly offered to lend it for the purpose of a public demonstration in favour of a national theatre. In the event, this demonstration was averted and the event transformed into a forum for collaboration, but the offer and acceptance of the Lyceum as a place appropriate for popular discussion and protest offers an insight into the role that the advocates for a national theatre hoped it might fulfil in terms of the nation as a whole. Significantly, the Lyceum meeting was also the place at which the idea of a public memorial was finally judged an inadequate embodiment of public feeling and the decision was taken to activate the past through the medium of a national theatre rather than commemorate it by means of a monument. This early indication of the gradual evolution of an understanding of the national theatre as a designated national place or space was given concrete reinforcement by the actual purchase of a site in Bloomsbury Road shortly after the House of Commons debate of April 1913. In autumn 1913, a site in the 'heart of the educational quarter in Bloomsbury, immediately behind the British Museum at the corner of Gower Street and Keppel Street, and within a stone's throw of the Royal Academy of Dramatic Art'[93] became available. Geoffrey Whitworth's detailed description of the site fleshes out the characteristics of this new place; its educational connotations, the potential for collaboration with the Royal Academy and the cultural kudos provided by the proximity of the British Museum.

The site was promptly purchased. However, a much greater territorial issue was soon to occupy Britain with the outbreak of the First World War. The aftermath of this international crisis eventually led to the sale of the Bloomsbury site in January 1923 for £52,000 to the representatives of the Rockerfeller Trustees. This place had only begun to take shape in the minds of the nation by the time of its sale but the sale itself brought an interesting issue regarding the nature of the Shakespeare National Memorial Trust to the fore. The sale of the Bloomsbury site was thrown into jeopardy by the implication, later to be confirmed, that the Shakespeare Memorial National Trust was, in fact, a charity and could not dispose of its assets without the assent of the charity commissioners. In the final analysis, the official definition of the trust as a charity did not halt the sale but it did establish the interesting and rather embarrassing fact that the popular drive for a national theatre was a matter of and for charity. On the other hand, this revelation of the trust's charitable status might also raise it to truly national status in the sense that it designated it as above the level of government control. After the war, the Duke of Westminster offered a series of sites, initially one by Victoria station then another on Horseferry Road. In the event, neither proposal took on any concrete form and subsequent developments did more to raise the question of whether such a national institution should be fixed in terms of place at all than to move towards a designated site. Nonetheless, the Drama League did launch an architectural competition for designs for the national theatre and irrespective of its physical location the emphasis was now turned to the theatre's outward appearance and its status as a place in its own right. The league proposed that the winning designs should be exhibited in the British Empire Exhibition at Wembley Park where they would form part of a display, 'designed to illustrate the past, present, and future of the National Theatre Movement'.[94] Concerns as to whether the traditional imperialist ideals of the British Empire could be reconciled with the idea of a national theatre intended to function as a vehicle for communal, egalitarian actions may account for the trust's failure to respond to this offer.

Whether or not this was the case, the trust's inactivity made it seem likely that the only territorial claims that the national theatre could make now, or in the foreseeable future, were virtual ones. Ironically, in 1921 Archer published a plan with the support of the British Drama League, entitled *The Foundation of the National Theatre: a Chapter in the History of England after the Great War*. This publication is particularly interesting on two counts. First, it proposes an audacious scheme for the subsidising of a national theatre from an endowment fund, based on Inland Revenue surtax statements. Secondly, it poses as a history published in 1950 rather than a contemporary proposal written in 1921. This manipulation of the temporal context in order to criticize current shortcomings is a scathing commentary on the perpetual virtuality of England's national theatre. In 1930, Archer and Granville Barker tried to tackle the unresolved issue of the national theatre by reissuing the Blue Book with a new proposal that the national theatre building should house two distinct stages on a new site on the South Bank of the Thames. Then in 1937, the Cromwell Gardens site was finally purchased. This positive act actually occasioned a shrinking in the space claimed for the national theatre by Archer and Granville-Barker because the smallness of the Cromwell Gardens site made a twin-stage project impossible. In the event, Edward Lutyens's designs for this project were compact, inclusive, imposing without being pompous and characterized by perfect symmetry and a distinctive porte cochère.[95]

Just as the national theatre was beginning to take definitive shape, the outbreak of the Second World War thwarted any formal consolidation. By the time the matter was next resurrected the attitude of public authority to art had been transformed in a way that secured the future of the national theatre campaign; the agent of this change was CEMA, Council for Encouragement of Music and the Arts. It was at this point in the history of the national theatre that the views of government representatives regarding the role of the arts, and in particular of a national theatre, came into line with those of the long-standing supporters of a national theatre campaign. Historically, the prominence and dominance of the middle class in this campaign was problematic on two fronts: first, it could be argued that whilst its claims were perfectly legitimate, they did not represent the voice of the general public; secondly, it could also be maintained that the fact that they identified themselves by contrast to the state rendered them powerless to achieve their aim from a financial standpoint at the very least. In the wake of the Second World War, the Arts Council became the beneficiary of a realistic appraisal of Britain's national and international standing. It was felt, Minihan claims, that 'if the glorious days of empire and naval hegemony were gone forever, and if the war had reduced Great Britain to financial dependence on the United States, there was still enough cause for pride in British cultural strength'.[96] The arts had suddenly come to represent the pride and prestige of a nation that had been stripped of its material ballast. It may well have been this realization that allowed the state to be persuaded of the viability of claims for a national theatre in England. Once this official seal of approval had been obtained, it provided the financial support necessary to power the movement forward in accordance with the desire of the general public.

New interest and input on the part of the state led to the designation of a new site to represent all that the national theatre was now to herald of British pride and honour. In 1942, a hint was given that this was an opportune moment to approach the London City Council for a site on the South Bank, between County Hall and Waterloo Bridge, in an area designated for post-war development. The national theatre was evidently considered by the council as a worthy candidate for such a developmental site, designed to restore some of the city's badly damaged pride. It is interesting to note the proactive role of the council at this point in the developmental history of the national theatre. The catastrophic destruction inflicted upon London by the bombing raids of the Second World War seems to have stung the civil strata into unprecedented action, transforming their relationship with the city and, by extension, the country as a whole. Ironically, these raids had also cleared new space for developments such as the national theatre venture. The London City Council was now intent on taking direct responsibility for shaping the fabric and structure of the city itself – the national theatre was evidently to form part of the master plan of reconstruction. Their assumption of a new role was not an isolated event but rather a reflection of the general drive with which the post-war Labour Party was manoeuvring the country towards nationalization. As Minihan points out, the national theatre scheme was particularly attractive to the Labour government because 'it provided an opportunity for ... the kind of joint effort between central government and local government which Labour sought to encourage ... throughout the country'.[97] As a result, a definite offer of a site was made and Sir Edward Lutyens and Cecil Masey drew up new plans that expanded on Lutyens's original compact design and included a much larger theatre with two auditoria.

In 1946, a development took place originating from a very different quarter but one that affected the idea of the national theatre as a place – the Old Vic proposed a merger with the Shakespeare Memorial National Trust. Whilst London City Council struggled to etch out a place for the national theatre that would signal its new role as an indicator of British cultural wealth, the merger between the Old Vic and the trust suddenly made a new declaration about the theatre's place in English society, both in concrete and abstract terms. The proposed national theatre was now connected with the actual, popular, reputable and successful theatrical creation of Lilian Bayliss – the Old Vic. It might well seem appropriate that this artistic venture that had begun life as a coffee tavern was now to play a formative role in the making and placing of the national theatre. It is probably equally significant, although less inspiring, to recall that the architect who succeeded Edward Lutyens in 1944, and carried the hopes of this new cooperative national theatre movement forward was chosen by a questionably democratic process that involved immuring a panel of experts in the Savoy Hotel. Despite Bayliss's conviction that her establishment was, in fact, the only rightful claimant to the status of a national theatre, the merger with the Old Vic was only ever considered as a temporary measure. The curious relationship between the Old Vic and the proposed new national theatre recalls the antagonism between the Comédie-Française and the Boulevard theatres when the latter challenged the former's traditional right to its position as the nation's foremost national theatrical institution. This latent competition never came to a head in England and with her re-entry into the affairs of the national theatre in 1948, the state proved a powerful new ally and the passing of the National Theatre Bill with very little objection, either at the level of the Commons or the Lords, was swiftly followed by the royal laying of a foundation stone at the site on the southern end of Waterloo Bridge, opposite the designated location for a new concert hall. The official designation of a specific site might have been expected to herald the rise of a building within a year or two. This was not the case. It was as if the laying of the foundation stone had put the national theatre debate to rest.

It was not until 1962 that the National Theatre Board was set up under the leadership of Oliver Lyttleton. In a review of a publication by Allardyce Nicoll in *The Times Literary Supplement* of 24 August 1962, an interesting criticism was levelled at the board with regard to the absence of theatrical artists of any kind amongst its members. Furthermore, a recommendation was made that members of the board might read Nicoll's conclusions regarding a possible link between the usurpation of the actor's authority and the decadence of contemporary drama. This recommendation may well seem partially if not wholly validated by Sir Laurence Olivier's subsequent appointment as director of a quasi-national theatre company that assembled at Chichester and gave their first performance at the Old Vic on 22 October 1963. It seems that Mr Butcher's argument during the Commons debate of the national theatre bill in 1949 was proving its validity. He argued convincingly that the:

> theatre does not only consist of the building. On the whole, that is the least important matter. We have the play in this country ... we believe that in this country we have players second to none ... we believe that given scope the audiences will be worthy both of the play and the players.[98]

However, it was also in 1962, when it seemed that the national theatre did not need to claim a new place in order to represent its public appropriately, that Denys Lasdun, the architect who would finally give form to the aspirations of decades, was appointed. It is interesting to note the combination of factors which induced the National Theatre Board to appoint Lasdun because they demonstrate the way in which both the ideology and the mechanics of the national theatre reflected those of the public sphere that it was ultimately designed to replicate. Lasdun was invited to apply for the vacant post because the board felt that they would prefer an architect who 'was prepared to work with them rather than one who would try to implant a fixed idea of his own as to what the National Theatre should be'.[99] Collaboration was a vital principle, but Sir Laurence Olivier pinpoints two other important factors in his recollection of the interviewing process for the position. He recalls:

> The thing was most of the architects came in groups with their partners and we were another group on the committee, but Denys Lasdun arrived... entirely alone. Very theatrical... He didn't have to answer, 'Well, the majority of us feel'... During the interview Lasdun put his finger on it, very cleverly. He said that surely the most important aspect of what we were talking about is the spiritual one. Oh, my dear. We all fell for that.[100]

What Sir Laurence Olivier is describing here amounts to a theatrical performance where creative interplay is activated between committee/audience members and Lasdun/the performing artist. The committee is a device designed to facilitate democratic and rational debate but the role it has played in the history of the English National Theatre reveals the fact that it often fell short of this ideal in practice. Designed to neutralize hierarchical systems of power representation, it was constantly in danger of losing the energy that translates intention into positive action. Denys Lasdun's ability to transform the committee into an arena for the performance of creative interaction overcame this difficulty.

It was not until 4 March 1977 that the three theatres of the national – the Lyttleton, the Cottesloe and the Olivier – were fully operational and the national theatre could be said to have acquired its final form. During the planning and building period many a financial crisis had arisen and been averted by interim government subsidy until the National Theatre Bill became law in 1973, enabling the government to remove spending limits on the theatre project. The legalistic way in which the national theatre eventually secured financial security – a process that was initiated by the proposal of this bill in 1949 and completed with its legalization in 1973 – is particularly interesting in both the light of Orwell's comment regarding the English respect for legality and Habermas's general observations on the need for the ruling sector to be held and seen to be held accountable to the public at large. When the building finally became concrete, reactions to it were mixed. The English National Theatre began its struggle for life in the midst of a controversy about monuments. The concrete commemoration of the past and its heritage was problematized by the articulation of the nation's resistance to this process. One might have thought that this argument had been put to rest in 1913 as a result of the gentlemanly cooperation between proponents of the memorial scheme on the one hand, and the national theatre project on the other. However, the terms of the discussion in *National Theatre: 'Architectural Review Guide'* of the national theatre building in 1977 bear witness to the continuing difficulties connected with the bridging between past and present that is an inherent part of the processes of accumulating and declaring national prestige. In that review guide, William Curtis testifies to the sensitivity of this topic when he points out that 'the theatre is a monument and at present monuments are regarded with suspicion in England – as if they were dinosaurs from a previous age ... Monuments ... are not what modern architecture ... is about.'[101] Furthermore, he argues that the 'standard means for monumentalising: the iconography of domes, porticoes, grand orders, of stressed entrances, axial symmetry and honorific materials'[102] (a description that may call some aspects of Edwin Lutyens's original designs for the theatre to mind) are inaccessible to the modern architect. As a result, it is almost impossible for him to evoke parallels with civilized ideals from the past that instigate a response from the public at the most instinctive level. Whilst the modern movement's tendency to disguise the reality of civic hierarchy behind 'uniform facades of glazing or strip windows'[103] may be a throwback to the desire for equality and unanimity current in the liberal public sphere, in architectural terms it makes the indication of national prestige a challenging task.

Modern architecture was in a state of moral crisis at the time of Lasdun's appointment due to a general mistrust of or distaste for professionalism, defined by Curtis as 'part of the present cultural transition'.[104] Curtis does not elaborate on the nature of this transition but Habermas's reflections on the cost of modernization in terms of culture may well be relevant here despite the fact that they do not make direct reference to this specific period in England. Habermas argues that in the modern world art is elitist and people have become alienated from the core values of their culture. This process, he says, has been accentuated by the insulating effect of the growth of the professional classes and by a loss of a sense of collective identity amongst the public that has, in turn, relieved the state of the burden of justifying its actions. The general trend identified by Habermas is contextualized in terms of twentieth-century England by Peter Hall's question 'have architects ever been so unpopular as they are today?'[105] Hall's comment captures the sense of public antagonism towards this representative of the professional classes but Curtis claims that Lasdun went some way towards combating this problem of perception by his creation of an 'urban landscape philosophy'[106] that avoided monumentality and sought to create an architecture that collaborated with its environment, as opposed to dominating it. Lasdun himself hoped that the theatre would be part of the life of the city, its strata were designed to be 'new levels of ground and they will become real places'.[107] The review conveys a general consensus that:

> the large scale of the towers, the uninterrupted treatment of the strata, the geometrical control of the whole form, the use of axes and processional routes, the elegance and forthrightness of the materials, the expression of hierarchy and partial symmetry ... these are all ways in which the theatre proclaims its importance in the city hierarchy. There is grandeur of effect with simplicity of means.[108]

What is more interesting from the point of view of our analysis of a national theatre as a reconstructed forum for the expression of concerns with questions of nationhood and nationality is the role played by the public in Lasdun's great scheme of things at the national. Marc Girouard's description of the way in which the audience becomes part of the building itself during performance intervals confirms the fact that the public are provided with the opportunity of making an active contribution to the architectural pose struck by the building itself by parading,

> up and down through a series of inter-connecting stage sets, striking conscious or unconscious attitudes and watching others do the same. One looks up at people leaning over balconies above one, or down through clefts, along valleys, or into pits, at the people parading below.[109]

Lasdun hoped the public would use the building as a fourth theatre in which the terraces and foyers would play a primary functional role. In Easter 1976, Tony Harrison's *Crucifixion* was performed on the terraces, clearly part of Peter Hall's attempt to save his theatre from accusations of insularity. Tim Goodwin's assessment that the theatre was in fact designed as 'an area of casual encounter, where the public provide their own entertainment ... a social centre, a theatre of the crowd'[110] underlines the importance of the principle of public involvement in and interaction with the theatre.

In 1979, a political statement made by National Theatre staff marked a significant development in the theatre's history when an unofficial strike over pay and work shifts, that was to cost the National Theatre over a quarter of a million pounds, completely closed all three theatres and disrupted the presentation of Galsworthy's *Strife,* a play about a strike in a Welsh tin works. Suddenly, the National Theatre had burst its bounds. By taking up their rights of residency, in the most literal sense, National Theatre employees had responded to the spatial challenge sketched out for them by Lasdun's urban landscape philosophy. The National Theatre had suddenly become the site for industrial action as opposed to a place where artistic reflections are made on such social phenomena. This moment in the National Theatre's history captures a problematic point of intersection between the real and the fictitious. In so doing, it reveals both the extent and the limitations of the theatre's achievement in terms of its reconstruction of a liberal public sphere of the type described in Habermas's account of the move from medieval to modern society. Initially, the theatre's long pre-history activated a rational egalitarian debate. Subsequently, its establishment carved out a definitive arena for the development of that debate. Finally this dramatic stage in its experience in existence brought about a crisis that revealed the illusory nature of that debate.

At the point at which the English National Theatre became the locus for real and unreasonable industrial action, it made a daring statement regarding its role in the life of the English nation whose life and concerns it proposed to mirror. Ironically, this was also the point at which it also lost its capacity to stimulate and foster rational, egalitarian debate simply because the assumption of greater rights by one section of its public – its employees – inhibited the rights of others and removed the opportunity for creative interpersonal exchange that is the core of theatrical performance. In a paper presented to the National Culture/National Identity Research Group at the 2004 ASTR conference at Las Vegas, Mechele Leon described a similar scenario at the Comédie-Française on 13 July 2003 when a production of Molière's *Le Malade Imaginaire* was cancelled in response to vociferous protests staged by casual entertainment industry workers enraged by recent changes made to their entitlements to welfare benefits. In this case, the consequences of the takeover were less problematic because the cancellation of the performance made way for a lengthy and lively discussion between audience members, actors and the theatre manager, Marcel Bozonnet, regarding a crisis in the theatre industry. The fact that in the case of the English National Theatre dispute, negative strike action substituted positive theatrical action without providing an interactive alternative as was the case in Paris, makes it possible to interpret this event as an emblem of the political disease afflicting Britain that the subsequent Conservative governments, led by Margaret Thatcher, were designed to and did overcome.

In the event, the English National Theatre survived a long period of Conservative government and continues to survive under the current Labour regime. Despite instigating and nurturing political debate by means of its plays and productions, the institution itself never lost its own identity in order to become an agent of political propaganda, as was the case in Nazi Germany, nor was its function and status rationalized in terms of a modern network of regional national centres as is the case in France. Instead, it exists as one of those 'mysterious phenomena' listed by Shaw amongst those national institutions which the English people do not actively claim, yet of which they are passively proud. Perhaps this is, in fact, the most apposite way in which the English National Theatre can maintain the illusion of its reconstruction of the lost opportunities of a Habermasian liberal public sphere.

~ 4 ~
The National Eisteddfod, the national pageant and the Welsh national theatre: friends or foes?

A discussion of the Welsh national theatre debate and its relations to Habermas's liberal public sphere is particularly exciting and challenging because, as we speak, the Welsh national theatre takes its first shaky but dramatic steps towards concrete realization in twenty-first century Wales. Wales – remarkable for the distinct sense of ethnicity that has persisted 'in so small a nation devoid of a natural frontier and with the might of England, like great sea waves dashing over a rock, ever drenching it'[1] – has always been in need of dramatic declarations. The year 2004 saw the most recent incarnation of Theatr Genedlaethol Cymru[2] – a flagship of national enterprise and ambition – as a representative of the nation's theatrical aspirations and probably equally indicative of the theatricality of those aspirations. In England, we saw the middle class construct a national theatre that allowed them to rediscover lost opportunities for national debate and discourse. In Wales, the process of construction, reconstruction and renewal is still in progress.

Despite Patrick Geary's cautious attitude towards cultural creation or creativity, Wales boasts an ancient literary heritage. The poetry of the Cynfeirdd, the Gogynfeirdd and Beirdd yr Uchelwyr[3] did much to establish and sustain the country's cultural and linguistic heritage, but modernization, industrialization and population movement have since done just as much to erode her national confidence. It might well be argued that in seventeenth- and eighteenth-century Wales, the country was one of Engels's 'unnarrated nationalities'.[4] By the 1880s, the Welsh historian Kenneth Morgan pinpoints a period of cultural regeneration[5] and it was at the turn of the nineteenth century that the idea of a Welsh national theatre began to germinate. In a vivacious address in 1894, Tom Jones argued that current conditions favoured the development of a national theatre in Wales. As a result he was inspired to make a direct and personal appeal to his fellow countrymen, 'now who wants to form a Welsh theatrical company?'[6] Jones's appeal was important for two reasons. First, it launched the idea of a national theatre into the public domain. This marked the genesis of a reasoned and reasonable debate about the nation's cultural life and aspirations, reminiscent of Habermas's liberal public sphere. Secondly, it located this national discourse, a discourse focused on defining and refining Welsh national life but, most of all, on driving it forward in a new direction within a pre-existing pattern of cultural activity, namely, the National Eisteddfod of Wales. In England, we have already seen that the Shakespearean theatrical tradition provided the initial impetus for the effort to establish the country's national theatre. In Wales, the National Eisteddfod[7] fulfilled a similar function by providing a potential forum for the development of a theatre that might mirror and serve the Welsh nation – that theatre that had first emerged in the eighteenth-century Welsh interludes.

The umbilical nature of the connection between the Welsh eisteddfod tradition and the national theatre debate in Wales is manifest in the fact that the earliest efforts to promote dramatic interest in the country's national life originated at an eisteddfod. In 1879, some years prior to Jones's appeal, a prize was offered at the Eryri Eisteddfod at Llanberis for the 'best Welsh play in the Shakespearean tradition'[8] [my translation]. This enticement evoked a positive response and the competition was won by Beriah Gwynfe Evans's important, historical play, *Owain Glyndwr*.[9] Years later, the importance of this eisteddfod-led development was summed up in Kitchener Davies's comment that 'if it were necessary to trace the modern Welsh drama movement to one particular date, it would be 1879'[10] [my translation]. Tom Jones did not doubt the fact that the Eisteddfod should build on this early success and lead the way in the process of establishing Wales's first national theatre company. The Eisteddfod should, he said, 'offer a grand prize, leave the subject open, and give one Eisteddfod night to have the prize drama staged and acted'.[11] The Eisteddfod, then, was to be the place where a Welsh national theatre was to develop.

The nomination of the Eisteddfod as the seed bed for a Welsh national theatre, a definitive site in which it might put down roots

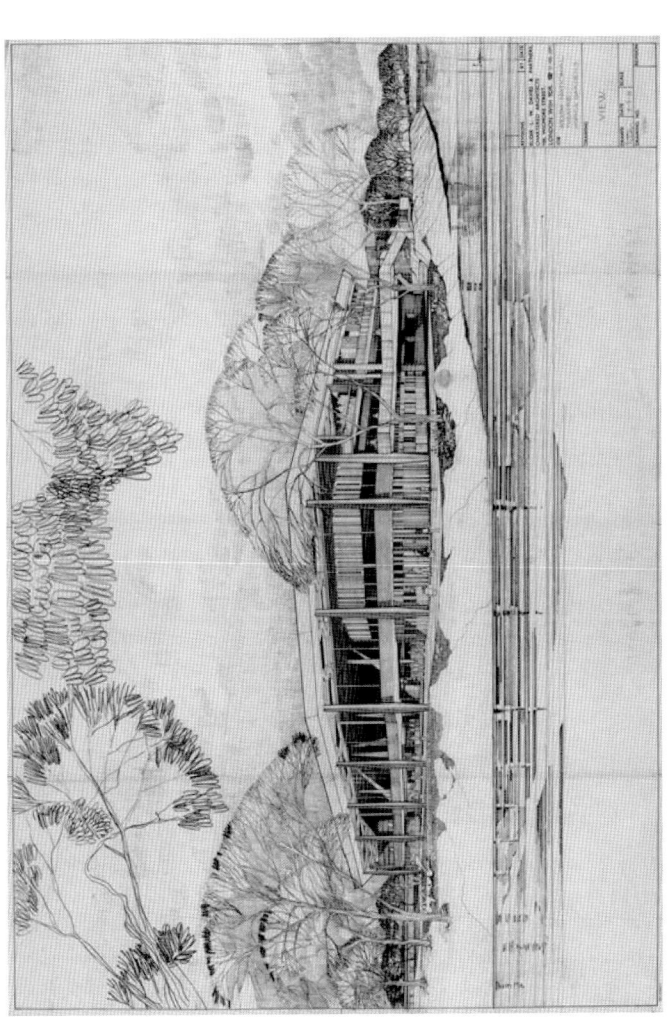

1. An external view of one of Elidir Davies's designs for a Welsh national theatre to be located at Sophia Gardens, Cardiff (1970). By permission of Llyfrgell Genedlaethol Cymru/The National Library of Wales.

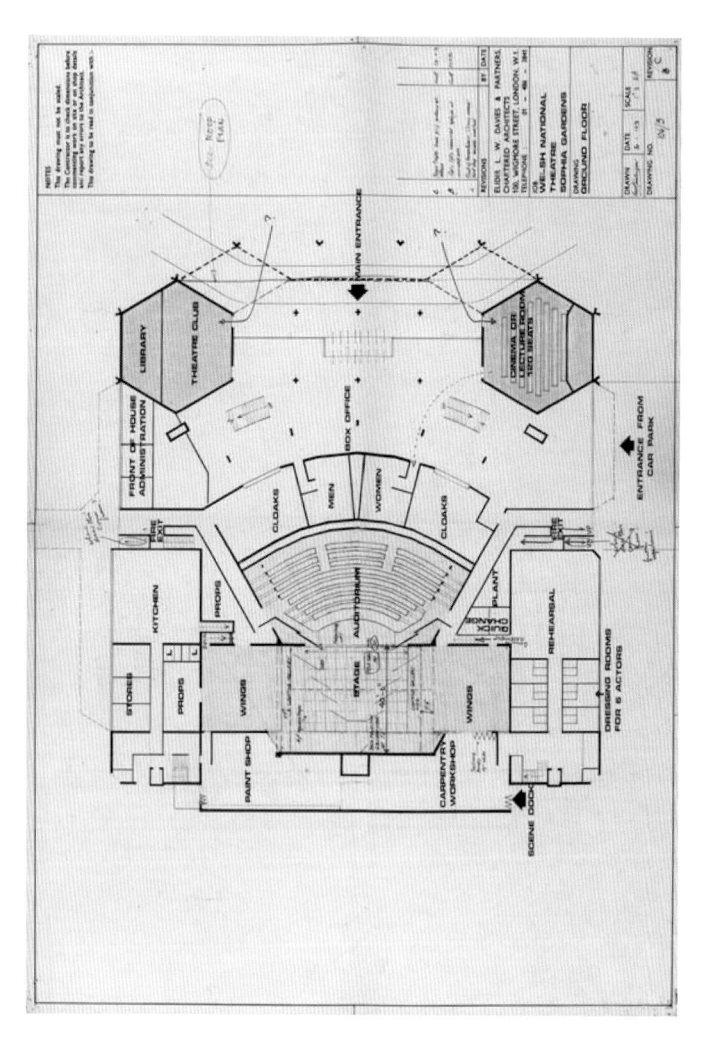

2. A ground floor plan of the Welsh national theatre designed by Elidir Davies for a site in Sophia Gardens, Cardiff (1970). By permission of Llyfrgell Genedlaethol Cymru/The National Library of Wales.

3a. A model of the trailer that was to carry the whole shell of Wales's first portable theatre designed by Sean Kenny c.1967. By permission of Gwynedd Archives Services.

3b. A model of Wales's first portable theatre as it might be on site. External view. By permission of Gwynedd Archives Services

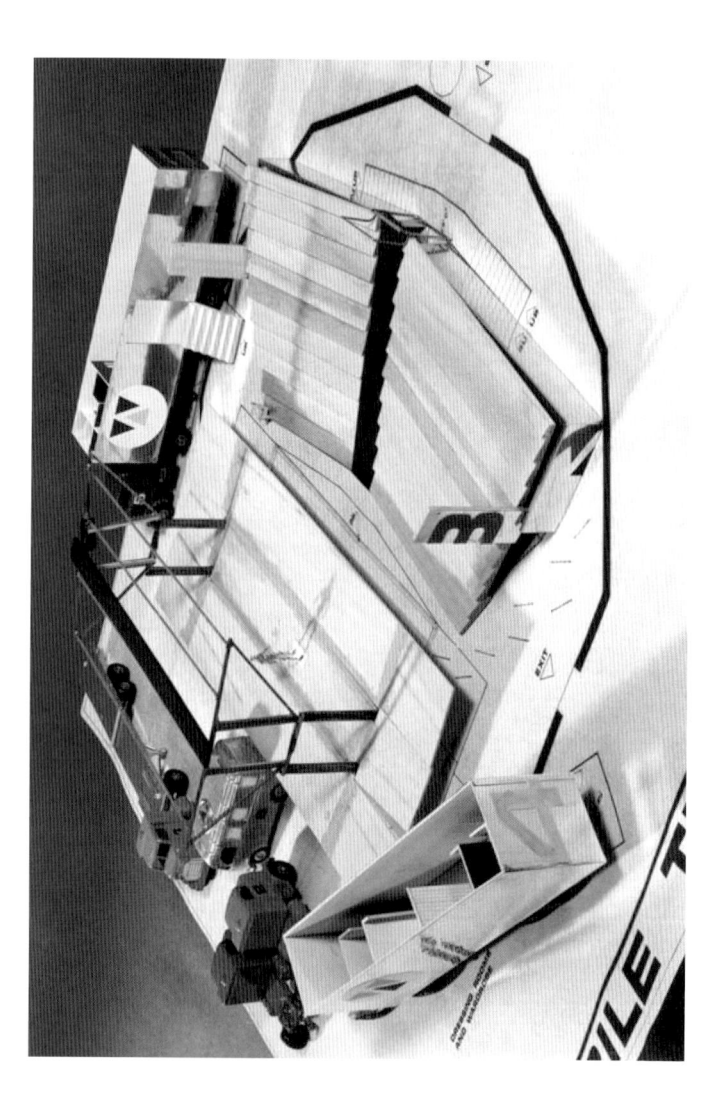

4. A model of Wales's first portable theatre providing an interior view of the stage, the auditorium, the dressing rooms and wardrobe. By permission of Gwynedd Archives Service.

5. David Lyn, Gaynor Morgan Rees and Eilian Wyn in a production of *Y Ffin*, Cwmni Theatr Cymru, October 1973. By permission of Gwynedd Archives Services.

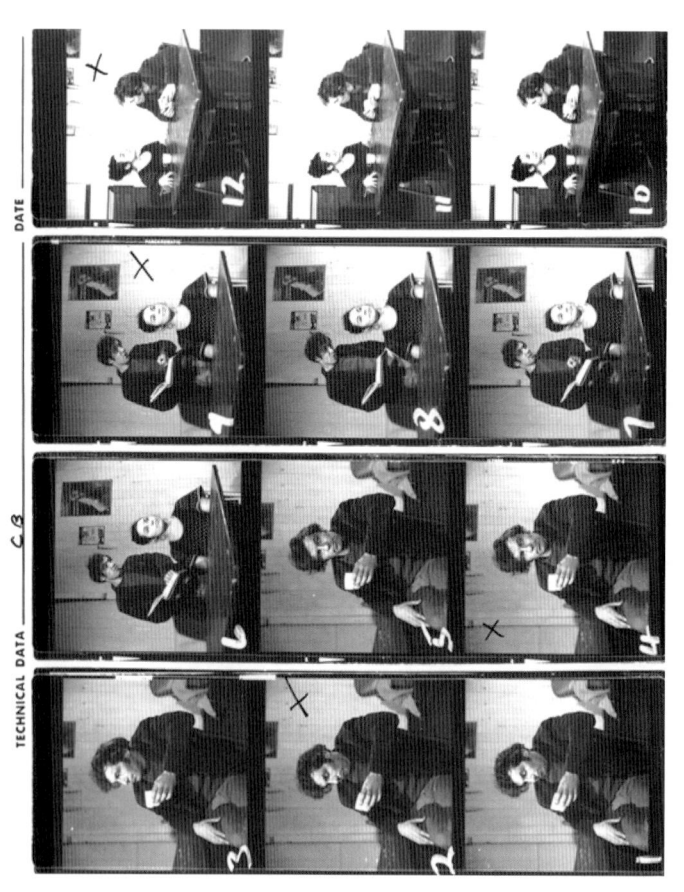

6. John Ogwen and Maureen Rees in a production of *Alpha Beta*, Cwmni Theatr Cymru, December 1974. By permission of Gwynedd Archives Services.

7. Carys Eleri Evans in Theatr Genedlaethol Cymru's production of *Plas Drycin* (January/February 2005). Photograph by Warren Orchard. By permission of Llyfrgell Genedlaethol Cymru/The National Library of Wales.

8. Rhian Blythe and Christine Pritchard in Theatr Genedlaethol Cymru's production of *Romeo and Juliet* (October/November 2004). Photograph by Warren Orchard. By permission of Llyfrgell Genedlaethol Cymru/The National Library of Wales.

before being nurtured into mature life, was problematic because the Eisteddfod, a travelling, cultural festival, was not rooted to a permanent place itself and therefore could not actually ground Welsh drama, in any concrete sense. Ironically, the place in which a Welsh national theatre was set to develop was an ideological construction, a point marked out on the horizon of the Welsh creative imagination rather than a definitive, geographical location. It is fruitful to compare and contrast this situation to that of the early German national theatre and the difficulties it faced as a result of the proliferation of small states that made up the national unit in eighteenth-century Germany. While the nomination of the Hamburg National Theatre as the country's first national theatre overcame this problem, albeit temporarily, the Welsh response to the equivalent challenge was to forgo a physical location in favour of a virtual one. This response constituted an innovative, imaginative feat, but the fact that the Eisteddfod was not, like the Hamburg theatre building, dedicated to and designed for theatre, brought a new set of obstacles to the fore.

There were those who accepted the link between the Eisteddfod and the idea of a Welsh national theatre as an inevitable and even a desirable connection. Some weighed up the Eisteddfod's own claim to support and patronage in terms of the good it could do by channelling its energies to foster and stimulate other national art forms, such as a national theatre. There were others, like Lloyd George, who suspected that the nation's cultural development would benefit from breaking free of the Eisteddfod establishment. In an address at the Caernarfon Eisteddfod in 1894, he argued that the festival's ancestral clout should not hold the nation spellbound and that it was the duty of every patriot to seek to expand his countrymen's desires, in this case towards a taste for Welsh drama,[12] that was not tied to the apron strings of any other, pre-established cultural institution, the Eisteddfod included.

Whichever may be the more appropriate response, any analysis of the Welsh national theatre debate in Wales would do well to begin by attempting to establish what kind of an artistic animal this age-old, cultural festival was and how one might account for its relation to the idea of a national theatre in Wales. Local and national eisteddfodau are a feature of modern Welsh life, but their contemporary manifestation is the result of a relaunch attempt made in 1789 as part of an effort to promote Welsh literature and, primarily, the Welsh poetic tradition. This effort was spearheaded by one Edward Charles. In an essay on the eisteddfodau, G. J. Williams records Charles's declaration:

> I have the vanity to say that I was the first Man that thought of reviving the Eisteddfod. It had engaged my thoughts from the age of 14 to my 26th year. Had not the Gwyneddigion[13] granted my request (which was in the form of a petition in 1789) the Eisteddfod might for what I know have remained dormant to this day.[14]

It is interesting to contrast the quietness of this cultural campaign to promote Welsh literature and arts and, ultimately, Welsh national identity, to the violence of the political upheaval occurring in France at the same point in time. At this stage in its history, the French nation had boasted a national theatre for over a century. Wales, on the other hand, had only recently begun groping toward the establishment of a formal, cultural identity, recognizable from both within and without the country, and was very far away from obtaining a national theatre. Just as the French set about deconstructing both their artistic and political institutions, Wales was facing the milder task of coaxing them into first life. The Eisteddfod provided a channel for the facilitation of this process of conception and construction; a forum in which the development of a distinctive Welsh literary culture could be practised and promoted.

Edward Charles may well have been responsible for resurrecting the tradition of the Eisteddfod in Wales.[15] Once he had done so, it became public property and opened up a new, cultural arena to the public. It was not long before one Edward Williams, or Iolo Morganwg,[16] grasped the new opportunities made available to him and set about transforming the Eisteddfod into a cultural engine of a most particular kind. The Eisteddfod, as envisaged by Edward Charles and as realized under the auspices of the Gwyneddigion society, aimed at promoting the arts and, in particular, the poetic arts. As such, it was a public forum in which a particular form of cultural interchange took place, namely, the reception of lyrical declamation by a listening audience. This reciprocal ritual was a strange medley of the active and the passive, the authoritarian and the egalitarian. The audience partook in a cultural activity but they did not do so as equal players. On the one hand, their active role was manifest in their physical presence at the event and their participation as listeners; on the other hand, their passivity was underlined, not simply by virtue of the fact that their input was restricted to listening, but because the election of the winning poet was a matter not for the public themselves but for educated adjudicators.[17]

In the context of the restricted nature of audience participation[18] at the Eisteddfod, it is interesting to note that Thomas Edwards,[19] the most famous and skilled exponent of the Welsh interlude, the nation's earliest documented form of drama, took part in these eisteddfodau not as a dramatist but as a poet. The fact that his interludes were relegated to the fringes of the Eisteddfod was not indicative of a lack of consumer demand, but reveals the fact that drama had, as yet, no place in the campaign for national cultural revival and refinement that centred on the Eisteddfod. The educated elite brought together at the Cymmrodorion and Gwyneddigion societies was not yet able to conceive of allowing the populace a fully active role in the process of cultural creation in Wales.[20] As a result, Edwards's interludes in which a merry, lively and vociferous audience entered into a creative compact with a band of players, who presented them with a pithy, dramatic debate, were consigned to the underworld of Welsh cultural life.[21]

When Iolo Morganwg took centre stage at the Eisteddfod, things were set to change. Iolo, a stoneworker by craft, was a charismatic, energetic and controversial figure in his own and later times. He played a fundamental part in the developmental history of the Eisteddfod, securing its transition from a minor, cultural force working at a regional level to that of Wales's most popular and influential national cultural event. In his study of Iolo's ideas and work, Ceri Lewis recognizes the achievements of those who sponsored Wales's regional eisteddfodau but argues that Iolo, more than any other man, created the Welsh people's Eisteddfod, the large, national festival with which we are familiar today.[22] Despite the fact that Wales's first national Eisteddfod, an event attended by thousands of people from all over the country in Llangollen in 1858 was held decades after Iolo's death, the event was cast in the mould prepared so painstakingly by 'the Bard'[23] himself.

Iolo put the Eisteddfod at the heart of Welsh culture and national identity. The means by which he did so are as important to our study of the origins of Wales's national theatre as is the central fact itself. What Iolo actually did was to introduce a core of ceremony and ritual to the Eisteddfod that quickly became its centrepiece and its raison d'être. These ceremonial rites were drawn from a treasury of literary secrets that he claimed had legitimate, historical validity. By today, he has been exposed as a literary fraud, but this does not diminish the importance of his role in the shaping of the modern-day Eisteddfod; the cultural festival that was to be the home of Wales's earliest national drama and theatre. The foundation upon which he based his elaborate system of literary status symbols was the identification of the Welsh bards with the ancient druids, vates and bards of Britain, documented by John Leland in his *Commentarii de Scriptoribus Britannicis* (1709). In the first instance Iolo developed an imaginative (and largely imaginary) infrastructure of bardic rites and rituals outside the Eisteddfod context;[24] at the heart of these rites he anchored *Gorsedd y Beirdd*. Originally, the word *gorsedd* meant a mound of earth, but Iolo soon began to use it to indicate a special, open-air assembly of bards. His ideas were seductive and they influenced many of his literary friends at the Gwyneddigion society, so much so that in June 1792 the first *gorsedd* ceremony was held at Primrose Hill, London.[25] Accounts of this event tell of the setting of a ring of twelve stones around one central stone. The ceremony was opened by the placing of a sword on the central stone, followed by Iolo's oration of his English-language poem, 'Ode on the Mythology of the Ancient British Bards'. It is also said that two adult members were received into the *gorsedd*, along with Taliesin, Iolo's five-year-old son.

Iolo had originally intended that the *gorsedd* should replace the Eisteddfod. Later, in view of the latter's popularity, he decided it should become a central component of the Eisteddfod experience. By conducting the *gorsedd* ceremony at the Carmarthen Eisteddfod in 1819, he instigated the symbiotic relationship between the two that persists in Wales to this day. Some critics attribute Iolo's cultural activity to regional pride and argue that it is inappropriate to claim that he had a national agenda in any sense. Cathryn Charnell-White exposes his prejudice against the inhabitants of north Wales and his insistence on the excellence of the south of the country in linguistic and cultural matters when she quotes a challenge he issued to the poet Goronwy Owen, 'And you, north Walian, go to the south where you will see and hear what their language is and take there [the poems of] Taliesin... in your hand and you will see if a south Walian or a north Walian will understand them best.'[26] However, Lewis argues for Iolo's importance to Wales as a whole on the basis of his success in capturing the public imagination by means of his invention of the ceremonial pageantry of the *gorsedd*.[27] I wish to argue that by placing the *gorsedd* ceremony at the heart of this pageantry, Iolo prepared the way for the development of drama and theatre alongside the Welsh tradition of oratory, recitation and musical and lyrical declamation. In this context, it is telling to hear a prominent critical commentator note in 1914 that whilst Hwfa Môn, the Eisteddfod's chief bard, may not have been the nation's greatest poet, he was, arguably, its finest actor.[28]

It was Iolo's popularizing of a central ritual of metamorphosis that established 'play-acting' as a legitimate cultural activity and opened the door for the development of a national theatre in Wales. Unbeknown to himself, and almost by accident, Iolo's tireless and enthusiastic cultural creativity in the service of his native region, Glamorgan, actually played a central part in the development of Wales's national theatre. Whether or not Iolo had intended it to do so, the *gorsedd* ritual achieved two things: first, it alerted the Welsh to their capacity for metamorphosis, or, in other words, for theatre; secondly, it alerted them to the fact that theatre could release them, albeit temporarily, from the constraints of real life and provide them with access to a world in which they might both investigate and articulate their national identity by means of an egalitarian process of dramatic debate. After Iolo's innovations it could no longer be claimed that the Welsh were a 'nation of listeners'.[29] Their participation in the Eisteddfod, the nation's central cultural event, was no longer a passive one since they, too, were 'changed, changed utterly' [30] by their personal investment in the *gorsedd*'s central rite of metamorphosis.

By participation in the *gorsedd* ceremony, individuals traded in their real identities for a new role and status, in a virtual society. A report of the initiation of His Royal Highness and other members of his royal party into the *gorsedd* at the 1894 Caernarfon Eisteddfod captures the central significance of the act of renaming and the adoption of a fictitious persona. It relates how:

The Royal party on leaving the Pavilion were driven through the crowded streets to the Castle Square, where a Gorsedd was formed under the direction of Clwydfardd, the venerable Archdruid. The druids, bards, ovates, all attired in their robes of white, blue and green, having arranged themselves in due order within the mystic circle, the distinguished visitors were called upon to witness that 'grave, innocent druidic rite done in the eye of light' ... Sir John Puleston and Mr. Lewis Morris then advanced to the Prince of Wales, and, conducted him to the foot of the Logan Stone. The Prince submitted his right arm to Hwfa Mon, who as chief bard, tied the green riband around it. Clwydfardd proclaimed that the bardic title of the new ovate was Iorwerth Dywysog. His Royal Highness withdrew, and made way for the Princess of Wales ... after which she was renamed in the Gorsedd circle as Hoffedd Prydain.[31]

Admittedly, there was always a hierarchical force at work in the constitution of the *gorsedd*, but the ceremony itself offered all members of the Welsh nation access to a new sphere in which they could function as equals. Whilst *gorsedd* members were selected on the basis of literary merit, their successful initiation into its mysteries was entirely dependent on those audience members who assisted their affiliation into a national circle of cultural excellence by means of a willing suspension of disbelief. Despite the fact that the Prince of Wales had been afforded the honour of initiation on the basis of his social status (the criteria regarding literary merit could not have been applied in this case), he too was divested of that in this new world in which human interaction was governed by a democratic process of negotiation and mutual consent, captured most emphatically in the exchange between the Archdruid and the pavilion audience, upon the crowning of the Eisteddfod bard.

The changes Iolo introduced to the Eisteddfod were important in their own right. They had further significance because they reflected the onset, in Welsh society as a whole, of a critical debate concerning matters of national interest that had hitherto been complicated by the country's subservience to England in terms of the structures and mechanisms of political power and social affluence. The shift from declamation to dramatization that occurred at the heart of the Welsh Eisteddfod marked the naissance of a desire on the part of the Welsh nation to play an active role in the articulation of her own identity, both within and without Wales. It remained to be seen whether a national theatre and, indeed, theatre itself, could ever achieve sufficient popularity in Wales in order to fulfil this promise, but the potential significance of a national theatre to Wales had been identified in terms of its ability to activate an egalitarian process of interchange between those at both ends of the creative process, players and audience. A national theatre, then, might function as an objective correlative for Habermas's liberal public sphere and as such could provide the nation with much needed practice in the art of debate, discussion and negotiation that would facilitate its survival in the modern world, beyond the theatre, and beyond Wales itself.

The affinity between the ceremonial transformation of the *gorsedd* and the practice of national theatre, when understood as a communal, cultural activity designed to express and strengthen a common identity, explains why the Eisteddfod was so prominent in terms of the genesis of the national theatre debate in Wales. More than a century after Iolo's innovations, comments made by J. O. Francis regarding his own experience of the *gorsedd* ceremony at the Corwen National Eisteddfod, suggest that the theatricality with which Iolo had endowed the ceremony remained a live and potent force. J. O. Francis was a young Welsh dramatist whose excellence as a creative artist was due, in the main, to his sensitivity to the changes that were transforming the 'social atmosphere'[32] of early twentieth-century Wales. However, despite the modernity of his approach to Welsh life, he thought and spoke of the Eisteddfod much like Iolo before him as a man of the theatre. Francis approved of Iolo's creativity and argued that the *gorsedd* had no need of any historical basis because it was, at bottom, 'a piece of ceremonial'. 'If we go out to play', he comments, 'it does not matter that the form of the game differs from that of our forefathers. What matters is that all generations should play it in the true spirit.'[33] The game that the Welsh choose to play at the Eisteddfod climaxes, as I have already mentioned, with the naming of the victorious bard. Francis valued this exercise as a communal celebration of artistic inspiration and artistry – a thrilling moment when 'eight thousand Welsh people rose to their feet in honour, not of a great politician or of a famous millionaire, but in honour of an unknown man who had written a poem'.[34] In his view, it was this that externalized the adherence of the Welsh nation to a system of artistic values that brings out the 'inward essence of a race – and mark(s) a people apart'.[35]

Regrettably, Francis complained, once the focus returned from the audience to the platform, it deteriorated. He felt that 'while the situation had its centre of gravity in the audience, it was a fine situation. As soon as the centre of gravity shifted to the platform, there was another slow collapse.'[36] Francis was not arguing that the centre of gravity should not be shifted from the audience to the stage, but that it must take up the characteristic discipline of theatrical art in order to carry the spirit of the people forward, rather than lose its effect on the platform of public committee meetings. In order to achieve this, he concluded that effective control of the *gorsedd* should lie not with the scholar but with the theatrical producer. 'What the *gorsedd* has to reveal', he insisted, 'is not the truth of History, but the truth of Pageantry.'[37] He was convinced that 'rites and ceremonies are governed by the deliberate art of the theatre, not the careless promptings of the platform'[38] and those who practice them must bow to the discipline of the theatre.

Francis's analysis of this central Eisteddfod event manifests the contradictions of Welsh life. The event celebrates some of the core values of Welsh society; it also reveals the danger to those values inherent in the process of affording them objective validity within an official sphere. Clearly, if the concept of a Welsh national identity is to gain credence in the world at large, the fundamental characteristics of Welsh life and the Welsh *geist* must be able to survive the rigours of this transitional process. Francis's recommendation that the *gorsedd* ceremony ally itself with the theatre, in order to secure its status as a vehicle for the expression of national characteristics and values, reveals his conviction that theatre possesses an innate ability to authenticate the internal values at the heart of communal activity and to decode them in a format that is readable, to both participants and onlookers alike. I have found no evidence of any immediate response to Francis's observations, but it is interesting to note that a newspaper report published a few years later, in 1923, refers to the presence of a particularly large crowd at the *gorsedd* ceremony in anticipation of changes under the new supervision.[39] It is noted that there were improvements to the organization of the ceremony, the committee had invested in new robes and the procession was much more orderly than previously. Whilst criticism of the residual custom of delivering ugly englynion and boring witticisms[40] as part of the ceremony implies that the desire for change had not been fully satisfied, it was evident that adherence to a theatrical formula had intensified the *gorsedd*'s appeal to and effect on its audience. Surely it follows that a national theatre that presented its dramatic debate in accordance with a specific and standard set of formal principles would be of invaluable worth to the Welsh nation in its attempt to externalize its own national identity in a permanent and accessible form?

There can be little doubt that Iolo's innovations at the Eisteddfod opened the door to future developments in the field of Welsh theatre. However, there had been other influences at work as early as the eighteenth century in the field of Welsh drama itself that had indicated both the kind of artistic interaction that a national theatre might foster and the significance of that dramatic activity to the idea of a Welsh national identity. Most scholars agree that modern Welsh drama emerged towards the middle of the eighteenth century with the appearance of the Welsh interlude. It is true that the practice of interlude playing in general was almost entirely confined to north Wales and therefore could not be considered a truly national cultural activity.[41] Saunders Lewis's argument that Thomas Edwards's interludes are written from a medieval perspective, based on the unity of a metaphysical vision of man's social life in the state and as a reflection of a greater, Christian world order, suggests that the concept of a distinct, national life in Wales, or anywhere else for that matter, was alien to the mindset that brought forth this particular form of dramatic entertainment.[42] Nonetheless, the fact that Edwards structured his work in the form of a dramatic debate meant that whilst the primary object of his interludes may not have been to reflect the life of the nation, they could not avoid contributing to the development of national life.

D. R. Davies is right to comment that modern Welsh drama grew 'pure and simply from the argument'[43] [my translation] and that this argument found its earliest textual manifestation in Edwards's interludes. Whilst this basic form of dramatic debate may well have been restricted in thematic and geographical scope, its national significance lies in its introduction of a forum for debate amongst sectors of the Welsh population that had very few alternative opportunities in this area. Captain Factor, one of Edwards's miser characters, rationalizes the magnetism of the interludes precisely in terms of their instigation of a dramatic debate, when he notes that the launching of 'some dispute',[44] either by a Methodist preacher or an interlude player, is a sure-fire way to draw a Welsh crowd. In this sense, Edwards's eighteenth-century interludes signalled the most appropriate and culturally profitable direction for any future Welsh national theatre. If it was to fulfil its potential to play out 'an identity that is publicly performed, constituted by certain practices of social interaction within a regular territory that strengthens collective identity',[45] a Welsh national theatre would have to instigate and foster a creative and democratic, dramatic debate in which all nation members had an active investment.

There has been much critical interest in Edwards's interludes, but Saunders Lewis's view that 'we have lost the key to his work'[46] [my translation] is a common one. In fact, it is generally agreed that it is difficult, if not impossible, to establish a line of continuity between pre- and post-nineteenth century drama in Wales. Dramatic critics often support this claim by noting that Welsh-speaking Wales witnessed almost no further dramatic activity between Edwards's death in 1810 and the renaissance of Welsh drama in 1880. I wish to counter the view that this hiatus is either the cause or proof of a fundamental rift between the dramatic genius of the two centuries, with the argument that Welsh drama was in fact in a cocoon-like state, awaiting a change in the national climate that would facilitate its winged emergence from its chrysalis. There can be no doubt that there was a revival in the field of Welsh drama from about 1880 onwards and that this surge of dramatic activity was part of the struggle, described by Kenneth Morgan as the transformation of a 'static sense of national consciousness' into a 'more dynamic sentiment of nationalism'[47] that began in earnest in Wales towards the close of the nineteenth century. Ioan Williams also locates the Welsh drama of this period within a more general cultural renaissance when he characterizes it as a dramatization of 'a celebration of the transformation of the old Calvinist Wales to the new country confident by virtue of bilingual education and social progress'[48] [my translation]. I agree with both commentators regarding the importance of this new dramatic development, but I would argue that when Welsh drama reappeared in the 1880s, it was not distinguished by its ability to establish a new dramatic tradition, distinct from Edwards's interludes, but by the fact that it could now take advantage of a process of cultural acclimatization that would allow drama its fullest significance in the country's national life.

Both Edwards's interludes and the moral and religious resistance they encountered[49] can be understood as opposite aspects of an early manifestation of the desire to establish and maintain a national Welsh identity. On the one hand, the practice of interlude playing instigated a communal dramatic activity that began the process of defining a Welsh national character. On the other hand, the association of immorality with interlude playing marked the beginning of an attempt to restrain the Welsh character by those in positions of moral, religious and economic superiority. Edwards's death in 1810 coincided with the onset of a barren period in the history of Welsh drama and theatre. This period of sterility suggests that the cultural climate of nineteenth-century Wales was unable to nurture the dramatic discussion instigated by Edwards because the battle to establish the legitimacy of a Welsh national culture had yet to be won. Iolo Morganwg's innovations at the Eisteddfod marked a significant stage in the development of this struggle: the flamboyant advances made by him enabled Welsh drama to reassert its entitlement to the instigation of debate and discussion and to extend the scope of that discussion to include the people of Wales as a whole.

On the threshold of the twentieth century, Wales was poised to follow through with these pioneering developments. In the event it proved to be a lengthy and difficult process. In a discussion of the forces that prepared the way for a Welsh national theatre,[50] Cecil Price argues that the famous composer Sir Joseph Parry was a significant early influence. Price argues that Parry's operatic compositions did much to counteract the moral prejudice against theatre in his contemporary Wales because music lovers set aside their distrust of the theatre[51] in appreciation of the symbiosis of both elements in Parry's work. My view of his importance has more to do with the evidence provided by the popular response to his work, regarding the failure of the Welsh to distinguish between drama and song at this stage in the nation's cultural evolution. Joseph Parry's operas were Welsh in terms of their interest, subject matter and feeling. The first opera, *Blodwen*, performed at the University College of Wales, Aberystwyth, in May 1878, had a Welsh libretto. The second focused on a central

Welsh historical figure, Llewelyn, the last prince of Wales, and Parry's final operatic work, *The Maid of Cefn Ydfa*,[52] took a familiar tale of Welsh folk mythology as its heart-rending subject. Along with Parry's other musical creations,[53] they did much to promote an image of the Welsh nation, albeit a rather romantic one.

The operas were important in that they employed the Welsh language as a medium of artistic expression and Price refers to the travelling operatic company, set up by Mendy Parry's son to tour his father's work, as a national opera company. However, whilst we can trust Price's assessment that Parry's operas counteracted moral prejudice against the drama in Wales, they did nothing to clarify the distinction in the Welsh mind between song and drama, opera and theatre. *Blodwen* is described as having little theatrical merit and a review of the Moody-Manners opera company's presentation of *The Maid of Cefn Ydfa*, composed towards the end of Parry's career, suggests that his theatrical skills had not undergone a tremendous development. The review is full of praise for the musical elements of the presentation but notes that the action was somewhat slow and a 'perfect knowledge of stage-craft was wanting'.[54] It may be that moral prejudice against drama in Wales had been assuaged by Joseph Parry's impressive musical talent but it is questionable whether those theatrical elements to which the audience were accustoming themselves in the interest of music were, by any critical standards, theatre at all. Where does this leave Joseph Parry? In the context of Williams's argument that the Welsh drama of the 1880s and 1890s heralded the transition from the old Calvinistic Wales to a new country, shaped by forces other than religious ones, Parry's destigmatizing role in relation to Welsh drama is clearly significant. I would argue, however, that his prime importance lay with his introduction of the Welsh nation, inhabitants of the Land of Song,[55] to both the splendours and the limitations of lyrical declamation, an experience that eventually alerted them to the possibilities inherent in dramatic action.

For a long time, Welsh dramatists failed to exploit the fact that whilst song might say important things about the Welsh nation, drama might let the Welsh nation say important things about itself. The early Welsh drama of the closing decades of the nineteenth century is a curious medley of the lyrical and the dramatic, neither element reaching the heights attained by Parry in his musical compositions. In his article 'Towards a Welsh National Theatre', Cecil Price notes that Welsh audiences appreciated references to their nationality and that the employment of a Welsh singer, who 'appealed to their nationality with a good song',[56] was a common method of pandering to a Welsh audience. William Haggar's succesful Llanelli theatre boasted the '"Williams" Welsh minstrels who comprised two ladies being dressed in Welsh costumes,'[57] as a feature of its variety programme in 1910. How Welsh these token Welsh performers were in truth is difficult to ascertain, particularly in view of the complaints of the 1860 Merthyr theatrical clientele that the Welsh clown at the annual pantomime failed to capture the 'Cymric accent'[58] adequately. Nonetheless, it is clear that the Welsh valued this lyrical declamation of their national identity and it is interesting to note that even Jones's appeal for a Welsh theatrical company estimated the harpist's wages at £3 a week, on a par with those of the actors themselves.[59]

Despite the rather disheartening nature of these musical tributes to the Welsh in the field of drama, there were more significant developments afoot. Beriah Evans followed up his initial success of *Owain Glyndwr* with the writing of another historical play, *Llewelyn ein Llyw Olaf*, published in 1883 in Llanelli.[60] Although they earned him the title 'the father of Welsh drama', Evans's early plays provide evidence of the difficult passage of Welsh drama from the realm of the lyrical to that of the theatrical. Williams's suspicion that the celebratory element he detected in the Welsh drama of the 1880s and 1890s was, in fact, a means of masking the pain of the socio-political changes sweeping the nation, provides insight into Evans's obstinate clinging to song and music and his timidity in embracing dramatic action and debate. The fact that the lyrical propensity of Evans's plays did not elicit much contemporary criticism was probably due to the fact that the Welsh populace had not yet developed a critical attitude towards drama as a distinctive art form. By 1911, things had changed and W. J. Gruffydd described a later version of *Owain Glyndwr* as a mongrel of a play, somewhere between an '*operetta* and a pageant'[61] [my translation]. A quick perusal of the play substantiates Gruffydd's criticism, but Evans's own notes to the original text suggest that he did not conceive of the lyrical elements as a weakness at all. The text is categorized as a drama cantata and the composer of its musical score, Alaw Ddu,[62] is afforded equal honours with the author. Evans's note that 'the play has been written and structured so that the narrative parts are subservient, and lead up to the musical parts'[63] [my translation], is an implicit admission of the fact that he lacked both an understanding and a command of that basic element of dramatic construction: theatrical tension.

Evans was not the only dramatist to compose his drama according to such hybrid principles. Lewis David Jones and John Lloyd Williams's joint dramatic creation, *Aelwyd Angharad*,[64] was another play that suffered from comparable confusion with regard to its own artistic pedigree. In the newspaper *Y Brython*, it is referred to, in a single article, both as one of the latest products of the Welsh folk song movement and as promise of the future emergence of a 'new faculty in Welsh art, – Welsh Operatic Drama'.[65] The writer, Elidir Sais, complicates matters further by going on to justify his preference for musical drama, as opposed to historical drama, in terms that lend credence to my argument that music and song were detrimental to the advancement of a national drama in late nineteenth-century Wales. Elidir may well be right in his indictment of Evans's early dramatic output, but his own response to the challenges inherent in the process of generating a Welsh national drama is to retreat into the national stronghold of music and song by arguing that,

> the half-dozen historical plays produced by us during the last decade are dramatically worthless ... We are as yet not sufficiently educated in stage-craft to produce history on the stage, – and stage-craft is the essence of the historical play. A musical play on the other hand can be made easily successful, because, if the music be good, many dramatic blemishes are thereby condoned.[66]

There were those critics who argued that, upon discovering song, the Welsh chose to sing 'with gusto, but as if there were no connection between song and art'.[67] Whether or not we agree with this indictment, it is evident that the nation's early failure to recognize drama as an art form in its own right played a significant role in thwarting the development of a Welsh national theatre.

It was the Eisteddfod's adventure into the arena of performance and production that would ease the nation towards an understanding of what drama really was. In his notes on the Welsh dramatic movement, T. O. Jones pinpoints 1906 as the 'first occasion on which the National Eisteddfod extended its official patronage to drama playing'.[68] He is referring to the performance of Beriah Evans's play, *Caradog: Pendragon Prydain,* by the Red Dragon company in the Guild Hall during the Caernarfon Eisteddfod week. In his study of the history of Welsh drama, Ioan Williams debates the advantages and disadvantages of the major role played by the amateur movement in the field of theatre production and performance in Wales.[69] But here, once again, the Eisteddfod can claim precedence because its decision to perform Evans's play effectively sanctioned performance as a legitimate, cultural pursuit. It was this development that began to manoeuvre Wales towards the realization that drama boasted not only the theatricality that they associated with song but the capacity to instigate a rational dramatic debate that would propel the nation into the twentieth century. Thereafter, the touring of plays like *Aelwyd Angharad* whetted the Welsh people's appetite for performance and instigated a debate about theatre as an independent art form. Testimony of the debate fuelled by the production of these plays is provided by an open letter written from Liverpool, in which a recent production of *Aelwyd Angharad* at the David Lewis Theatre in the town is discussed. The particular significance of this correspondence lies in its revelation of the naissance of a popular desire to engage in a dramatic debate in Wales. It also exposes the fact that the linguistic terminology that might facilitate a debate of this kind was, as yet, crude and undeveloped.

The writer's choice of the informal and pseudo-private form of an open letter to deliver his thoughts on the production, manifests his nervousness concerning the transition from a private zone to the realm of public affairs and, indeed, public opinion, in a way reminiscent of Jean Loret. The Welsh writer's comments lack critical perspicacity and his language according to his own assessment is downtrodden. Nonetheless, he displays awareness that the piece is, in fact, a play and advises the company to learn from the English way of laying out the stage and placing characters upon it. He tempers his praise with the admission that he is 'neither an editor nor a regular reporter'[70] [my translation]. but simply the son of a Mona farmer.[71] This admission, along with his definition of the players themselves as members of an extended family group, 'Angharad's tribe', is evidence of the modernity of his critical approach. However much he is hampered by the lack of a terminology adequate to the task in hand, here is one Welshman who is determined to discuss a theatrical production in terms of a democratic communal activity. It is no coincidence that this letter appeared contemporaneously with an attack on Elidir Sais's criticism of the same production. Elidir himself seemed to have moved with the times and was now urging the removal from the play of precisely those musical elements that he had praised for concealing the blemishes of Welsh drama, some four years earlier. Possibly the most convincing proof yet that the Welsh public was inching towards a drama of national dimensions and character is provided by the correspondent who is not outraged but inspired by Elidir's advice to 'cut down the Overture ... Cut down *Modryb*'s song ... it spoils the play'.[72] This reader receives the change in Elidir's critical viewpoint as evidence that the nation is benefiting from an increased acquaintance with Welsh drama to such an extent that it may be acceptable to concede that 'the fault of *Angharad* is, that it is no drama, – in the true sense-at all; and to advertise it as such is a '"terminological inexactitude".' [73]

Despite encouraging signs that Wales was sharpening her critical skills on the grindstone of live theatre, there was also a feeling that development in the field of performance and production was slow to fulfil its potential. As a result, a contributor to *Y Brython* took the initiative by urging the national drama movement to take the next logical step forward: the establishment of a Welsh theatre. Drama, he argues,

> has a purpose beyond that of the awdl or pryddest – at least beyond its publication in the press. It is intended to be acted, and its worth cannot be fully evaluated in any other light. Wales has been reticent in fashioning anything in the likeness of a playhouse ... but it is essential to move with the times, and adapt ourselves to new circumstances, in as far as that is beneficial to the general good[74] [my translation].

Whichever way one looks at the history of the Welsh national theatre debate, it is impossible to ignore the dependence of Welsh drama and theatre on the Eisteddfod institution. It is equally difficult to avoid the fact that this relationship was as problematical as it was productive. As early as 1898, E. Derry Evans had counterbalanced his recognition of the 'inestimable service' rendered to the nation by the Eisteddfod, an institution that had, in his view, fulfilled 'the functions of an University', with the view that the artistic rules and regulations promoted by this 'conventional body' had arrested the development of the Welsh national character and particularly the Welsh artistic genius.[75] His argument that other art forms such as the novel had only been able to prosper in Wales outside the pale of the Eisteddfod supports my identification of the poetic and the lyrical with the Eisteddfod. His criticism of the institutionalizing effect of the Eisteddfod on the Welsh idea of lyric beauty, both in relation to its promotion at the expense of other art forms and to the quasi-neoclassical straightjacketing of its own format and function, has obvious relevance in terms of the curious hybrid that was Welsh drama in the 1880s and 1890s. It was not that Wales was unaware of this dilemma, only that she did not know how to solve it.

As the century drew to a close, it eventually became evident that Welsh theatre needed a new place beyond the Eisteddfod, wherein it might attain its fullest, national form – the discovery and definition of that place became an inherent part of the movement to establish a Welsh national theatre. Despite being one of the earliest of its kind, Jones's appeal identifies one of the distinctive features of the endeavour to establish a national theatre in Wales from its inception at the close of the nineteenth century to its latest realization at the turn of the second millennium – the diversity of Wales's geographical constitution. Mr O. M. Edwards, who presided over the evening concert at the 1894 Caernarfon Eisteddfod, recognized this factor when he spoke of his vision that a future Eisteddfod might set aside part of its own territory as a suitable place dedicated to Welsh theatre. His proposal centred on the allotment of at least one Eisteddfod night to the nation's drama.[76] Jones, on the other hand, was prepared to make a break from the Eisteddfod. He insisted that whilst a successful play might well be staged at the festival, it should then be toured around the whole country. In the absence of a focal centre, accessible to both the rural and urban areas of Wales, he was convinced that the country as a whole could hardly be served by any system other than a travelling repertory theatre which carried with it its own 'space', so to speak, in the form of a marquee or a 'portable theatre'.[77]

Despite the infectious nature of Jones's enthusiasm, the problem of place was not to be resolved so easily. Whichever way the scales were tipped in an evaluation of the 'deficiences' and 'excellences'[78] of the Eisteddfod, no other national space existed to rival it and any attempt to move in on its territory inevitably led to a stalemate. One of the first efforts to lay down the footings of a separate and distinct national space came, not in the shape of a Welsh national theatre or theatre company, but in the form of a national fête or pageant. The staging of Wales's first national pageant, in Cardiff in 1909, is important to our discussion in two ways: first, it established another place in which the Welsh identity could find expression; secondly, it highlighted one of the major difficulties involved in that process of articulation: Wales's position as part of a multinational British confederation in which the balance of power was unequal. We have already discussed the rationale that inspired the French national fêtes of the revolutionary years, in terms of their consecration of a new national order by means of public and communal acts to be played out in a virgin space, free from any vestiges of the past and orientated towards a future of creativity and construction. The Welsh pageant can be understood as a similar attempt to reorientate Wales positively within a British framework, by means of public and communal activity in a distinct and novel location.

According to Hywel Teifi Edwards, the Cardiff pageant was modelled on Louis Napoleon Parker's English pageants and as such was 'a combination of the masque, the medieval pageant and the drama ... the most important of these three elements was drama'[79] [my translation]. Kirsti Bohata describes how in the Welsh National Pageant of 1909, Lady Bute, representing the Welsh nation itself, opened the pageant, along with thirteen other women, each representing one of Wales's thirteen shires.[80] This kind of allegorical scene graced with a mixture of symbolic figures and fairies was typical of the historical *tableaux* presented at the pageant. But if Wales wanted drama, why did it opt for this kind of spectacular *tableau vivant* rather than pursue the 'truly national production ... adapted to the traditions of the Welsh people'[81] called for by E. Derry Evans and Lloyd George, and the idea of a national theatre championed by Tom Jones? The answer, I believe, lies in Parker's own description of the pageant as 'drama lifting up our souls to God and our hearts to the

King'.[82] What Wales (or at least those sections of Welsh society that interested themselves in the arts) wanted at this point in its history was to articulate Welshness as a distinct but integral aspect of Britishness. In revolutionary France, it was the fear of mimesis that rendered the national pageant preferable to the national theatre. In Wales, it was not fear of theatrical artifice that secured the promotion of the pageant at the expense of the development of a national Welsh theatre, but nervousness regarding the development of a rational and egalitarian, theatrical debate that might well raise questions as to the value of Wales's affiliation to the overarching British framework within which it had traditionally taken its place.

Edwards's account of the 1909 Welsh National Pageant at Cardiff reveals its significance as an international advert for Wales, a vehicle for the rekindling of national pride and a means of locating Wales as a nation. The location of the pageant at Cardiff Castle, wherein all the splendour of the country's geography could be encapsulated along with the wealth of its historical past, was an indication of the fact that this new national space was not to be free of the past, but shaped by it. There would be no Bastille-style hordes of stamping feet to obliterate the vestiges of history here. Patrick Geary's argument that 'the past . . . is a foreign country, and we will never find ourselves there'[83] held no sway with the pageant makers. The place that was to be Wales in the Welsh National Cardiff Pageant was not a clear, open space in which a Welsh national identity could be debated and negotiated by means of creative, communal activity but a place impregnated by the heritage of Wales's past, a past that included the country's contribution to a British, colonial project. In view of this mindset, it is no coincidence that the immediate inspiration for the pageant came from Warwick, beyond Offa's Dyke.[84] There was a contemporary force at work here, but it consisted in the effort to orientate Wales positively within the overarching infrastructure of the British Empire.

The shoulders upon which the Parkerian mantle fell in Wales were those of pageant-master, Mr G. P. Hawtrey, and scripter, Owen Rhoscomyl, or Captain Owen Vaughan. The latter, a fascinating character in his own right, was an ardent Welsh patriot, but had no difficulty in articulating his love for Wales within a British imperialist framework. The Cardiff pageant he enthused would, mark to all the world that Wales is a special country in the Empire, with a proud past behind her, resolved to bring her to the front of the Empire, to make her a land to which the Empire may look for help and strength in the hour of temptation and in the day of danger.[85]

This imperialist breed of Welsh nationalism was not confined to the mindset that brought forth the pageant but had long since informed attitudes towards Wales, both within and without the nation. Andrew Davies's discussion of the representation of Wales in the antiquarian and historical fiction of the Romantic period, in terms of a process of re-representing the nation both as a fictional and historical entity, reflects this trend.[86] He attributes a rise in British nationalism towards the close of the eighteenth century to the disturbing influence of the French Revolution and argues that the manufacture of a collective national identity, formed under the auspices of the British nation state in the fiction of Scott and his ilk, was a reaction to this crisis. Davies concludes that this fictional project came to a close after Walter Scott's days, but an address delivered by Lord Mostyn at a meeting of the Caernarfon Eisteddfod provides evidence that it remained a valid national viewpoint at the close of the nineteenth century. Welshmen, Lord Mostyn urged,

> must not forget that they in common with the English, Scotch, and Irish had taken no mean part in building up the Empire now presided over by one of the most beloved and powerful of sovereigns that had ever reigned, and it behoved them to promote its welfare, for upon it the wealth, strength and prosperity of the Cymric race depended.'[87]

The historian Aled Jones points out that whilst Wales was considered to be an essential part of imperialist Britain from the sixteenth century onwards, its importance came to a height towards the middle of the nineteenth century when it was considered the 'metropolitan core of the British imperial project'.[88] He argues that during this period the founding of the country's national institutions and its cultural and linguistic renaissance all thrived within a British imperial framework. The national pageant marked the height of this process. It also functioned as its watershed.

The national pageant was a positive influence in as far as it established the Welsh people's claim to a new space, defined, in part, by their physical presence within it. Nonetheless, the episodic and emblematic nature of pageantry playing denied them access to any sustained dramatic debate. A pageant, after all, is not designed to stimulate debate but to evoke wonder at the exploits of a heroic past. As the opening decade of the twentieth century drew to a close, it became clear that the Welsh national pageant, first dreamt up in 1906, had failed to provide a satisfactory theatrical vehicle for the articulation of a national identity in Wales and the residential status of Welsh drama remained that of the vagabond, 'of no fixed abode'. A return to the Eisteddfod environment, however, seemed a retrospective step in terms of the search for a new place for the drama of Welsh life and Welsh identity. In a rather aggressive article in *Y Brython*, Elidir Sais suggested a way forward. He attacked the Eisteddfod and the University of Wales for their failure to take up the cause of Welsh drama[89] and suggested that 'a group of enthusiasts join together, with a high and determined purpose, and ... begin in a quiet and small way'.[90] This is in fact what happened when Lord Howard de Walden gathered together a select group to form a Welsh national theatre company that staged its first run of performances at the New Theatre, Cardiff, 11–16 May 1914.

The Cardiff 'production of Welsh plays by Welsh players'[91] was the culmination of an advertising campaign for the Welsh national drama that had begun some twelve years earlier with Lloyd George's appeal for support from the Eisteddfod platform at Bangor. Lloyd George's public prominence played a major role in the promotion and publicizing of the Welsh drama movement but it was Lord Howard de Walden who first realized the idea of a Welsh national theatre. A correspondent in the *Western Mail* in December 1913 is at pains to draw the nation's attention to the fact that 'amid all the present stir about Welsh drama in Wales, it is just as well to keep an eye on the man to whom the chief credit is due for all this dramatic ferment, and that man is Lord Howard de Walden'.[92] The writer refers the reader to de Walden's sponsorship of Welsh drama in 1911, when he established an annual £100 prize at the Eisteddfod for 'the best play, in Welsh or English, suitable for the repertory of a Welsh national dramatic company touring in Wales'.[93]

This invitation encapsulates the moment at which Wales stepped forward into the new cultural arena of a Welsh national theatre. Lord de Walden had made use of the Eisteddfod framework to issue his invitation to Welsh dramatists but it is of vital importance that he stipulated that the plays should be written with their performance in mind. The precise terms of his challenge make it clear that the 'Welshness' of these plays would not be judged according to their thematic or linguistic criteria alone, but would hinge on their suitability as performance material for a national Welsh company of players intent on playing to a Welsh audience:

> In pursuance of the scheme to establish a Welsh National Dramatic company, a prize of £100, with other advantages, is offered for the best play, in Welsh or English, suitable for such a company. The subject may be of any period – ancient, modern, or a 100 years ahead – so long as it deals with things Welsh – dream, facts or fantasies, history, legend or grim realities.[94]

The Eisteddfod was still the springboard of Welsh national drama but, once launched, it was clear that the new national art form would not confine itself to this familiar cultural forum but would carve out its own identity and occupy an independent territory negotiated by means of its interaction with its audience.

There can be no doubting the success of Lord Howard de Walden's experiment. The initial meeting held to pursue his plan took place in the offices of Messrs Richard and Morris, solicitors, High St., Cardiff on Friday, 30 January, when it was decided to form a company under the name of Welsh National Drama Co. Ltd with the unregistered title Welsh Players.[95] Despite the respectability provided by this auspicious start, it was not long before the Welsh effort abandoned the office in favour of the box office. There was a public appeal in the press, a process of selecting suitable players and a board of directors made up of 'seven everyday men',[96] but this was all considered mere mechanics beside the theatrical spectacle of the Cardiff Drama Week itself. In the light of Lloyd George's talk of the climate of change sweeping over Wales, it seems no coincidence that one of the plays heading the bill at the Cardiff Drama Week was J. O. Francis's *Change*.[97] *Change* is described as a play that,

> deals with modern education and the conflict of young ideas with the old – between the present and the passing generation. Religion, labour, conduct, the Celtic temperament, the all-absorbing parental pride of the Celtic people, the ambitions and the bitterness of what the gossips call 'fortune'. The drift of the new play is that of Ibsen – the

conflict between the old and the new, with the new generation knocking at the door.⁹⁸

Lloyd George was present at the New Theatre, Cardiff, on the evening of Friday 15 May and his comments regarding his experience convey the extent to which both the performance and its audience were central to the Welsh national theatre movement. The chancellor remarked that both the play and the manner of its acting were a powerful manifestation of the changes coming over Wales and that these changes were equally manifest in the audience's reaction: 'one section cheered one sentiment, and another section another sentiment, and then there was a perplexed section. I think the audience itself was quite as emblematic of the change coming over the country as the play itself was.'⁹⁹ The fact that the chancellor read the audience's response to the play as an indicator of the condition and kind of Welsh experience in general confirms the fact that the process of activating the nation at the heart of Lord de Walden's campaign had begun in earnest. In answer to Abel Jones's argument that drama was unnecessary in Wales on the basis that it lacked intrinsic worth because it came to us with little or no effort,¹⁰⁰ it could be shown that the Welsh idea of a national theatre was a place where an active and reciprocal process of discovery and debate was undertaken by means of the interaction between the play, the players and audience members themselves.

Lloyd George was not alone in his praise for the play and its performance. The contemporary Welsh press was littered with positive reports. A report in the *Western Mail*, May 1914, captures the spectacular effect of the Cardiff Drama Week in terms of its launching of the idea of a Welsh national identity into the public domain. The writer remarks:

> Friday night at the New Theatre, Cardiff, will long remain an evening of memories. Every nook and cranny of the playhouse was filled to the utmost.
>
> Several elements contributed to this unequivocal success, but the principal, without doubt, were the spirit and determination of the ardent friends of the Welsh drama to give the movement a hardy and shapely national character.¹⁰¹

It is significant to note this flattering report appears alongside an account of a visit to the Welsh capital by Mr Lewis Casson, a tremendous force in the American advertising business and by coincidence, Sybil Thorndike's husband. Mr Casson had come to advise Cardiff on the matter of advertising and his address focused on the argument that,

> nations have got to advertise, too – they are already beginning. All the great nations are reaching out for the international trade – there is a great competition of the nations for the markets of the world – and it is tremendously important that every nation should have its advertising well organised. This is a matter of national importance – it is not the concern of advertising people.[102]

Lord Howard de Walden's Cardiff venture was a hugely successful artistic advert for Wales. Mr Casson's reference to his Cardiff visit as part of a project to get 'England to take on the benefits'[103] of the American methods of advertising highlights the urgency of such a national undertaking.

In an essay in *Y Beirniad*, E. Morgan Humphreys notes that the function of national literature is to 'picture the life of the nation to herself or to explain and demonstrate that life to the English'[104] [my translation]. We will return later to his identification of a vital aspect of Welsh identity embodied in its complex relations with neighbouring England. My current interest lies with Humphreys's definition of a nation's dramatic art as a vehicle for representing a national identity within the country itself. However vital the importance of national advertising might be, whether on an artistic or a purely commercial level, Wales would need to get to know herself before she could project her identity elsewhere. The surge of interest created by Lord de Walden's Cardiff venture highlights the importance of production and performance in this process of self-discovery. The production of a play was clearly intrinsic to its claim to represent the nation and its concerns. In fact, it was the most efficient means by which the nation as a whole could verify and validate those interests. As the reporter in the *Western Mail* maintained:

> No movement of vital importance is ever made. It must grow. The men must be in evidence before they congregate in a league, as there must be national leaders before manifold causes bring the needed men to the front.
> The ... drama in Wales is no new thing ... but most of these plays were never acted ... Today Wales is fortunate in the friends she has

attracted to her new cause, and right gladly she has accepted their proffered aid. The new-born delight and magic taken hold of her sons and daughters ... were on Friday accorded a warm welcome.[105]

The report leaves us in no doubt regarding the precise nature of the role played by the Welsh players and their production in the dramatic enquiry into the nature of the Welsh national identity. The players themselves were 'the men in evidence'. It was their small-scale gathering in the form of a band of national players that instigated the congregation of a greater and more representative league: the audience itself. It was they who fulfilled the role of 'national leaders' who brought the 'needed men to the front', so that the articulation of a Welsh national identity could be achieved not only in play but also in practice. When viewed in this light, the claim that 'a representative and a democratic ... Welsh audience welcomed what has been described as "the birth of the Welsh National Drama", at the Cardiff New Theatre tonight'[106] gains its full significance.

The launch of Lord de Walden's Welsh National Theatre Company closed an era in which Wales had sought to establish a new form of national, cultural activity – Welsh national theatre – through the agency of pre-established national festivals and fêtes, namely the Welsh National Eisteddfod and the Welsh National Pageant. These ready-made fora had both facilitated and restricted a process of discovery and definition, designed to propel the nation forward into pastures new. However, the time had come for Wales to cut itself free from other artistic institutions in order to commit itself to a process of national redefinition and rediscovery that might eventually bring forth its own, unique dialectical form – the Welsh National Theatre itself.

~ 5 ~
Fragmented reflections and shattered fragments: the mirror image of Welsh national life?

Once Wales set about investigating and debating her identity by means of direct theatrical presentation and representation, the challenging nature of being Welsh in the twentieth century began to surface. W. A. Humphreys celebrated the fact that Lord de Walden's theatrical venture had brought the nation to the threshold of a new epoch,[1] in which a national theatre could play a vital role in stimulating and shaping a national debate. However, there were others, like Thomas Richards, who feared that it was no longer possible to produce a 'pure Welsh Drama, due to the fact that modern Welsh life was such a complicated affair'.[2] The wave of new plays and productions that were stimulated by and provided for Lord de Walden's Welsh national theatre venture reflected this complexity. The Welsh national theatre pioneered at Cardiff by Lord Howard de Walden offered the nation a way forward, but one of the conditions of progress was that the nation undertook a thorough process of self-analysis and ultimately self-criticism that would enable it to grapple with the many contradictions with which its sense of identity was riddled.

One of the imperatives resulting from the emergence of a Welsh national theatre company was the need for Wales not only to accustom herself to criticism but to cultivate the skill of self-criticism. George Bernard Shaw took a moment's respite from his efforts to secure an English national theatre to offer some good advice to Wales. Wales, he said, with his customary acidity and wit, would have to embrace criticism in her national theatre 'if Wales will not have the best that Wales can produce, she will get the worst that the capitals of Europe can produce; and it will serve her right'.[3] Llewelyn Williams, MP spoke in a similar vein when he commented on the capacity of a national theatre to hold the mirror to nature:

The mirror image of Welsh national life? 157

Up to now the beauty of Welsh life has been that it is unconscious of its own virtues and its own defects. A Welshman will always pride himself upon the possession of qualities which don't seem to be admirable to people outside. The real reason is that the Welsh have been without standards. They have no fiction nor drama to hold the mirror to life. Now for the first time they are going to be shown themselves as they appear to be.

How this will affect the Welsh nation it is impossible to say. They have never had self-criticism, so it is impossible to say what will happen. One thing is certain. The national life of Wales will never be the same after this.[4]

His linking of Wales's insularity with a certain innocence, or naivety, echoes the rather hysterical comment by the eighteenth-century writer of the *Torrington Diaries* who claimed that their language had kept the Welsh 'innocent and at home', but that once they became bilingual, 'they read, hear plays, debauch and emigrate'.[5] Despite the element of exaggeration in both these views, it is evident that the pioneering effort to establish a Welsh national theatre would end an era of Welsh ingenuousness and bring the nation to a more objective awareness of itself and of its relation to others. The question of whether or not the Welsh nation could equate how it appeared to be with how it felt itself to be was yet to be answered. Likewise, the question of whether a Welsh national theatre should, or indeed could, move beyond appearances in its attempt to discover a valid, Welsh national identity remained in the balance.

The need for change in the field of Welsh drama was urgent. In recent years, the writing and staging of English-language plays of Welsh interest, such as *Miss Llewelyn, The Bells of Lin Lan Lone* and *The Jones's,* had caused much alarm in Wales. This dilemma was heightened by the reticence of those who were 'possessed of a close knowledge of the country, and a clear insight into the ways of the people, and who can view the national aspirations and ideals, if not with approval, at any rate with sympathy'[6] to take up the cause of Welsh drama. An upsurge of interest in Welsh plays from the direction of London made the question of why it should 'be left to the Borrows, the Watts-Duntons, the Bradleys and the Friths to mirror the genius of Wales' all the more pressing.[7] Cecil Price cited the role played by one London manager who raised the Welsh national theatre question during the course of his promotion of Allen Raine's dramatic output with the comment 'what we want today in London is "Wales With the Lid Off". It certainly seems incredible to me that Wales should be the only part of the British Isles without its national dramatist.'[8] Despite the promising tone of this interest, the warning delivered in *The Welsh Outlook* with regard to the flirtation of mainstream London managers with Welsh drama was probably a timely one. The paper points out that whilst the subject of Welsh drama may have 'touched the hearts of some London managers, it has also touched their pockets'.[9] J. Tanad Powell compounds reservations concerning the value of this interest to Wales with his expression of contempt for the superficiality and wrongheadedness of attempts to fashion an imported Welsh drama leading to 'a banquet of burlesque' wherein 'Welsh is used for the garnishing'.[10]

The staging of plays such as Francis's *Change* by the Welsh National Drama Company put an end to this tradition of misrepresentation. Not only did the new drama[11] speak of Wales in its attempt to face the pain of the 'transformation of the old Calvinist Wales to the new country confident by virtue of bilingual education and social progress'[12] [my translation], but its performance and production by the national company enabled it to speak to Wales, on a level never achieved before. One reporter's comment on the performance of *Change*, that heralded the onset of the drama week hosted by the national company at Swansea, highlights the fundamental importance of production and performance in the process of instigating a dramatic debate on a national level. *Change*, he argues, is,

> a significant piece of work. It portrays a stage in Welsh life ... a change in outlook and sentiment which is destined to leave lasting marks on the nation. And it could have been portrayed in no other way. We had to have it visualised.[13]

The scale of this achievement is somewhat reduced by an acrimonious event that marred the performance of D. T. Davies's *Ble Ma Fa?*[14] on 15 May at Cardiff. The fact that the suffragettes who heckled Lloyd George on this occasion with calls of 'the villain of the piece is in that box there'[15] were ejected from the theatre with such enthusiasm and force, testified to the fact that Wales had some way to go before she could lay claim to the credentials of a fully subscribed member of an egalitarian public sphere.

The Cardiff Drama Week of June 1914 saw the first in a series of visits by the Welsh National Drama Company to the major towns of Wales. As the national theatre extended its geographical scope beyond Cardiff, the debate regarding the relevance of the dramatic fare on offer to the nation's identity gathered steam. Many argued that the writers providing for the new Welsh national theatre movement, such as J. O. Francis, D. T. Davies and W. J. Gruffydd,[16] had set about matters in the right way by asking social questions and locating their dramatic action firmly within their social environs. This, it was felt, was the recipe for a drama of national proportions and significance.[17] J. J. Williams linked the growth of a Welsh middle class, represented by these dramatists, and the provision of material for dramatic debate of national interest. He was of the opinion that Wales had lost out because she had no truly middle class, other than in Liverpool and that it was the 'growth of a middle class that has given rise to some of the major questions of our age'[18] [my translation] and made them matter for drama. Saunders Lewis's description of the dramatists who answered Lord de Walden's call as 'young intellectuals ... schoolmasters and ... ex-students of Universities'[19] is heartening evidence that a new Welsh middle class was on the rise. However, there were those who felt that the drama produced by Wales's new National Theatre Company was exclusive, by virtue of its allegiance to the emerging middle class and that it would do well to take heed of a 'life that doesn't always reach the publicity of the parish council'[20] [my translation]. By comparison, it is interesting to note the absence of public protest at the overwhelming middle class feel to the drive to establish a national theatre in England. A comment by one Welsh reader, contrasting the tabloid tone of English papers to the earnest discussion common in the array of Welsh periodicals available to the ordinary Welshman, suggests that the Welsh benefited to a greater extent from a democratic representation in and democratic distribution of the press. There were drawbacks to this press, but it may well be that it provided the everyday Welsh reader with a means of expression that was denied his/her English counterpart at this point in the history of the two countries and their respective efforts to establish national theatres. The prominence of the ordinary Welsh *gwerin*, or folk, at the performance of D. T. Davies's *Ephraim Harris*[21] at the inaugural Cardiff Drama

Week suggests that they were both eager for and equal to the task of taking up their rightful place in the new Welsh national theatre and were arguably 'the most responsive to the nation's most beneficial movements'.[22]

Whoever made up the Welsh theatre audience, it was felt that modern Welsh drama arose from the need for an organ through which the emerging Welsh middle class 'might utter their impatience and disgust at the unseemliness of our time. [Thus] the theatre became the platform of revolt, and nearly all the Welsh plays bear standards of rebellion.'[23] This spirit of rebellion, 'this delight in sweeping the social floors from every direction',[24] provoked plenty of reaction. The paradoxical positions held by advocates and denigrators of the Welsh national theatre adventure found vehement expression during the Swansea leg of the Welsh National Theatre Company's tour. The launch of the Welsh National Theatre Company at Cardiff was a vital step in the history of the Welsh national theatre debate. However, I would argue that the company's subsequent visit to Swansea was as important in that it carried the blushing bride that was Wales over the threshold of a new era. In the *Cambria Daily Leader* of 15 June 1914, it was noted with some consternation that, despite Wales's fitness 'by generations of preparation for an outburst of something higher and better', despite the fact that 'her schools and colleges are as numerous, as active and as well equipped as any nation could desire ... There – for the moment – she has stopped.'[25] This stoppage was cleared by the Swansea event. In preparation for the event, Harley Granville Barker accompanied Lord Howard de Walden on a visit to Swansea where he commended the Welsh effort. At a magnificent reception hosted by Swansea's mayor, he confirmed the Welsh in their conviction that the 'development of their national art was a thing of vital and great necessity to their national life'[26] and added that Wales's greatest service to the rest of the world was to remain true to herself in her drama to the last drop of her blood. The Swansea success, however, was not without its drawbacks. Reservations were expressed with regard to the selectivity of the social niveaux and the somewhat middle-class manifestations of democracy and decorum that characterized the campaign, such as the great banquet at which the wives of local dignitaries displayed their 'pretty toilettes'.[27] These weaknesses are as important to our discussion as is the success of the Swansea event in as far as they testify to the fact that the effort to discover an inclusive formula for a national theatre in Wales had begun in earnest.

The most striking characteristic of the Swansea event was the way in which it laid bare the contradictory views regarding the development of a Welsh national theatre in Wales. J. D. Williams summed up his experience of it as a distressing and perplexing one. He regretted that:

> The writer confesses to a worrying week! On the one hand assailed for doing devil's work; on the other, commended for a little done on behalf of the Welsh drama; yesterday accused of assisting a movement destined to carry Wales along the broad road leading to ——, to-day, told that such help (small as it may be) is upon the right lines leading Wales to intellectual freedom! In the multitude of such council is confusion.[28]

Despite the obvious benefits of the bitter pill of criticism, John Colwyn was amongst those who sought to sweeten its taste by advocating 'kindly criticism of a constructive kind',[29] it was not to be swallowed without a great deal of puff and gusto; a great deal of drama, in fact. The significance of the Abbey Theatre to the Irish nation was evaluated by one Welsh commentator in terms of its capacity for self-criticism, but the Abbey audience's hysterical reaction to J. F. Synge's *Playboy of the Western World* provided ample evidence of the difficult process of negotiating a national image and identity. The Irish theatre might have seemed 'one of the finest forces for the expression of nationality that Ireland ever produced'[30] to outsiders, but its audiences clamoured out against its representation of their nation. In the same way, the representation of Wales by the Welsh national players stirred up a fiery debate regarding the nature of the Welsh identity.

The opposing views that were voiced most vehemently can be broadly separated into two distinct camps. On the one hand, there were those who welcomed the new liberal vision of modern Welsh drama, even with its accompanying materialism. On the other, were those, such as the Reverend W. Morris,[31] who sought to protect the perceived religious and moral purity of the non-conformist Wales of the recent past. The alacrity with which objections to the dramatic portrayal of deacons, preachers and the chapel itself were raised suggest that Elidir Sais's view that the value of a national drama was not dependent on its moral qualities but simply a matter of supply and demand, was not a common one. An amusing announcement of the forthcoming visit of the Welsh national players to Swansea revealed the fact that although the chapel had already lost its battle to suppress Welsh theatre, contemporary Wales still found it difficult to make an ideological distinction between the idea of a national theatre and the spectre of the nation's main spiritual institution, the chapel. The Welsh people, it was reported,

> are preparing for the advent of the new messiah – the messiah of the Welsh nation. Next week, has been appointed 'The Holy Week' of the drama. On Sunday next, we suppose, prayers will be offered in our churches and chapels for a blessing upon the promoters, actors, scene shifters, Mrs Price, Lisa Ann, and the rest who rally around the Welsh drama. Prayer meetings, services, cyfeillachau crefyddol,[32] will be suspended, that the ministers, deacons ... and young people may gather within the 'hallowed walls' of the Grand Theatre.[33]

W. A. Humphreys made the same connection from the opposite end of the spectrum when he expressed his conviction that the pulpit had been Wales's theatre, but that its scope was confined to a depiction of the nation's spiritual life.[34] His comment implies that, in the past, the nation had used the quasi-private forum of the chapel environment to dramatize its inner, spiritual life. This argument throws new light on the tradition of non-conformist opposition to Welsh drama and theatre because it suggests that it was driven not by prejudice, but rather by a sophisticated understanding of both the chapel and the theatre as alternative national frameworks for social interaction that were in competition with each other. If theatre and, more specifically, national theatre could embody the fictitious, if it did not confine itself to the representation of one central spirit but introduced the much more expansive concept of a national spirit, if it could maintain an emphasis on the validity of internal experience and yet allow modern man to see himself in his life and judge his own behaviour objectively, then it might be a vehicle for the substitution of the spiritual values at the heart of religious behaviour for those social values at the heart of interpersonal interaction. In brief, it threatened to provide Wales with a different kind of conversation, not a confidential and privileged exchange between the individual and his God, but a rational debate between equals that took place in the public arena of theatrical performance.

The Swansea event had clearly spurred Wales on to a passionate inspection and discussion of its national past in the immediate and exciting context of its national future. However, there had been another notable occurrence in the build-up to the event that prepared the way for public discussion, debate and even dissent on a new and refreshing scale. This was 'the issue of a manifesto signed by well-known citizens calling upon the Swansea people ... to march abreast of the times by supporting the Welsh Drama'.[35] Despite the feeling amongst some that there was much too much fuss and trouble[36] surrounding the Welsh drama movement, the issue of the manifesto instigated a furious debate. The manifesto made its appeal to the patriotism of its citizens, calling on those inhabitants of the 'Metropolis of Welsh Wales' who 'are Welsh in origin, or who have Welsh sympathies' to declare their support for the 'Cymric' endeavour towards national theatrical excellence.[37] Earlier that year, prior to the launch of the national company, Owen Rhoscomyl had issued an open invitation to all those who wished to declare their support for the Welsh drama movement. Some comments he made at the time explain the rationale behind the more formal Swansea manifesto. Rhoscomyl argued that,

> if one man came running to this Welsh drama alone, like a voice crying in the wilderness, the busy crowd might pass by because it was nobody's business but that one man's. If, however, a sufficient number of representative men of Wales came together ... suspicion would be disarmed.[38]

A significant section of the Swansea populace was determined to bring together these representative men in order to promote the efforts of another band of representative men – the Welsh national players themselves. Another section was equally determined to resist all efforts at the representation of a common desire or design by anyone, but most particularly by the 'medicine-men of creation.'[39] In fact, it was not only medicine-men, but medicine-women who were called upon to play their part in the promotion of the 'senseless, silly incantation',[40] of the Welsh national theatre movement at Swansea. Whilst Cardiff had ejected its vociferous ladies from the theatre, the Swansea and District Organization Committee was eager to enlist the support of its female contingent in the form of an auxiliary ladies' committee.

It seems curious that a manifesto should instigate such heartfelt opposition in Wales. In England, the lively response to the publication of William Archer and Granville Barker's Blue Book had focused not on the propriety of the publication itself, but on a discussion of its contents. In Wales, the issue of the manifesto, accompanied by an array of illustrious signatures, including those of schoolmasters, the secretary of the Cymmrodorion society, Glamorgan's High Sheriff, vicars and newspaper editors and managers, caused an outcry in itself. To its signatories, this public manifestation of and call for support was simply an opportunity to declare solidarity and determination in the cause of the national Welsh theatre. To others, it was an outrageous exercise in the manipulation of the public. The promoters of the Welsh drama movement were accused of 'girdling land and sea in search of supporters'[41] [my translation] and of forcing the public hand. There had been earlier intimations that all was not well with the way in which Swansea was proceeding. Despite the general rejoicing in the reception afforded to Granville Barker and Lord Howard de Walden on their visit to the city, one reporter felt that there was a fundamental incongruity between this sort of public ritual and the traditional character of Welsh social intercourse. He noted with no little sarcasm that there had even been 'so Welsh a thing as a reception'[42] [my translation] held in Swansea last week. The same discomfort is voiced in a less forthright manner by another report which sought to de-anglicize the reception by referring to it as a *cwrdd croeso,* or welcome gathering. There were, however, other critics who urged Welsh dramatists to recognize that the locus of debate had shifted from an informal, private arena to a formal, public one and warned them against the perils of dreariness, resulting from the confinement of Welsh drama to the 'collier's cottage'.[43] The Swansea campaign had come up against the difficulties that would have to be negotiated if Wales was to move forward in her journey towards a Welsh national theatre that would be both worthy and representative of the nation as a whole.

The Swansea theatrical venture beat a path that led Wales into a new arena where she might investigate and articulate her national identity by means of creative and communal interplay. Further progress was hampered by the nation's doubts regarding whether she had either the inclination or the necessary credentials to force an entry into this forum. One of the main issues that manifest this combination of indecision and insecurity was the question of whether Wales preferred to abstain from professional theatre in favour of a commitment to amateur theatre. Beriah Gwynfe Evans's claim that 'the national talent of Wales does not take kindly to professionalism'[44] encapsulated this resistance. The target of Evans's attack was Lord Howard de Walden's company of professional Welsh players, but he was not alone in his detection of an essential antipathy between professionalism and the country's national dramatic genius. Abel Jones expressed appreciation of the fact that 'amateur acting will "draw out" certain types of young people as nothing else will'[45] yet he felt that the danger of insincerity and inconsistency in real life was almost inevitable in the case of the professional actor. His conviction that the professional actor's life is one of insincerity, of 'make-believe, of emotional dissipation, of travelling in mixed companies away from home',[46] echoes the seventeenth-century prejudice against the acting profession in France that justified the exclusion of the actor from the rights of citizenship. It is interesting to hear the same dilemma approached from a different perspective when the editor of *Tarian y Gweithiwr* argues that we have nothing to fear from mimesis in the theatre, but that it is a dangerous force when suffered to go unmasked in life.[47]

Evans sought to turn the grist of Lord de Walden's mill away from professional acting towards the promotion of amateur Welsh drama by urging him to reconsider his current policy and set about ensuring that 'every village, every remote rural hamlet' had an amateur dramatic society 'as much as a matter of course as its local choir'.[48] Despite the fact that the choir and the dramatic society are now seen as distinct institutions, his comment recalls the good old days of the hybrid drama cantata. The failure to rise to the challenge of professional theatre seems a similar attempt to evade meaningful discussion of the condition and crisis of modern Welsh society. In fact, Evans's aim is somewhat more complex in the sense that he sees the amateur dramatic movement as a means of 'revivifying rural life by popularising drama'.[49] His instinct is to sustain the communal values that fed the intellectual flame of rural Welsh life:

> the family circle – and the 'family' then, as in patriarchal days, included the manservant and the maidservant, and every stranger within the gates – provided an entertainment, beside which the

grinding gramophone of the town-dweller to-day is a weariness to the flesh. Gathered literally around the kitchen fire ... the company was a merry one ... Song and story followed each other in quick succession, and light-hearted laughter accompanied nimble wit. Those days are gone. The bright hues have faded into a dull, depressing monotonous grey, making the spirit sombre and the intellect dwarfed. Why not, at least in part, revivify rural life by popularising the drama?[50]

His advice to the Welsh National Theatre Company to support the amateur movement by means of the provision of sets, costumes, advertising posters, scenery and plans of how to fit 'up a model stage in the village schoolroom'[51] might well be a retrospective step in terms of the development of a Welsh national theatrical art, but he clearly felt that it was the only way to sustain the Welsh culture from which he and many other Welshmen drew their life blood.

Evans's attack did not cast too great a shadow over the launch of the Welsh National Theatre Company, but it was of much greater significance in terms of the effort to foster that national theatre once it had been successfully launched. Owen Rhoscomyl was dismayed by the ferocity of his adversary's assault on the proposals for the establishment of a professional Welsh theatre. His description of it as an onslaught of 'carronades and twenty-pounders, Long Toms and muskets'[52] is not an indication of his awe of the attacker but rather a recognition that his was not a lone voice. In fact, Evans's promotion of the amateur cause represented a general and overwhelming fear that entry into the liberal public sphere would mean the loss, rather than the discovery and strengthening, of a Welsh national identity. At the heart of this dilemma was the Welsh language. The fundamental question was how was Wales to maintain its own national character and yet establish meaningful discourse with its foreign friend, England? This dilemma was at the heart of the Welsh national theatre venture. On 18 June 1914, a report appeared from Merthyr claiming that Lord de Walden's effort was flawed because performances of the Welsh National Theatre Company were advertised in English and their programmes were published in English.[53] The report is important because it identifies both the urgency of the effort to sustain and foster the Welsh language and the link between that effort and the amateur drama movement in Wales. The Englishness of Lord de Walden's National Theatre

The mirror image of Welsh national life? 167

Company is taken as evidence that a Welsh-spirited and Welsh-medium drama could only be fostered by promotion of the Welsh amateur movement. The writer's reference to the current healthiness of the amateur movement in Wales indicates his view of the Welsh National Theatre Company as an attempt to fix something that was not broken.

Wales is a unique case in the context of the current study in that it is the only country undertaking the analysis and definition of its own national identity by means of a national theatre within the context of an overarching framework in which another language reigned supreme. Tom Jones's 1894 appeal to establish a national company of Welsh players – one of the earliest steps in the direction pursued so ardently by Lord de Walden – promptly identified the importance of the language question. Jones's appeal recognized the linguistic diversity at the heart of Welsh society by noting that any national theatre catering for the populace as a whole would have to be a bilingual one. Whilst a Swansea audience at the Albert Hall was happy enough to applaud Lord de Walden's few Welsh words, 'Mr Cadeirydd, Foneddigesau a Boneddigion',[54] the nation at large found the question of the relationship between its national theatre and its national tongue much more problematic.

A report in *Y Darian* in 1914 highlights the value of amateur theatre as a means of 'maintaining and securing the language'.[55] By 1919, the point was being made more explicitly and with direct reference to Lord Howard de Walden's National Theatre Company:

> Our suggestion to Lord Howard de Walden would be the following: let him set about perfecting his Welsh, and begin calling those who could form a drama company in the villages around him, and let him get them to learn Welsh plays, not English ones, and he will thus help to restore the Welsh language and the best Welsh life in his area. He could perform a great service to Wales if he were to follow this course of action[56] [my translation].

In the same issue, a report on W. J. Gruffydd's discussion of the challenges presented by the English presence within Wales singled out two types of Englishmen from amongst many, 'the ill-disposed and the well-disposed'.[57] Gruffydd's suggestion that 'of these two – the worst is the latter'[58] is intended as humorous, but it indicates the fact that Lord de Walden, despite his undeniable honour and commitment to the cause of Welsh theatre, might appear, to some at least, in the guise of a 'patronising'[59] influence on a healthy nation. Many prominent and worthy Welsh figures came under attack for similar reasons. J. O. Francis became the focus of an onslaught on the very idea of English-medium Welsh drama. The attack was championed by J. Tywi Jones who regarded the amateur movement as a means of sustaining the Welsh language against the incoming tide of Englishness sweeping the country. The portrayal of Francis as a Caradoc Evans type character, guilty of the vilification of Welsh culture and society[60] was unjust, particularly in view of Francis's sensitivity towards the Welsh language issue. Francis had demonstrated an awareness of the linguistic shortcomings of writing an English play about life in Wales from within the Welsh drama movement when he admitted in his 1922 foreword to *Crosscurrents* that 'written altogether in English, this play must, I know, have now and then an awkward air'.[61] Nonetheless, despite its unfairness, the attack itself demonstrated the central importance of the language issue in the context of the definition of Welsh identity and the articulation of that identity by means of the establishment of a Welsh national theatre.

For a while, it seemed that Wales would shirk the responsibility of developing a national drama and theatre that might reveal her, both to herself and to the world at large. The path forward seemed too precarious and the consolidation of a Welsh past was afforded precedence over a foray into a Welsh future. As Lord de Walden's initiative ground to a halt, amateur theatre rose, phoenix-like, from the ashes of the Welsh national theatre venture. If, as reports in *Y Faner* suggest, there were between twenty and one hundred amateur companies dotted around the country in 1913, by 1930, Rhys Puw[62] claims that there were hundreds, possibly as many as five hundred. In 1919, Francis noted that whilst in England drama is professional and in Ireland it is not of the people, in Wales 'the children act; the colliers act, the shepherds act; the quarrymen act; the students act – and, not to be outdone, the deacons act as well'.[63] Whilst Francis considered the country's commitment to a national theatre as an inevitable part of the process by which 'a small and intimate nation' would change 'old lamps for new',[64] the amateur movement fought hard to preserve precisely that closeness and intimacy. In so doing, it appeared to have solved the problem of place or space that had hindered the successful establishment of a Welsh national theatre from its earliest beginnings.

The amateur movement in Wales located itself at the heart of Welsh rural and urban communities and slotted in to the spatial infrastructure of those towns and villages. The village or town hall became the natural locus of the drama. Its central but organic geographical locus within the community was a physical manifestation of its role in the confirmation of pre-existing practices of social interaction and patterns of being. The family focus of the movement, manifest in 'the huge delight of relatives'[65] at performances is evidence that it was, indeed, the perfect tool for the mission to revivify rural life outlined by Beriah Evans. By March 1920, the term 'Welsh Drama Week' had been adopted by the amateur movement as a title for the hundreds of week-long drama competitions that dotted the country. The *Western Mail* and the *Cambrian Daily Leader* were littered with reports on and announcements of Welsh drama competition weeks all over the country. It is hardly surprising that Rhys Puw talked of the amateur Welsh movement in Bismarckian terms, as a revolution, not from above but from below, 'racy of the Welsh soil'[66] [my translation].

T. Rowland Hughes's account of the rational debate that followed a popular local performance is a heartening one. He describes the village hall:

> the village hall full to the brim because a play is being staged; at the end crowds of eager people collecting together at the roadside to criticise, to praise, to argue furiously, and almost unconsciously, to try to discover the needs and necessities of the art – this is the scene that is often witnessed in Wales today[67] [my translation].

His description certainly captures the modernity of the Welsh people's engagement with their amateur drama movement. It also points out the limitations of that engagement and, ultimately, the shortcomings of the amateur movement itself. Hughes was right to celebrate the freeing of the Welsh voice manifest in the local enthusiasm for discussion and debate. What was missing was the launching of that debate onto an international footing so that Wales might talk of herself to others, rather than to herself. In a consideration of the future of Welsh folk drama, D. T. Davies argues that drama arises from the need for the individual's perception of his relationship with a higher and future life to be supplemented by 'intelligent comprehension of his social adjustments on earth'.[68] He feels that Wales's chief failings, both individual and national, are due to the neglect she has suffered with regard to training in the latter skill. The remedy, he is confident, is provided by drama's ability to present both the individual and the nation 'with a more expansive reflection of his environment, wherein he will see how his daily traffic acts upon his fellow man and eventually re-acts upon himself'.[69] His argument corroborates my interpretation of the non-conformist antagonism towards Welsh drama and theatre as a desire to avoid the substitution of the spiritual values at the heart of religious behaviour for those social values at the heart of interpersonal interaction. The question remained whether the Welsh amateur movement could foster drama of this kind. Its status as an artistic medium for national preservation suggested that the answer might well be in the negative.

J. Tywi Jones was one of the main spokesmen for the value of amateur theatre as a vehicle for language revitalization. He believed, like Goethe before him, that 'the best way to interest people in a language is through the theatre ... it is not necessary that the plays should be literary. Small homely plays will do better.'[70] However, it was not long before the amateur drama movement in Wales came under attack for its brilliant success in the production and promotion of small homely plays in a secure, family atmosphere. As early as 1914, drama critics and commentators had been directing the nation's attention to the 'mechanical rules'[71] of drama. Yet, in 1920, D. T. Davies voiced his exasperation at the fact that 'Welsh audiences, at present, display a lower capacity for the appreciation of form, pure and simple, than for any other component of stage-writing'.[72] In a review of the Cymmer drama competition, he noted that J. Tywi Jones's play *Dic Shon Dafydd* was fatally flawed on the level of form: 'However sound its sentiments might be, it is,' he argued, 'a striking example of how not to write a play.'[73] Its twenty-one scenes, all in one act, were in flagrant contravention of the principles and practices of modern technique.

The Welsh dramatist's reluctance to abandon the 'multiplicity of scenes' and the 'absurd use of the soliloquy and the aside'[74] was an indication of a general immaturity in the field of scriptwriting skills.[75] However, Davies's argument that the existence of formless plays was due to the belief that a play was simply an elongation of the old *dadl ddirwestol*,[76] reveals the fact that the true source of this deficiency was, in fact, more complex. Davies provides a rationale for the Welsh dramatist's tardiness to foster new skills, when he accuses him of a 'fear of the inevitable, as shown in a refusal ... to permit the natural bias of a character or situation to eventuate in a consistent issue'.[77] This comment is particularly interesting in the context of Wales's transition from an era in which non-conformism had dictated the form and function of social interaction in Welsh society to a new era, in which the Welsh spirit was freed to discover its own natural bias. This freedom was clearly a daunting prospect to those schooled in the disciplinarian mindset of a Methodism that ordered society according to a set of inclusive and decisive rules. It would require great courage on the part of Wales's dramatists if their work was to reflect the identity crisis gnawing away at Welsh life and experience during this transitional period. A positive response to the structural demands of the new dramatic genre actually required an acceptance of a new framework of intellectual and social activity in the everyday lives of the Welsh people. Saunders Lewis recognized the controversial nature of Davies's artistic demands, but was equally convinced that this new challenge would have to be met. He confessed to his suspicion of the term village drama and his fear that it might, in fact, be a refuge for incompetence. In his view, 'an incompetent drama has no more right to a thatched home in a Welsh village than to a marble theatre in Athens'.[78]

Despite the performance of some good dramatic material, such as R. G. Berry's *Ar y Groesffordd*,[79] structural weaknesses were a common fault of drama competition fare. In one of his reports, Davies regrets the failure of a certain amateur dramatic company to tackle the structural defects of Mr Bryn Davies's *Colli ac Ennill*.[80] In this case, Davies's criticism is directed towards the dramatist rather than the company itself, but his efforts to educate companies and their producers in the art of theatrical form reveals the fact that the problem of form was not confined to the field of playwriting. He addressed this weakness in his remarks on the practice of production and his criticism of the failure of producers to treat the play as 'an organic composition'.[81] Saunders Lewis, however, took heart from the performance of *Ephraim Harries*, a play by Davies himself, at Swansea on 24 October 1919. His praise for the writing and production of the play suggests that the problem of form had finally been resolved, both at the level of production and writing. His tribute could hardly have been more flattering, either to the dramatist, the producer, or the company itself:

> In all the Welsh plays I had seen or read previous to last night the interest has been, I confess, only in the experiment, in noting the tentative efforts of our writers to accustom themselves to a new form. It was the interest of watching a pupil scanning a new instrument, and trying what sound he might draw from it. But when Mr. D. T. Davies wrote *Ephraim Harries,* he fashioned a work of art, something which has not a relative importance, a merely historical interest, but a separate and independent value – an interest for its own sake and by its own right. As emphatically as I may, I desire to salute a work of genius, and for me the full beginning of Welsh drama dates from last night's performance of this play by Dan Mathews's company.[82]

Lewis was evidently inspired by Davies's lead and a few years later, a new effort to establish a Welsh national theatre under the aegis of the Cardiff Cymmrodorion Society opened with a short play by Davies, Y *Dieithryn*[83] and a longer play by Lewis himself, *Gwaed yr Uchelwyr*.[84] This new attempt at establishing a national Welsh theatre differed from Lord de Walden's venture in that it had clear links with the amateur movement. The officers of the company included many of the dramatists who wrote for the amateur movement as well as the well-known and widely respected producer heavily involved in the amateur movement in Wales, Dan Mathews. The beneficial effects of amateur participation in this effort were manifest in the fact that at least half the company's officers were listed in terms of their practical and professional roles in the everyday workings of the company itself, as opposed to in terms of any externally imposed social criteria. Amongst the usual listings of chairman, secretary and treasurer were found those of Lewis and Mathews as stage managers and Davies as artist. Alleged ineptitude in matters of form evidently did not bar these representatives of the amateur tradition from a thorough knowledge of the basic, practical needs of production.

Despite a positive report on the performances at the City Hall, Cardiff, by Mr John Phillips, a further difficulty emerged as a result of this new initiative. There was no longer any conflict regarding the preponderance of English plays or promotional material, as in the days of Lord Howard de Walden, but contradictory opinions began to emerge regarding the linguistic mode and register appropriate for a national Welsh drama and theatre. Both the plays staged were in Welsh. D. T. Davies wrote, according to his wont, in the Rhondda dialect to which he was accustomed. His expression was deemed 'natural and free from affectations' and his 'capital trifle'[85] was applauded. Saunders Lewis's effort, on the other hand, was harshly criticized for its stiff, archaic language in which Luned, the play's heroine, 'throws stiff bits of icy Welsh'[86] at her lover. Lewis's attempt to establish a formal literary linguistic standard for Welsh drama had been presaged by W. J. Gruffydd's writing of his ground-breaking play, *Beddau'r Proffwydi,* [87] in 1910. This four-act play was welcomed because it set new standards of stagecraft, but criticized for the formality and stiffness of its language. It seems to me that the struggle between those who sought to escape 'the oppressive question of dialect'[88] and those who fought against linguistic standardization was a different version of the conflict between those who sought to instil an awareness and understanding of the formal demands of western European drama into Welsh dramatists and those who maintained that it could thrive outside the pale of the modern principles of practice and technique. The essential debate was the same – should Welsh theatre operate as a protector of cultural distinctiveness or according to imported aesthetic principles that would put the nation in touch with a world beyond Wales?

The lukewarm reception of the Cardiff Cymmrodorion-led initiative to re-establish a national Welsh theatre made it clear that the fundamental issue of how to retain the best of the amateur tradition and yet gain access to a brave new world remained unanswered. Despite some opposition, Saunders Lewis's textual input manoeuvred Welsh theatre towards development of a professional linguistic norm, yet, at the same time, productions were criticized for maintaining amateurish standards, manifest in the absence of scenery, 'except in the curtain which only worked with a will of its own'.[89] What was the way forward? The establishment of a national dramatic union at Cardiff, in May 1927, can be seen as an attempt to respond to this challenge by channelling the energy of the amateur movement into a semi-professional framework. Rather than inventing a new, professional national theatre company to rival or lead amateur production, it was decided to work on grafting professional standards onto the existing amateur movement. The idea of the National Dramatic Union was to draw the work of all the Welsh amateur companies under its wing and foster the highest dramatic standards at all levels. It was evidently felt that a national union was the 'only medicine capable of securing, keeping and perfecting the drama'[90] [my translation].

It was with Conrad Davies as secretary and Lord Howard de Walden as president that the Union of Welsh Drama drew up a list of its main aims and objectives as follows:

1 to provide help and training for its members and secure their links with drama in general;
2 to support the formation of new companies;
3 to hold festivals of drama similar to the British Drama Festival in England;
4 to organize educational courses and conferences;
5 to facilitate the study of drama at secondary and tertiary level in Wales;
6 to organize ways of promoting the use and distribution of the necessities of the stage to companies within the union;
7 to publish an official, bilingual booklet;
8 to set the foundations of a national drama company;
9 to clear the way for and stimulate interest in the eventual foundation of a national Welsh playhouse.[91]

Some of these aims were realized with the establishment of a drama school at Llanfairfechan and with the welcoming of Ellen Terry to Caernarfon to give a series of lectures on the craft of the theatre. An educational programme was run by the Union, the Worker's Education Movement and the Department of Continuing Education. Its success resulted in sixty people attending a two-day course at Caerleon in January 1930 and to the increasing prominence of drama in the curriculum of schools and colleges. As the Union matured, it became evident that its main aim was to foster the organic growth of a national Welsh theatre from the amateur movement, so to speak. Gwernydd Morgan expressed his conviction that the drama union would lead naturally to the foundation of a national playhouse:

The mirror image of Welsh national life? 175

There was a lot of talk some time ago about getting a National Playhouse for Wales, but the thing is as if forgotten by now. Others insisted that the Welsh Drama should remain in its feebleness. They say that Welsh Drama should be 'village drama'. We believe that the village should have drama at its best, and it is certain that this will be ascertained with the aid of the playhouse. If a National Union of all the country's dramatists and companies was obtained, a National Playhouse would be in evidence in Wales in the near future[92] [my translation].

The aspiration towards a professional national Welsh theatre may well have accounted, in a strange way, for the union's desire to de-nationalize itself. This impulse was manifest in its choice of the title the Union of Welsh Drama over and above that of the Union of Drama in Welsh. The decision was made on the basis that some English-medium Welsh plays were more Welsh in spirit than their Welsh-medium counterparts and that unifying the Welsh and English contingents would make the union attractive to English companies and allow it to benefit from their skills. The vote was won in favour of the former title at 31 votes to 30.[93] The English feel to this venture was compounded by the fact that, very early in the union's history, it was proposed that an approach be made to the British Drama League (Geoffrey Whitworth, its secretary had delivered a lecture at Caerleon in 1930) in order to arrange a Welsh branch of the British Drama Festival. Ifan Kyrle Fletcher was at pains to point out that any festival allied to the British Drama League would not act as an incentive to the production of plays in Welsh. He also suspected that any attempt on Wales's part to orientate her own dramatic development within the pre-existing order of things in England might well be disorientating from an English viewpoint. As a result, he advocated 'that a separate Welsh Festival be organised on the lines of the British Festival ... open to both Welsh and English plays'.[94]

In the event, the union did not realize either of these aims: despite the fact that Kyrle Fletcher urged Wales to accustom herself to 'certain confusions'[95] occasioned by the state of bilingualism in the country, the nation itself did not respond with the recommended passivity. By 1928, despite the battles won from within the Union on behalf of the Welsh language, Saunders Lewis felt that it was fast becoming an English drama union in Wales. Two years later, the reputable Welsh newspaper *Y Faner* felt justified in pronouncing to the nation that the Union had succumbed to the fate of any institution that seeks to merge two elements that do not sit comfortably together, in this case, the English and Welsh languages.

The history of the Union of Welsh Drama is important, not on account of its own successes and failures, but because it includes the moment at which the debate about Welsh national theatre entered the arena of politics. Kyrle Fletcher's comment that the state of bilingualism in Wales had been brought about by economic conditions and would, in all likelihood, be regulated by economic factors, is clearly related to Michael Hechter's theory of the Celtic fringe. Hechter argued that the reappearance of Welsh nationalism in the twentieth century was due to the failure of any state body to invest sufficiently in the Welsh periphery or hinterland.[96] Saunders Lewis's view that drama's dependence on state aid or government sponsorship should fuel a national struggle towards political autonomy is an indication that political independence might be a prerequisite of the Welsh claim to adequate representation in all aspects of her national life, including the successful establishment of a Welsh national theatre. In 1932, the scholar Idwal Jones had characterized Welsh life as divided. He shared Lewis's view that the dilemma of the Welsh dramatist was an artistic echo of the reality of Welsh life in general:

> The dramatist who wishes to find expression for Welsh life ... cannot spread his wings, because large parts of social life are outside his reach. Our country is administered through the medium of English, and the most important part of our trade is conducted in English. A large part of our entertainment is English and there is a tendency to turn to English in our political discussions. It is English that is spoken by our aristocracy, and by the Welsh branch of the Army and Navy. In truth, it is difficult to express national conflict between the Welshman and the Englishman save in the language of the foreigner[97] [my translation].

George Moore voiced similar fears when he noted that the Welsh language was retiring before the language that 'will soon be the business language of the world'.[98] However, his distrust of the apparatus of government as a potential avenue for the resolution of this crisis is evident from his comment that if the first act passed by a future Welsh parliament should be 'that all debates shall be conducted in Welsh, my opinion of the value of Parliaments will need to be reconsidered'.[99]

In this context, the Union's launching of its own periodical, *Y Llwyfan*, as an open vehicle for the 'expression, in Welsh and English, of the opinions, aims and ideals of any person or group of persons interested in the art of drama in Wales',[100] was an event of national significance and one that counteracted accusations of an English bias. Both the denominational and non-denominational Welsh papers of the past had generally succeeded in offering a 'fair and gentlemanly lead on important Welsh questions'[101] [my translation]. Nonetheless, this approbation was mixed with reservations regarding their mimetic tendency in relation to English papers and the more serious objection that they had no political influence. It is unclear whether this deficiency was the responsibility of newspaper editors or whether it was due to the fact that 'Welsh Wales has not taken the question of her representation seriously yet and her representatives do not sympathise sufficiently with the need to prepare themselves for public service in Wales'[102] [my translation]. Either way, it demonstrated the fact that the Welsh nation had not yet been educated in the skills of citizenship. *Y Llwyfan* did not have a lengthy lifespan,[103] but it did go some way towards remedying this situation and establishing the value and viability of a bilingual debate about the future of Welsh drama and theatre.

Whatever its shortcomings, the amateur drama movement in Wales did draw the attention of the Welsh nation to the necessity of sharpening its citizenship skills. Proponents of the idea of a professional Welsh national theatre company felt that the amateur movement could not see beyond itself. In fact, it succeeded in bringing about a realization of the incongruity of applying the administrative infrastructure designed for the gov-ernance of one country to another country, with a flagrant disregard for national differences. In a newspaper report of 1931, under the heading 'Unlicensed Drama',[104] it is noted that the Talysarn Drama Company stood accused at Caernarfon county court of performing G. R. Jones's *Y Crochen* without a licence. The company was reputedly in contravention of section 15 of the Playhouses Act 1843 because it had staged a play that had not been licensed by the Lord Chamberlain. The matter was im-portant because it highlighted the inadequacy of the English administrative infra-structure for dealing with things Welsh. J. Ellis Williams took advantage of the columns of *Y Darian*[105] to alert the nation to the inappropriateness of the regulations that were restricting her right to free dramatic expression. He notes with some sarcasm that it is only an English synopsis of a Welsh play that needs to be presented in order to satisfy the censor: could this really be called responsible censorship? In Wales, it was not a question of disputing the need for national censorship, as was the case with the English revolt against the censor at the turn of the twentieth century, but in claiming the Welsh people's right to adequate censorship and ending the farcical situation where,

> a Welsh author is forced to apply to obtain the licence of an English official before he can perform a Welsh play in Wales ... This ridiculous present method is just as if a doctor tried to guess whether a patient is ill or not by looking at the size of his hat.[106]

Before this dilemma could be adequately addressed, the Second World War brought the amateur drama movement in Wales to a halt. According to J. E. Williams, he had 350 amateur Welsh companies on his mailing list before the war. By 1946, only one in ten remained active and no more than thirty were in rehearsal for the forthcoming winter.[107] In 1933, the National Eisteddfod production under the direction of Dr Stefan Hock drew some of its players for an adaptation by T. Gwynn Jones of a play by Hugo von Hoffsmanstahl, *Pobun,* from the amateur ranks at Wrexham, but the 1930s in general were characterized by a resurgence of interest in the idea of a professional Welsh national theatre.[108] The latest drive was headed by the familiar figure of Lord Howard de Walden, but the fact that this company gave its first performance, not in Wales, but at the Arts Theatre, London, on 26 January 1933 suggested that the old difficulties surrounding the national affiliations of Lord de Walden's very first initiative remained unsolved.

O. Llewelyn Owain's assessment of the aims of this new national endeavour reveals nothing new, other than a professed respect for amateur drama in Wales as a means towards the foundation of a permanent professional Welsh national theatre establishment.[109] After an initial English-language performance of *A Comedy of Good and Evil* by Richard Hughes (1924), that was honoured with the presence of Lloyd George and other dignitaries, the company set up residence in Llangollen, under the direction of Evelyn Bowen. Its location in Plas Newydd,

Llangollen, was a heartening indication that the Welsh national theatre might at last benefit from the permanence afforded by physical and geographical definition. Moreover, the company's intention to stage Kitchener Davies's *Cwm Glo*[110] – a play that bravely uncovered some of the more sordid aspects of modern Welsh life and was castigated as a result[111] – suggested that they were committed to the revelation of Welsh life in all its complexity and variety. This plan had already been presaged by a decision that indicated the company's desire to afford the Welsh people ownership of the company itself, by means of a plan to sell annual membership shares at a price of a guinea each, giving each member a say in the election of officials to run the company from day to day. Nonetheless, when it came to it, the company cast aside any real hope of establishing a democratic and creative relationship with their audience. Rather than following through with the plan to stage *Cwm Glo,* they chose instead to stage a mixed programme of original Welsh plays, adaptations and translations. Despite Evelyn Bowen's public insistence that the company was committed to the development of Welsh medium drama in Wales, she was accused of an English-language bias. A report in *Y Brython* regrets that English elements were thwarting the Plas Newydd effort in the same way as they had previously hindered the Welsh Drama Union project. Interestingly, the main attack came from the prominent literary figure, Cynan, who accused the company of operating in English in rehearsal, in in-house training, in the delivery of its educational programme and in its official correspondence. He raged:

> For shame that such a place be called either 'National' or 'Welsh'. What wonder if the majority of our Welsh companies want nothing to do with it? What wonder that its generous sponsors have recently had to express their disappointment, in public, that it could not claim the support of the nation? It is too late in the day any longer for any 'national' institution to be viable in Wales and it guilty of neglecting the Welsh language[112] [my translation].

The immediate cause of Cynan's wrath was a claim by Meriel Williams, who had succeeded Evelyn Bowen at the company's helm, that drama was more popular than poetry in Wales: the poetic heritage of Wales was one that celebrated the link between the country's cultural wealth and a respected social system of royal and aristocratic patronage of the arts. Ms Williams's comment that drama had superseded poetry was particularly tactless in view of contemporary fears regarding the gradual erosion of the traditional values of Welsh and, particularly, Welsh-speaking society. Cynan's partiality to poetry may well have cast some suspicion on the veracity of his accusations regarding the company's neglect of the Welsh language. Indeed, the decision to employ the Austrian director, Dr Stefan Hock, to stage an adaptation of Hoffmanstahl's work by T. Gwynn Jones in Liverpool was a popular one. There were some expressions of dismay at the importation of foreign dramatic material into the Welsh arena, reminiscent of Matthew Arnold's reservations regarding the visit of the Comédie-Française to London, but Dr Hock's expertise, along with his constructive attitude towards the Welsh nation, was appreciated. It was the company's attempt to entice English actors and actresses to take part in the production by means of a public meeting held at Liverpool, in which the proceedings were conducted solely through the medium of English, that really caused outrage. The company could hardly argue with one attendee's assessment that:

> This was a novel meeting, and I learnt, at any rate, that the National Playhouse has no desire to be Welsh. It is not by getting a company of Welsh and Englishmen to play a German drama under the direction of an Austrian ... (although that gentleman is a better Welshman than many of Liverpool's Welsh – to all appearances) that Welsh Drama will be propelled forward[113] [my translation].

There can be no doubt that Wales and Welsh drama and theatre, in particular, had risen to the challenges of self-criticism and that self-criticism had led to increased self-awareness. In turn, self-awareness had brought about an impasse, a polarization of those who opted for cultural and linguistic promotion and preservation and those who advocated an ecumenical acceptance of the variety of different cultural and linguistic perspectives and experiences that combined to constitute twentieth-century Wales and, ultimately, put the nation in touch with a wider world, beyond its own national boundaries. Both viewpoints were valid and valuable. Both were presented, problematized and promoted in the debate surrounding Lord de Walden's Welsh national theatre. Lord de Walden's pioneering work in the field of Welsh national theatre was invaluable because it instigated a public debate about modern Welsh identity and modern Welsh drama and theatre. The failure of these ventures was equally important because it saw the Welsh national theatre debate go public in a whole new sense as it entered the novel realm of government planning, policy and politics.

~ 6 ~
Changing old lamps for new: private patronage gives way to public subsidy

The end of Lord Howard de Walden's patronage of Welsh drama and theatre marked the close of a definitive phase in the history of the Welsh national theatre debate. Lord de Walden's death, much like that of Thomas Edwards before him, ended an era in which Welsh drama and theatre had grown, more or less organically, from within the life of the nation. The next benefactor of drama and the theatre in Wales was neither one of the country's leading cultural institutions nor the leader of a 'group of enthusiasts ... with a high and determined purpose'[1] but an official government body, operating in the name of a Westminster parliament. From the latter half of the twentieth century onwards, the Welsh national theatre debate would be shaped, in part at least, by the British Arts Council. It was under the patronage of the Welsh Committee of the British Arts Council that Wales finally realized its dream of a national theatre company that was 'forward-looking and missionary'.[2] The journey towards this national theatre was a difficult and hazardous one. The main obstacles of accommodation, availability and quality were compounded by the country's linguistic diversity – a factor that made it necessary for the Arts Council's Welsh Committee 'to consider Welsh as well as English Theatre'.[3]

Initially the Council was confident of its ability to solve the 'problem which is Wales'[4] by setting up an English-medium professional touring company, with the pious hope that 'at least some of the members ... will be bilingual'.[5] Later, it reassessed the situation and conceded that it might, in fact, be necessary to create a Welsh-medium company that had a 'separate existence to the English company'.[6] What became increasingly apparent during this process was the fact that the Council was no more master of the difficult task of discovering a national theatrical formula that would reflect the cultural and linguistic diversity of Wales than were its predecessors. The Arts Council report for the year ending 24 March 1969 openly admitted the fact that the Council found that 'the need to purvey drama in two languages instead of being complimentary and even profitably abrasive, tends to be divisive, both artistically and administratively'.[7] It might be argued that it was through wresting its independence from the Arts Council's Welsh Committee, whilst continuing to benefit from its subsidy, that Wales secured the success of her most influential official national theatre to date, the Welsh-medium Cwmni Theatr Cymru.

Cwmni Theatr Cymru earned its reputation by virtue of its popularity, its productivity and its professionalism but its status as an exclusively Welsh-medium national company curtailed the scope of its appeal both to non-Welsh nationals resident in Wales and to non-Welsh-speaking Welsh people. Despite this shortcoming, its success marked a vital phase in the history of the drive to establish a Welsh national theatre because it highlighted the fact that the culture of power in Britain was more often than not – even in the case of the invaluable cooperation between the BBC, the Welsh Theatre Company and later Cwmni Theatr Cymru – detrimental to the power of culture in Wales. With this paradox in mind, it is difficult not to concur with the conclusion reached by the Arts Council's Welsh Committee that 'nowhere are the problems inherent in the Welsh situation more vividly seen than in the provision of drama'.[8]

In the earliest days of the drive for a Welsh national theatre, Tom Jones had acknowledged the 'difficulties imposed by geography'[9] in Wales when he noted that the population was dispersed up and down the country in small rural or urban centres. His answer was to propose the idea of a portable theatre as the best means of servicing these diverse areas. Owen Rhoscomyl and Lord Howard de Walden had also originally envisaged a travelling theatre as part of their plans for a national theatre network in Wales.[10] In the event, they found it was a difficult and expensive idea to put into practice and in 1932, the call for the building of suitable theatres in Wales was still being made by people like J. J. Williams who hoped that one of these buildings would fly the flag as a national playhouse.[11] Idwal Jones echoed Williams's sentiments when he attributed the fact that Welsh drama reminded one of 'a young and lithe, mountain pony, unable to pull its cart forwards because he and his cart are trying to traverse a bog' to the fact that there is in Wales 'no urban focal point, nor playhouse, nor players either – with nothing but the drama as the main interest of their lives'[12] [my translation]. Several decades later, the Arts Council's Welsh Committee noted that by 'English standards'[13] Wales had no long-established metropolitan centre and was 'a country of small towns, of strong national feelings, nowhere stronger than in these small towns'.[14] The Committee's initial response to this challenge was to instigate a policy of touring the 'theatreless centres of Wales'.[15] However, when it eventually concluded that this policy was ineffective it began to engage with the idea of a national theatre in the hope, voiced many years earlier by W. C. Elvet Thomas, that such a centralization of national life would stimulate the country's 'intellectual and artistic vitality'.[16]

By the middle of the twentieth century it was generally agreed that Wales should never again put her dramatists in the position endured by Thomas Edwards who had reached out 'blindly for the stage that was not there'.[17] The two main players that came to the fore at this vital stage in the struggle to establish a Welsh national theatre were the Arts Council's Welsh Committee and the St David's Trust – the former an official government organization, the latter an independent and voluntary one brought together by high profile figures such as Saunders Lewis, the actor Clifford Evans, Lord Aberdare and Col. C. G. Traherne, in order to lobby for the establishment of a national theatre at Cardiff.[18] Both the Welsh Committee and the St David's Trust agreed with J. J. Williams that 'the future of Welsh Drama was tied up with a problem of bricks and mortar'[19] [my translation]. They also seemed to be in agreement that the answer was the establishment of a concrete cultural centrepiece of national dimensions in the country's capital, Cardiff. However, the zeal displayed by the St David's Trust in putting flesh on the dry bones of this concept was sufficient to put its government ally to shame. The architect Elidir Davies[20] was commissioned to design the new national theatre and the building itself was regarded of fundamental importance to the success of the venture as a whole. The St David's Trust choice of another theatre, the Mermaid Theatre, as the venue from which to launch their manifesto highlighted their understanding of theatre as a venue for a communal struggle towards a definite goal that had political, cultural, social and artistic consequences.

The building sketched forth in Davies's plans was an expansive and flexible resource. Davies himself described it as a living, comprehensive scheme in which separate units came together to form a centre which provided facilities for study, leisure and amusement day and night. It was a multi-purpose building in line with the Trust's aim of fostering the growth of all the performative arts in Wales and included an oriel, a library, a studio theatre, a luxurious restaurant, rehearsal space and design facilities. A stipulation by the actor Clifford Evans – one of the Trust's founding members – that he wanted there to be a hall of poets in the theatre, on the walls of which all the Eisteddfod's chaired and crowned bards were to be noted, provided a reminder of the Eisteddfod's influence on Welsh theatre, both in terms of its patronage of drama and its domination of the space available for cultural activity and articulation in Wales.[21] However, despite this nostalgic reference to the Eisteddfod establishment, the Welsh national theatre building proposed by the St David's Trust was not unlike the eventual home of the English National Theatre, particularly in terms of the functional and practical bias of its architectural structure. Not only was there an emphasis on the practical needs of production, of education and of leisure requirements, but Evans stipulated in a draft letter to the architect that in order to keep the actor's energies fresh, it would be necessary to ensure that his daily professional life was centred in the theatre as another man's is at his office.[22] In his Blue Book, William Archer drew a similar parallel between the actor's working life and the workings of life in general when he requested that members of the acting profession be granted access to all aspects and avenues of social life and intercourse. Just as the post-revolution government of France had granted full rights of citizenship to actors and actresses subsequent to the political upheaval of 1789, Archer sought to place English actors and actresses on an equal footing with their fellow citizens. Evans's aim was the same but he adopted a different approach by attempting to secure a healthy environment for the actor/actress through the direct agency of the national theatre building itself. Both men were striving towards the same aim – the fulfilment of the individual by means of his/her integration into all aspects of the life of the nation – but their methodological approaches were different. What Archer was requesting was a change of attitude towards members of the acting profession, a commitment to a process of social fine-tuning. Evans, on the other hand, clearly saw the physical environment of a Welsh national theatre as a means of providing an alternative structure for the process of personal fulfilment through a full and expansive engagement with and in the nation.

Evans's linking of the pragmatic and mechanistic framework of modern existence orientated towards and emanating from the work place, and those artistic ideals that provide life with its sacramental core, must have appealed to the Cardiff Town Council. It may well have been the hope that just as the actor would be centred in the theatre, so the theatre would be central to the life of the city that prompted the Council to donate a piece of ground by the castle for the venture. The project took upon it a civic identity when Evans presented his report to the mayor and members of Cardiff Civic Council in the town hall on 30 March 1961. Evans intended to seek the funding of some £300,000 necessary for the building and early maintenance of the theatre from the unions, from industry and from church tithes. His pricing policy was in line with that outlined by Archer in that it sought to make the national theatre an available resource to as wide a section of the populace as possible. Prices were to range between 3/6 and 15/- with at least three hundred seats at 5/- . At this point, however, the Welsh Committee of the British Arts Council stepped in. Under the leadership of Professor Gwyn Jones and Dr Roger Webster, the Committee resisted the St David's Trust's plans on the basis of practicality. Past experience had taught representatives of the Committee the validity of D. T. Davies's observations regarding the failure of Cardiff, with its population of nearly a quarter of a million, to sustain even one permanent and well attended theatre.[23] They were convinced that no more than 2 per cent of the population of Cardiff could be lured into the theatre. Despite Lord Aberdare's conviction that 'mediocrity in conception has little appeal in the arts today',[24] a report in Cwmni Theatr Cymru's archives documents the Welsh Committee's preference for a 'smaller theatre only centre'[25] over the trust's proposal for a multi-purpose building. However, as time went on the Committee seemed to become more and more convinced that a Welsh national theatre should be based on a company, as opposed to a building.

Private patronage gives way to public subsidy   187

In a discussion of the National Theatre Campaign in the 1960s in Wales, Elan Closs Stephens confirms that there was, in fact, a discrepancy between the views held by the British Arts Council's main body and its Welsh Committee with regard to the idea of a national theatre building. Closs Stephens claims that whilst the British Arts Council report of 1959 can be read as a call for the establishment of a national theatre building, this was not echoed in the Welsh section of the report, *Housing the Arts in Wales: Report of the Committee of Enquiry set up by the Welsh Committee of the Arts Council of Great Britain*. This, she tells us,

> is a puny report and argues a lack of confidence in the Welsh Committee of the period. It makes no reference to actual money at all, though the London and Scotland reports do so. More interestingly, in comparison with the 1961 English report, it does not talk about building *one new theatre* other than giving its support to the idea of a National Theatre in the distant future.[26]

It is difficult to account for the Welsh Committee's lethargy with regard to this issue, particularly in view of the fact that it had been granted autonomy from the British Arts Council since 1 April 1953 in recognition of the fact that it spoke on behalf of a 'nation with its own language and way of life'.[27] A sympathetic interpretation suggests that the committee was striving to remain true to opinions emanating from within Wales. Cross currents of contradictory feelings had been stirred up by the proposals of the St David's Trust. There were fears that a Cardiff-based theatre would be exclusive both in social and linguistic terms. There were also indications of paranoia from other artistic institutions, such as the Welsh National Opera Company, which had been identified by the Trust as co-inhabitants of the proposed building. Finally, there were reservations regarding the negative effect a Welsh national theatre might have on Cardiff's existing theatre, the New Theatre. One newspaper report that branded Evans as the inhabitant of a comfortable zone of professionalism, asked the question 'how can people be so blind? Closing a theatre – the only live theatre in the capital – and intending to build a new national theatre, in the same city?'[28]

At this point, it seemed that different attitudes towards the issue of a national theatre building constituted an irreconcilable rift between the trust and the Arts Council's Welsh Committee and there can be little doubt that there were unresolved differences between the two bodies when the Welsh Committee finally beat the trust into retreat. I believe, however, that it was not the national theatre's external characteristics but its inner qualities that constituted the main bone of contention between the two. The St David's Trust wanted to restore the theatre to the centre of Welsh cultural life and thereby to secure the survival of the nation. Its understanding of national survival was not in line with the mindset that had made linguistic preservation a national imperative earlier in the century. It did not shirk its responsibility towards the Welsh-speaking parts of Wales and included in its mission statement the declaration that it would 'have a special responsibility for the occasional performance of plays in the Welsh language and for the general encouragement of dramatists working in that language'.[29] But it directed its appeal 'to all Welshmen as well as to all sections of the community in Wales'[30] and aimed at bringing the best of European theatre to Wales as well as fostering native talent. Under the Trust, the national theatre was to be a concrete manifestation of the vivacious and undying spirit of the nation. Evans's statement that he hoped the national theatre would be a means of replenishing the nation's spiritual reservoir stipulated the precise nature of the service it might offer and the Trust's symbolic association with Wales's patron saint, St David, underlined the importance of spiritual mythology to its members. The retelling of myths about St David are in a sense dramatizations of eternal national truths of a spiritual nature in a widely accessible form and, as such, were a blueprint for the kind of inspiration that Evans and Lewis hoped the national theatre might offer the Welsh nation. It is probably a coincidence, but no less interesting for that, that the land offered by Cardiff City Council for the building proposed by the trust was sacred ground associated with the interests of the city's Catholic contingent. On the basis of this evidence, the Trust's clash with the Welsh Committee of the Arts Council for Britain can be understood in terms of a polarity between two different perceptions of the role and function of a national theatre – one driven by a pragmatic desire to accommodate national differences and diversity, the other by an exuberant ambition to make that very depth and diversity the driving force of the nation's theatrical creativity.

Whatever the truth of this hypothesis, the Welsh Committee certainly used its political bulk to manoeuvre the Trust into a position of subservience. In its annual report for 1962, the committee publicly abandoned its policy of ad hoc touring. Over the previous decade, some twenty professional companies had been assembled to tour the theatre-less centres of Wales, presenting plays ranging from those of Shakespeare to those by contemporary playwrights in both English and Welsh. By 1962, it was felt that this policy 'did little towards creating a permanent organisation for professional drama'.[31] As a result, it was resolved that 'as soon as possible a permanent touring company should be formed'.[32] Faced by this opposition, the Trust finally admitted defeat, gave up its dream of a national theatre building at Cardiff and renounced its independent status in favour of membership of a working committee in conjunction with the Cardiff City Council and the Welsh Committee of the Arts Council. The Trust did feature occasionally in connection with the Welsh national theatre debate over the next two decades – a *Western Mail* report of 17 February 1972 refers to the Trust's input into plans to build a national arts complex in the redeveloped area of south Cardiff[33] and Clifford Evans presented plans of a theatre for this site to the minister of state for Wales, John Stradling Thomas, as late as February 1984 – but the campaign gradually fizzled out and the Trust never regained its original importance and influence.

The Trust's withdrawal from the active pursuit of a Cardiff-based national theatre company did not bring about a swift resolution of the Welsh national theatre dilemma. In fact it was at this point that the conflict between an appreciation of the artistic benefits of a centre of national dramatic excellence in Wales, and the overwhelming fear that any such centre would marginalize the interest, values and input of a significant section of the Welsh populace, came to a height. When the Arts Council came into existence in 1945, it did not encounter a theatrical wilderness in Wales but, as we have seen, an amateur tradition that flourished despite the inadequacy of theatrical accommodation that meant that 'few, if any, of the amateur companies in Wales have homes in which they can act whenever they want to'.[34] The novel principle of the availability of government monies that accompanied the introduction of the Arts Council had repercussions throughout the different strata of dramatic life in Wales, including the amateur arena. During the late 1950s and 1960s, press reports reveal a consistent call for subsidy by Welsh-language amateur companies such as Cwmni Môn and Cwmni Drama Llangefni who were already servicing reputable Welsh drama festivals. These requests, designed to enable companies to tour their plays to a wider Welsh-speaking audience, had to be filtered through the Arts Council's Welsh Committee. Newspaper reports discussing appeals by Cwmni Môn for financial support to aid tours of Saunders Lewis's play, *Esther,* indicate both the confidence of Miss Myra Owen, the Arts Council's Welsh director, that the council was well equipped to assess the company's quality, and her apparent lack of confidence in her proficiency in the language of performance. The fact that Miss Owen conducted a discussion of the matter of Arts Council sponsorship of a Welsh-medium play, with the reporter of a national Welsh-medium newspaper aimed at a Welsh-language readership, in English suggests that fears regarding the negative effects of the encroachment of national professional standards on the country's indigenous amateur theatre, often regarded as a vehicle for Welsh-language maintenance, were not unfounded.

The attitude of the Arts Council towards the amateur movement did little to allay these fears. In its early years the Council demonstrated irritation, if not antagonism, towards a tradition that it identified as one of the 'many problems confronted by theatre in the provinces'.[35] As Clos Stephens points out, the creation of the Welsh Committee did not improve matters much. She highlights the lack of imagination demonstrated by the committee with regard to existing theatrical activity when she quotes its advice to companies playing in village halls regarding means of 'insulating stages from the noise of backstage lavatories'.[36] Ioan Williams is more openly critical of both the Arts Council and its Welsh Committee's stance when he comments:

> For a good part of the last hundred years theatre in Wales has been prejudiced by the dominance of one imported model – 'good, quality mainstream theatre in the literary tradition from Shakespeare through Ibsen and Shaw to our contemporary writers' – and by the widespread assumption that no indigenous theatre existed until the Arts Council assumed the responsibility for creating it.[37]

This assumption held no sway in Wales itself and if the Arts Council really did wish to follow its professed policy of supporting 'regional roses'[38] it would have no difficulty in finding worthy candidates amongst the Welsh amateur companies. In an article in *Y Llwyfan* in 1969, Enid R. Morgan celebrated the achievements of Theatr Fach Llangefni,[39] a small theatre company described by the Welsh Committee itself as a 'model of what a little theatre should be'.[40] Morgan offers an inspiring account of how this well-respected and well-housed amateur theatrical establishment had been producing drama for twenty years. An earlier report in *Y Cymro* boasted the Llangefni theatre's achievement in staging over forty plays over a five-year period from 1955 to 1960, ranging from the work of Arthur Miller to Ibsen, Eliot and Saunders Lewis himself.[41] Morgan's report confirmed the adventurous nature of the theatre's choice of dramatic material and recorded the fact that it was soon to reach a crescendo in a celebratory week of performances of a specially commissioned translation of Molière's *Le Malade Imaginaire* by Bruce Griffiths and Gwenllian Tudur. She went on to argue that Theatr Fach Llangefni had obtained its ultimate triumph and claimed its rightful place at the forefront of amateur theatre by obtaining the theatre chairmanship of the Little Theatre Guild of Great Britain for 1969. What we had at Llangefni, she argued, was,

> a group of people who, despite being amateurs, aim at the highest possible standards. As a result they stand between the wholly professional theatre that requires only ticket sellers and listeners of the local community, and the small local company that produces one play over the winter season and often presents it under terrible circumstances in village halls and chapel vestries[42] [my translation].

According to Morgan's assessment, one of the main advantages of Theatr Fach Llangefni was that it had overcome the 'problem of bricks and mortar' that J. J. Williams had associated with the National Theatre Campaign. In 1969, the Llangefni theatre was a proud edifice, housing all the modern requirements of theatre production. The company had begun in 1949 as a result of the efforts of a small group of enthusiasts who wanted to produce a play by George Fisher, a local secondary school mathematics teacher. The makeshift accommodation provided by school and town halls at Llangefni soon proved inadequate and when in 1955 the old school was condemned, a barn with a set of eight adjacent rooms, four of which were hired, provided the company with new accommodation. In 1955, after a good deal of renovation work and the installation of a lighting rig, the building was opened to the public. As a result of a rise in membership from 80 to 400 over a two-year period, coupled with fundraising efforts and some Arts Council grant aid, the building had a theatre, a vestibule, an auditorium of 111 seats, dressing rooms, a wardrobe and a workshop. In 1961, another major fundraising effort and various grants facilitated the building of a new roof and tower, the addition of more dressing and storage rooms and the installation of a fifty-five way lighting exchange. Enid Morgan's recommendation that there should be more little theatres like that at Llangefni in Wales, particularly in the light of the dominance of discussions about a national theatre, is evidence of her conviction that this small-scale indigenous Welsh theatre was more national than anything produced or promoted in Wales hitherto. The popularity of this opinion is confirmed by the common practice amongst newspaper reporters of referring to the annual Llangefni Drama Festival as 'Wales's National Drama Festival'.[43] The presence of the Arts Council's players at the 1955 festival, where they were commended on their production of Saunders Lewis's *Gymerwch chi Sigaret?* with no less an actress than Siân Phillips in the title role, could even be interpreted as an implicit recognition of the festival's national status by the council itself.

Theatr Fach Llangefni succeeded in affording its artistic aspirations concrete, material substance – something that had yet to be attained by any officially sanctioned Welsh Theatre Company. Theatr Fach Garthewin established a similar feat, but its physical status as a national, theatrical landmark – a distinct and distinctive place for Welsh theatre – was second to its importance as the location for an ideological debate about Welsh theatre and its significance to the nation. R. O. F. Wynne's account of Garthewin's beginnings presented the venture in terms of the crisis of theatre accommodation in Wales. He noted that 'it was with a view to providing at least one ... building as a temporary home for the Welsh National Theatre that the work of converting the eighteenth century stone and brick barn at Garthewin'[44] into a playhouse was carried out in 1937 under the direction of Mr Thomas Taig.[45] The Garthewin theatre, approached 'via a wide entrance under an old clocktower ... until you reach the far end of a spacious courtyard'[46] [my translation] certainly made a captivating architectural statement and the high standard of the artistic activity that took place within these walls compounded its attractiveness. However, Roger Owen's definition of the theatre as the locus for 'a debate of sorts ... in favour of giving precedence to theatrical transformation in an evening of drama'[47] rather than accepting the homely standards of folk drama, provides a more insightful indication of the theatre's national importance.

R. O. F. Wynne claimed that the Garthewin theatre had always had nominal national status and this is supported by the fact that its first production was presented by Lord de Walden's National Welsh players.[48] However, I think it is fair to argue that there had never been a contradiction in the minds of those who championed the Garthewin venture, namely R. O. F. Wynne and Saunders Lewis, between Wales's amateur theatrical tradition and the development of a Welsh national theatre. It was Lewis, after all, who had claimed that the only way to foster theatre in Wales was by continuous work and presentation on the part of an amateur company that had a little theatre and workshops.[49] From 1947 onwards, the Garthewin theatre adopted this model by establishing its own band of players who performed there annually under the direction of Mr Morris Jones. Furthermore, from 1950 to 1968, the theatre hosted a bi-annual national festival that was sponsored by the British Arts Council.[50] The programme for the 1952 festival provides a typical example of the mix of productions and lectures that formed the backbone of these festivals. It included performances of a translation of Molière's *Tartuffe* by D. J. Thomas, *Gan Bwyll,* an original work by Saunders Lewis, as well as Welsh- and English-medium lectures on various aspects of drama, production and dramatic criticism by Thomas Parry, John Moody, J. C. Trewin and Saunders Lewis himself. These festivals played a major part in the realization of the theatre's main aims as set out in its mission statement:

> to foster an appreciation of the Drama in Wales;
> to organise drama schools and lectures;
> to support Welsh authors;
> to organise regular performances of companies in this playhouse.[51]

These aims seem worthy national aspirations, but it is neither their definition nor their realization that gives the Garthewin Little Theatre its true significance in terms of the national theatre debate in Wales.

Newspaper reporters and critics often depicted Garthewin as a comfortable little theatre, similar to that described by Saunders Lewis as his ideal national theatre, 'a house in one of our villages, built pleasantly like an old farmhouse, and sheltered by trees'.[52] It was not, however, homely in the more familiar sense of the word. A report in *Y Cymro* reveals the fact that Garthewin cultivated a specific audience: a Garthewin festival, it is explained, was characterized by the absence of the *miri* of the Eisteddfod great crowds and was attended by just over one hundred and fifty people every day.[53] Owen's comment regarding the local people's reluctance to enter estate property because they had been excluded from it by its aristocratic owners for centuries provides a possible explanation of this phenomenon. The fact that no efforts were made to overcome this resistance or to recruit actors from the theatre's immediate vicinity makes his subsequent suggestion that the festival was aimed at the creation of an entirely new sense of Welshness seem plausible. According to Owen, the Garthewin theatre did not aspire to the creation of theatre as a community event, but rather to the creation of a community that would elevate the theatrical event. The theatre did not seek 'to declare her "national" title on behalf of the people, so to speak, but rather on behalf of those who supported the theatre across the country, more often than not, the educated middle class'.[54]

Owen describes the plays by Lewis that were performed at Garthewin as dialogic, vocal theatre in which the characters are their voices and experience no conflict between their inner experience and their external articulation of that experience. In this kind of drama, he argues, the stage has no function other than to elevate and collect the voices together and an empty space of any size will perform the task adequately. There were many contemporary complaints regarding the restrictive nature of the Garthewin stage, but Lewis was clearly at home with this sort of 'straitened stage'.[55] The reason for this is that his interest lay in stimulating and shaping a dramatic debate in a language that was not suited to the 'common Welsh drama companies'.[56] It was his commitment to the discovery of a suitable space for the conducting of that dramatic debate that inspired his interest and input into the Garthewin theatrical venture. What Saunders Lewis and, indeed, all those who had invested in the theatre at Garthewin, were prepared to admit was that the geographical, political and linguistic hybrid that was Wales made it an antagonistic environment for the development of rational, democratic and egalitarian debate. The limitations of Lewis's own drama and of the kind of theatre cultivated at Garthewin bear testimony to the cost of this courage. Owen argues that 'the desire of the audience at Garthewin was to see a piece of theatre create its own world, and it was this desire that was the starting point for the process of creating an aesthetic and an identity of the Welsh theatre'.[57] I would add that the Garthewin theatre created its own version of the Welsh nation in order to conduct a lively theatrical debate regarding Welsh identity. Whilst that debate was seriously compromised in terms of scope and scale, it was nonetheless a national endeavour of a startlingly new and brave kind.

Whilst the Garthewin theatre busied itself with what Owen rightly terms experimental theatre, there were other more mainstream developments afoot, namely the establishment of the Welsh Theatre Company in 1962 by the Welsh Committee of the Arts Council for Great Britain. This bilingual company – 'a national theatre ensemble serving directly, in active performance, the whole of Wales'[58] – secured £20,000 per annum for the first three years of its existence from the Welsh Arts Council. Warren Jenkins – the company's first director – referred to the development as part of a schedule of 'planned action'[59] necessary to ensure that Wales and the Welsh language were to survive, and it seemed that this might well be the beginning of an exciting era in which the country might benefit from having finally secured its long-awaited national stage. This was not to be the case. At the end of the initial three-year period, Jenkins provided a report that set out to identify the main difficulties facing the national company and inadvertently offered some indication of the reasons behind its difficult history and its ultimate failure in 1978. In his report, he highlighted the lack of accommodation as a vital issue and declared that 'without its own building the Welsh Theatre Company cannot long continue to exist, that stalemate will have been reached and the Company will start to disintegrate'.[60] Clearly, the problem of bricks and mortar continued to haunt the Welsh national theatre. Despite the ardency of his call for a home for his company, Jenkins dismissed the plans of the St David's Trust as too ambitious. As evidence, he cited the failure of Olivier and the National Theatre to 'barely fill the New Theatre for one week with three plays.'[61] Although his report manifested a sensitivity towards the difficulties faced by a minority culture that has had 'cultural and linguistic dualism forced upon it by a powerful and pervasive neighbour', his ideal that a national theatre could be at one and the same time 'classical in nature' but 'national in effect'[62] and that this effect could be obtained by the paltry figure of the four Welsh-medium plays that the company had succeeded in staging between 1962 and 1965 seemed somewhat unrealistic.

Whether or not this is a fair criticism, 1965 saw another quieter but equally significant development – the formation of a nucleus of Welsh-medium quasi-professional actors and actresses under contract to the BBC. The four Welsh-medium productions that Jenkins had staged were produced in conjunction with the BBC and, despite his annoyance at some Welsh actors' fondness for its cultural overtones, he admitted that 'the modern professional creation'[63] of public performance in Wales originated with the BBC. These passing remarks actually gloss over both the importance and the difficulties of the relationship between Welsh theatre and the BBC: it was in relation to the emergence and history of the Welsh National Theatre Company's sister company, Cwmni Theatr Cymru, that the full significance of this alliance was to become evident. The Welsh Theatre Company was intended as a bilingual company but it gave birth to Cwmni Theatr Cymru, an exclusively Welsh-medium company, under the directorship of the BBC's Wilbert Lloyd Roberts. By 1965, Cwmni Theatr Cymru was employing a group of some six full-time professional actors to perform exclusively Welsh-language work, at a guaranteed annual salary of £600. In 1968, Roberts left his employment with the BBC to become the company's full-time director. There can be little doubt that this company was the most successful national theatre that Wales has had to date and it was certainly an influential cultural vehicle in the service of the Welsh nation for a period of over a decade. I have already noted the fact that the company's monolingual performance policy curtailed its scope but it is useful to remember that, for a considerable part of its life, it coexisted with its founder company, the English-medium Welsh Theatre Company, in a national partnership. Unfortunately, the Welsh Theatre Company ran into difficulties from 1974[64] onwards due to its failure to complement its success in mounting small-scale productions at the Casson Studio Theatre[65] in Cardiff with the 'mounting [of] large-scale touring productions in co-operation with the New Theatre, Cardiff and the Grand Theatre, Swansea which in turn will justify its inclusion in the plans of the Arts Council of Great Britain's Touring Committee'.[66] It was its closure in 1978 that left Cwmni Theatr Cymru as the sole company operating in Wales under a national title and with a national remit.

In a report in the Gwynedd County Council Archive, it is noted that 'amateur acting in Welsh was catapulted into an alien professionalism in the sixties'.[67] The main impulse for this reaction was the advent of BBC Wales. The second half of the twentieth century was both an exciting and an alarming time when changes were sweeping over the cultural landscape of Wales. Theatre had been overtaken in a sense by the advent of radio and television and the repercussions of this were many and varied. It might well be argued that radio had a positive effect on Welsh-medium drama in that it stimulated a surge of writing that provided a platform for the work of many up-and-coming playwrights, such as W. S. Jones and Saunders Lewis who broadcast several of his stage plays on the radio, most notably *Buchedd Garmon*.[68] The advent of television in the 1960s was not as kind in terms of its influence on Welsh drama on or off screen. It was an expensive medium to televise and the seven hours of Welsh-language broadcasting at which the BBC Wales service aimed did not allow much scope for drama. Under these adverse conditions, the achievement of the BBC's drama department was considerable but, despite this contribution, Clos Stephens felt that television was destroying the traditional hinterland of community drama in Wales and not giving rise to any new talent.

The relations between the broadcasting media in Wales and the Welsh national theatre were characterized by paradox: on the one hand, they were interdependent, on the other antagonistic. Roberts notes that by 1961 it was becoming increasingly obvious that the 'television machine could not function effectively without the sustained concentrated effort which belongs to professionalism'.⁶⁹ The long debated shift from amateurism to professionalism in Welsh theatre had finally been necessitated by the coming of television – a medium that, according to Closs Stephens, like Cleopatra 'makes hungry, where most it satisfies'.⁷⁰ Initially, the demands created by the BBC stimulated the activity of Cwmni Theatr Cymru. Up to 1965, the Welsh-language theatre had been a pretty haphazard amateur activity; this presented difficulties to the establishment and health of a national theatre because actors and actresses were unable to sustain themselves in economic terms without other employment. It was to be Wilbert Lloyd Roberts who would overcome those difficulties, seize the moment and establish a working company of Welsh-medium theatre professionals to serve the nation on a regular and reputable basis. Roberts notes that the change from a 'native and natural amateur activity to a self-conscious professionalism'⁷¹ was in fact a horizontal rather than a vertical move because many of those enthusiasts working in the theatre were highly accomplished and experienced actors. He was able to bring these actors together to form an ensemble that possessed a 'new inner awareness of the disciplines accompanying high standards' and could satisfy the 'expectations of a more discerning public'.⁷²

From 1968 onwards, Cwmni Theatr Cymru operated as a full-time provider of Welsh-medium theatre. By 1970, the Welsh Arts Council's annual report recognized its status on a par with the English-medium Welsh Theatre Company and reported that although there was still no permanent repertory theatre in Wales, the two units of the Welsh Theatre Company had given a total of 244 performances in a period of forty-two playing weeks. By 1974, its annual report noted that Cwmni Theatr Cymru had become a 'fully independent organisation with its own board of management'.⁷³ The Welsh Theatre Company, by contrast, had been subsumed into the Welsh National Opera in order to form what Richard Fawkes described as 'the largest body of its type in the British Isles' but what actually proved to be one of the least effective bodies of its type in Britain.

The establishment of Cwmni Theatr Cymru and its subsequent success marked a new era in which the tables were turned in terms of the relations between the nation and the Welsh Arts Council. Wilbert Lloyd Roberts was keen to recognize and pay tribute to the fact that 'the central and major force in the development of the Welsh theatre from its tiny limping beginning to its present large scale professional operation was the support of the Welsh Arts Council'.[74] He was also particularly adept at securing the company's ideological independence whilst maintaining a firm grasp on the funding opportunities it provided. The Welsh Committee was firmly convinced that if Wales was to 'catch up artistically on other European countries',[75] she would need to secure a fully engaged opera company, a high quality national theatre, a full sized national symphony orchestra and a major arts exhibition centre. It took a three-pronged approach to this dilemma: first, it sought to raise the standard of the country's artistic products and productivity; secondly, it determined to provide and stimulate the provision of adequate and worthy accommodation to house this product; thirdly, it sought to stimulate and cultivate a culture of economic involvement based on an ethos of cooperation between other funding sources and the Arts Council itself. For the first five years of its existence, Cwmni Theatr Cymru not only collaborated with the council in the pursuit of these general objectives but attained them on its behalf.

The journey, however, was not a smooth one and the first disruptive incident came in the form of a dispute between the dormant St David's Trust and Cwmni Theatr Cymru. In 1967, the latter decided to register itself as a formal company and was promptly sued by the St David's Trust over its adoption of the term 'national'. The fire that disrupted the company's production of Lewis's *Cymru Fydd* in August 1967[76] burned with little fury in comparison to the row sparked off by the company's registration of its national title with the registrar of companies in October of the same year. It was clearly felt by both parties that it was national or nothing. Cwmni Theatr Cymru had the Arts Council's full support in this matter. On 3 March 1967, the Council resolved as follows:

> The Welsh Arts Council having considered the question of theatre in Wales in general and the future of the Welsh Theatre Company in particular, resolved, in accordance with earlier declarations of policy, that the work of the Welsh Arts Council, in directly providing drama, be taken over by an autonomous body, to be known as the Welsh Theatre Company. The Welsh Arts Council is prepared to recognize the existing Advisory Panel of the Welsh Theatre Company as an appropriate body to receive Arts Council grants of money.[77]

Cwmni Theatr Cymru responded with alacrity to this new challenge and within months had set up an advisory panel and then management committee. The fact that Lord Aberdare declined an invitation to become one of eight possible vice-presidents might have been an early indication of the Trust's furious defence of their claims to the title 'national'. When 'bearing in mind the Company was the only one in its field, that there would be need of building audiences... and that the Company had the full support of the Welsh Arts Council, it was resolved to register the Company as the 'Welsh Theatre Company Limited'[78] the storm broke. The press, namely the *Western Mail,* played some part in stirring up trouble by omitting an important clause from its report of the incident, but with the mediation of the Lord Mayor of Cardiff's representative[79] the Trust's Continuation Committee eventually pledged their support to the Cwmni Theatr Cymru cause. It seemed that a compromise between national life at an organic grass-roots level and national life as part of an overarching sphere of British officialdom had been reached – Cwmni Theatr Cymru, which had been stimulated by an Arts Council initiative, had developed in its own right, survived the all-important popularity test and had now assumed its place as a representative of an official national consensus in theatrical matters. This is not to forget that provision for English-medium theatre at a national level had been left in the lurch by the closure of the Welsh Theatre Company's English-medium company and that Cwmni Theatr Cymru had not stepped in to fill this void but only to claim that the company's achievements deserved the epithet 'national' as a hallmark of quality within the sphere of Welsh-medium theatre in Wales.

In the years to come Cwmni Theatr Cymru went from strength to strength and responded directly to the main aims and objectives of national progress as identified by the Welsh Arts Council reports of the period – the development of a worthy national theatrical product, suitable accommodation and an ethos of co-operation at a national level. In the mission to raise standards identified by the Welsh Arts Council there were three main difficulties – a scarcity of players, plays and places. Cwmni Theatr Cymru tackled each of these issues with impressive success. We have already noted that the BBC instigated a demand for professional performance in Wales but by 1973 the Welsh Arts Council report felt that in terms of the 'perennial dilemma ... whether raising standards in the arts in Wales is to be achieved by spreading the arts, widely, or by concentrating on the narrow front of high quality, professional arts',[80] the role of the BBC had shifted from one of raising to one of spreading.

This spreading was in fact threatening the healthy development of the Welsh national theatre by making it impossible to sustain 'a balanced strength of actors ... committed to live theatre'.[81] Roberts's polite refusals of requests for employment from part-time non-equity actors and actresses in the company's early years make it clear that he was intent on building up a steady repertoire of full-time dedicated theatre professionals. His comments that 'all the requirements of casting could not be met from the small pool of professional players, who were often otherwise engaged, or were not prepared to exchange their television availability for the doubtful benefits of an arduous tour'[82] outline the difficulties encountered in such an endeavour. Roberts was both diligent and successful in his efforts to attract actors such as Cefin Roberts,[83] then a student at the Cardiff College of Music and Drama, and one of those that the director was adamant would not be 'snatched up here and there, thereby bringing about the loss of an element particularly valuable to Welsh theatre'[84] [my translation]. Cwmni Theatr Cymru was not alone in its attempts to bridge the gap between the past and future of Welsh theatre. As Roberts himself noted, the 'outward concomitant teething troubles'[85] of the transition from an amateur to a professional status was now a matter of public interest and his correspondence[86] with the Welsh Arts Council director, Bill Dufton, during this period testifies to his willingness to shoulder part of the burden.

In a conference held by the North Wales Arts Association in the Normal College, Bangor on 7 May 1971, it was noted that any country with a professional national theatre needed training opportunities in its native language. It was resolved that a proposal made by Lloyd Roberts at the behest of the society's drama panel towards the establishment of such a course at Bangor should be considered at the society's next meeting. It is interesting to note that Lloyd Roberts had intended a short course on the Welsh system of the *cynganeddion*[87] as part of this training. Evidently, the Eisteddfod had not lost its hold on the national imagination and Closs Stephens's conviction that 'what has kept Welsh-language theatre aware of its critical standards has been the National Eisteddfod'[88] suggests that, despite its many drawbacks, this might have been at heart, and possibly remains, a healthy situation. Bill Dufton was equally convinced that in the 'long-term development of a national tradition of theatre in Wales there can be no substitute for a Welsh college providing training for Welsh actors'.[89] This training opportunity was ultimately realized by the provision of a course at the Cardiff College of Music and Drama in 1974. The one-year course was run by Owen Garmon and D. J. Thomas, the former head of television in BBC Wales, and in a letter to Bill Dufton, dated 9 October 1975, Lloyd Roberts admitted his suspicions that it was not designed to cater for theatre but for television. D. J. Thomas, he claimed, had suggested that were the course to throw up 'one or two new faces for television' it would have served its purpose. As a result, he added, 'you will therefore understand that I have some misgivings about the value of the course to the theatres'.[90]

In the event, the course foundered due to a lack of interest on the part of prospective students. Dufton continued his efforts to facilitate a dialogue between the various interested parties, Cwmni Theatr Cymru, the Welsh Joint Education Committee, up-and-coming theatre groups such Theatr y Werin and Theatr yr Ymylon and the College of Music and Drama, but it gradually became clear that Cwmni Theatr Cymru was itself providing a fertile training ground for professional actors. When it invited applications to the company from Welsh-medium performers, through the medium of the Welsh Equity publication *Deialog* in March 1974, it could be relatively confident of an adequate response. The company was well aware of the fact that 'the response to this appeal will be extremely important to the future of professional Welsh Theatre'[91] and by 1972 it had set up Theatr yr Ifanc[92] with Arts Council aid. Theatr yr Ifanc's significance as a training ground that provided opportunities for experiment and development for the growing body of young actors emerging from amongst the ranks of Cwmni Theatr Cymru was vital. The extent of its success is clear from the impressive profile of steady increase in the number of performances staged from 1965–73, starting at two per annum from 1965–7 and rising to four per annum from 1967–71 (barring 1969) and then to six per annum in 1972 and eventually to eight per annum by 1973. Despite, or perhaps on account of, this success, Lloyd Roberts was still complaining to the Welsh Arts Council about an acute shortage of actors in 1974. The Arts Council response was to facilitate cooperation between the BBC, the great poacher of potential theatre players, and Cwmni Theatr Cymru. The company's dealings with the broadcasting corporation manifest a willingness to cooperate but are equally indicative of its own growing standing as a national institution of some repute and status. On 24 July 1971, there had been a meeting between company representatives and the BBC at the Llandaff centre, where it was established that cooperation was a matter of both 'principle and desire'[93] [my translation]. In a letter dated 18 January 1972, a cautious but amicable schedule of cooperation was instigated with 'no commitment from one side or the other'[94] [my translation]. In the event, this alliance did not always run smoothly, as is clear from correspondence between John Hefin and Lloyd Roberts concerning collaboration on a production of Gwenlyn Parry's play *Y Ffin* in 1973.[95] Cwmni Theatr Cymru was clearly under no duress in terms of its relations with the country's other national institutions, but was effectively staking its claim to national respect and renown.

Cwmni Theatr Cymru was by now in a position to commission new plays by established authors and to apply to the Arts Council for funding to nurture new writers. The criticism of Welsh playwriting identified by the compilation of evidence from Eisteddfod competitions prior to 1969, citing a 'never-ending and directionless chatter' and 'basic ideas, craftsmanship and linguistic skills'[96] as characteristic of entries to the drama competition, were long gone. It is true to say that Gwenlyn Parry complained, with some justification, that commission payments for theatre scripts were too low, but even he admitted that by 1971 'the period of charity'[97] [my translation] was over in the history of Welsh drama. In 1971 Arts Council grants of £6,150 were obtained for three Welsh writers connected to the national company, including Eigra Lewis Roberts and Emyr Humphreys. The following year, the company obtained a total of £1,650 for six commissions that would enable it to 'replenish its larder with new plays now that the ones we are holding have been used up'.[98] By 1974, they were in a position to offer a commission fee of £500 to Saunders Lewis for a new play.

The one remaining problem was, yet again, that of place. Cwmni Theatr Cymru remained homeless and although its success can be attributed in large part to its brilliant record of touring – from an opening rate of sixty-five visits between spring 1965 and autumn 1967 the company had attained steady rates in the region of 201 in a similar time period from spring 1968 to spring 1971[99] – the Welsh Arts Committee report of 1959 had associated accommodation with progress and professionalism. Both were necessary attributes of a national theatre company. The Arts Council's original decision to grant autonomy to Cwmni Theatr Cymru was motivated in part at least by its desire to see someone press ahead with the original project for a travelling theatre that had been designed by Sean Kenny.[100] According to a newspaper report of 1967,[101] this portable theatre could be erected by five men in eight hours. It boasted a stage 40 x 23 foot and could seat 350 audience members comfortably. Its shell was of double aluminium and it had dressing rooms and electric lighting. The comparative costs of the travelling theatre and the Cardiff theatre were £500,000 to £125,000. Despite noting the objections of those who described the portable theatre as a huge sardine tin to be dragged around Wales, the reporter was enthusiastically in favour of the project. On the other hand, by 1969 the same paper was reporting the imminent onset of building work at Cardiff of a new Welsh national theatre building that would house 750 people. Emyr Humphreys's pledge to serve on a pursuance committee might well have been taken as a practical means of expressing his conviction that the only viable avenue for the articulation of a Welsh national identity in modern times was a cultural one. In actual fact, the scheme never materialized, cooled, according to Closs Stephens, by the wind of economic change and the looming prospect of the English National Theatre's packaging of art in 'concrete anonymity'.[102]

What did happen was that Cwmni Theatr Cymru took on the 'tremendous undertaking'[103] of Theatr Gwynedd, the newly built theatre that resulted from a cooperative funding effort by the Welsh Arts Council and the University College of North Wales, Bangor, that was to be run by Cwmni Theatr Cymru. In 1959, the Welsh Arts Council had pledged itself to improve accommodation for the arts in Wales. The need was greatest in relation to the theatre and discussions had been underway concerning the Bangor development since April 1968. A note in the Theatr Gwynedd working committee minutes commenting that it was desirable for the planned building to be compatible with that of the new national theatre building proposed for Cardiff by the St David's Trust indicated the national dimensions afforded this development by those most intimately involved in bringing it to fruition. In its report for the year ending March 1971, the Arts Council regretted the fact that the lack of improved facilities for professional theatre was only slowly being overcome. It noted with appreciation that newly built theatres were beginning to take shape at the University Colleges Aberystwyth and Cardiff and at Coleg Harlech but progress, it felt, lacked pace. By the year ending March 1972, it launched a more forthright attack on the lack of match funding in response to the acceleration in Arts Council funding from £30,000 in 1953/54 to £840,000 some twenty years later. Upon opening the new Theatr y Werin at Aberystwyth in 1973, it was hoped that this 'mixed programme theatre with plans to accommodate an ever-increasing amount, range and improved standards of production'[104] would stimulate the building of a whole circuit of regional theatres. This development did take place and Lloyd Roberts's prediction that some £6,000,000 would have been spent on the renovation of village halls and the erection of purpose built theatres by the end of 1974 was not far from the truth. The Arts Council remained adamant that 'if the Welsh people wanted a living growing theatre ... they must demonstrate their willingness to pay money for value, both at the box office and through the various channels available to Local Government'.[105] When Cwmni Theatr Cymru took over the management of Theatr Gwynedd, the nation was finally provided with a chance to demonstrate its support for its national theatre, both as a touring and as a theatre-based company.

In 1974, the Arts Council noted that Cwmni Theatr Cymru had become a fully independent organization with its own board of management.[106] In the same year, it set up an apparatus for self-promotion and an apparatus of national support at a minimal cost that was as important as the independence that it had been granted by the Welsh Arts Council in securing its long-term success and status as the national theatre of Wales. This apparatus was a network of local committees brought together under the umbrella of Cymdeithas Theatr Cymru.[107] This was the brainchild of Lynn Owen-Rees, who sought to avoid paying a national organizer to act on behalf of the company by establishing a national circuit of committees with eight to ten members – a chairperson, a secretary, a financial secretary and most importantly, a programme of work.[108] They were set up to meet at monthly intervals and to undertake all aspects of advertising and promoting the visits of the national company to local venues. In return for their efforts, they would be awarded an annual Christmas dinner at the company's expense. The benefits to the company are clear and the Welsh public responded to this call with verve. They accepted the importance of their role in the workings of the company and the society and realised that 'their evangelising was essential to the Company's future'[109] [my translation]. In the society's draft constitution, it is noted that the aims of the society were:

- to foster and promote the Welsh language presentations of *Cwmni Theatr Cymru* and in particular to ensure the highest standards of performance and appreciation and a more widespread support therefor [sic].
- to commission new literary or dramatic works for presentation by Cwmni Theatr Cymru and to award bursaries to authors who in the opinion of the Association or Cwmni Theatr Cymru are competent to produce literary or dramatic works suitable for presentation by Cwmni Theatr Cymru and also to give prizes and awards for any work whether literary or dramatic or stage performance [sic] which in the opinion of the Association or Cwmni Theatr Cymru merits such prize or award as being an outstanding contribution to the Welsh Language Presentations of Cwmni Theatr Cymru or as having won a competition organised by the Association or Cwmni Theatr Cymru.[110]

This organization, designed to carry through the aims and aspirations of the company, was hugely successful and whilst it was clearly not theatrical activity per se, it did involve the public in a creative interchange with the company in which it came to feel both entitled and empowered by its contribution to a collaborative pursuit of national dimensions.

The success of this venture enabled Cwmni Theatr Cymru to wrest its independence from its original source of funding – the

Welsh Arts Council. By 1974, it had its own network of regional committees that secured the success of its many tours and it was about to take over management of its own theatre. It was this independence that allowed it to undertake a role that extended beyond the expectations placed upon it by its alliance with the Welsh Art Council – a role unique to its position as a legitimate and legitimized Welsh national theatre. This role was described most effectively by the company's director, Wilbert Lloyd Roberts. Theatre, he argued,

> is not buildings, nor finance, nor equipment – these are the necessary adjuncts, but not its core. It is in essence a concerted creative effort by writers, actors, directors, technicians to create a relevant dialogue between images and reality – between characters and people. It is the creation of an experience unique to those who are present in a particular place at a particular time. Cwmni Theatr Cymru is fortunate in being enriched by the added significance of its existence in a language which is struggling for survival ... The present perilous state of the Welsh language gives a new dimension and a new meaning even to the craft of acting. It can become a deep emotional and intellectual involvement and identification with a language and a culture which is in danger of extinction. Nowhere else in Europe today do actors have this sort of significance. It is an experience entirely unknown beyond Offa's Dyke.[111]

Whatever Wilbert Lloyd Roberts's shortcomings,[112] he gave the Welsh nation a Welsh-medium national theatre company of which they could be proud.

Ironically, Cwmni Theatr Cymru's success sowed seeds of future developments that would eventually strip the theatre of its central national status – one of these seeds was the formation of its Adran Antur.[113] This ensemble of young players – Sharon Davies, Dyfan Roberts, Grey Evans, Valmai Jones and Iestyn Garlick – was an experimental splinter group established in 1965 that sought to extend the national company's work into different directions and new areas. A newspaper report of 1965 introduced the company to the nation as 'a brand new branch of Cwmni Theatr Cymru ... who will present a special programme in local halls across Gwynedd and Clwyd'. In their opening production, it reported that 'the players will be on the hall floor with the audience and the audience, so close to them, that it will be a part of the performance'.[114] The work of Adran Antur was representative of a discernible move to 'establish smaller, specialist companies with strong links with a local theatre or a particular community or part of a community' manifest in the 1970s in Wales.[115] It was probably also an indication that the choice between the promotion of 'large-scale, expensive traditional arts, representative of masterpieces and ... contemporary protractions of traditional forms' or those 'socio-educational artistic enterprises which are small-scale, inexpensive ... favoured by younger generations'[116] was no longer a matter for Arts Council deliberation.

Ioan Williams and Roger Owen both agree that the 1970s saw the regeneration of Welsh drama by means of the artistic efforts of a third theatre, comprised of the work of community theatre companies (both subsidized and unsubsidized), and highly innovative, devised work that was often site-specific and had a strong emphasis on the physical. According to Williams, this work injected 'a new sense of the relevance of theatrical practice among the increasingly fragmented Welsh-speaking communities'.[117] Owen goes so far as to refer to the work of companies such as Bara Caws[118] as 'dispersed national theatre.'[119] The Bara Caws company actually included many of the young actors who had worked with Wilbert Lloyd Roberts on innovative shows such as *Byw yn y Wlad*[120] undertaken by the national company's Adran Antur which had become frustrated by the lack of central funding to pursue such community based projects. Its work had a political edge that had not been characteristic of the national company from which it had grown and Owen contextualizes this development in terms of the political turbulence of a period in the history of Welsh language and culture that witnessed the referendum on Welsh devolution that was lost so decisively in 1979. The work of companies like Bara Caws established the legitimacy of a network of loosely connected but essentially fragmented communities, representative of modern Wales and perhaps of the post-modern world in general. The company presented its work in Welsh, in the pubs, clubs and school halls of Welsh villages. It put on show after show, continually rethinking its theatrical mission in terms of the changes in its contemporary environment and its success inspired others. According to Gill Ogden, 1979 was the year in which Wales's first Welsh-medium theatre in education company, Cwmni Theatr y Werin, founded at Aberystwyth in 1979, was set up.[121] By 1988, Charmian Savill reported that there were eight

Welsh-medium or bilingual theatre in education companies at work in Wales, funded by a combination of grants from local authority, Welsh Office, regional arts associations and the Arts Council.[122] These companies all had specific and different remits and cannot be considered to have fulfilled a national function, either individually or collectively, but the proliferation of companies during this period clearly encouraged the Welsh Arts Council to rethink its past funding decisions. By the year ending March 1982, it had cut funding for Cwmni Theatr Cymru from £253,000 to £175,000. In the same year, Wilbert Lloyd Roberts resigned, without finding an opportunity to account to the Welsh Arts Council for the 'quality of the Company's artistic work and the cost effectiveness of its organisation'.[123] These were heavy blows to a struggling company and by 1984, despite the positive influence of director Emily Davies and her new group of actors, it finally closed its doors to the public.

The loss of Cwmni Theatr Cymru was not one the nation felt too severely. A public meeting at the Eisteddfod in 1986 manifested the general sense that it had been superseded in Darwinian fashion by the marginal theatre groups that thrived in Wales during the 1980s. Opposition to Thatcherism may well have accounted for some of the creative energy emanating from Wales during this exciting period but it is also equally possible that the Arts Council's funding policy, its receptivity and support for the emergence of new companies like Brith Gof[124] and Bara Caws in the early 1980s, was paying dividends. In terms of the national theatre question, Arts Council support for these companies may not have seemed particularly helpful, particularly in view of the fact that these marginal companies all challenged the theatrical status quo and weakened notions of a national theatrical consensus. Nonetheless, I think it could be argued that the broadmindedness characteristic of Arts Council funding in this period facilitated a process of natural selection that led to the indication of a national theatrical preference in late twentieth-century Wales.

Cwmni Theatr Cymru's demise coincided with the onset of a post-modernist period in which Brith Gof commanded centre-stage in the Welsh theatrical arena. Although the difference between the two companies was marked – Cwmni Theatr Cymru, a text-based, traditional theatrical institution, Brith Gof, a group of theatrical specialists concentrating on experimental, site-specific, physical work – a closer look at Brith Gof's aims and objectives reveals significant similarities between them. In fact, Brith Gof's desire to employ theatre as a means of activating an experience of 'total community ... a satisfying, dignified, personal/political arrangement'[125] might be understood as a postmodernist equivalent to the idea of a national theatre. Whilst Cwmni Theatr Cymru employed theatrical standardization as a means of expressing national values, Brith Gof applied uncommon theatrical methods to an analysis and exploration of the common values of Welsh life. During the period of their co-existence, there were points of contact between the two companies that provided concrete evidence of their collective interests. One such an occasion was their collaboration on an Eisteddfod production in 1983 when Brith Gof identified its vital interest in 'the central preoccupation of Welsh culture with its own survival'[126] – a concern that was shared by Cwmni Theatr Cymru. Similarly, Cliff McLucas's[127] declaration that 'any kind of cultural activity in Wales is inevitably political, as is the decision to speak Welsh',[128] brings to mind Wilbert Lloyd Roberts's declaration that Cwmni Theatr Cymru was fortunate in being enriched by the added significance of its existence in a language which is struggling for survival.[129] McLucas's list of those 'cultural and historical customs' clustered around a 'repressive notion of Welshness'[130] might well have included Cwmni Theatr Cymru, but his desire to provide an alternative for those young Welsh people who sought to articulate their sense of self by other, less oppressive, means suggests that Brith Gof provided an ultra-modern alternative to a traditional national theatre. Indeed David Adams argues that the company established theatre as a place 'where identities – personal, artistic, national – are actually created, contested and altered and not just reflected or represented'[131] – a truly national theatre.

The lack of confidence and interest in Cwmni Theatr Cymru manifest by the complacent response to its demise was due, according to Ioan Williams, to linguistic factors. He felt that the continuing crisis of the Welsh language, combined with a cultural shift towards the Americanized interests of young, urban, Welsh-speaking groups, necessitated the development of a new theatrical terminology. This theatrical language should appeal to a generation of Welsh speakers facing new challenges and opportunities that demanded a new vocabulary. In the event, this new vocabulary was provided by the innovative work of Brith Gof itself and its appeal was not restricted to the Welsh-speaking community alone. As part of its programme of work, the company undertook a re-analysis of some of the central tales of Welsh history and mythology, but its emphasis was not on the creation of normative meaning. An extract from one of the shows staged in a forest in west Wales reveals the adventurous role afforded to language in their work. The play, first presented at Esgair Fraith, an abandoned farm in a conifer plantation in Llanfair Clydogau, Lampeter, in October 1995 was called *Tri Bywyd*. It featured three different life stories presented episodically in three sections of thirteen two-minute parts including physical work, commentary and spoken source materials. The action was presented on a 16 metre scaffolding interspersed with floors, stairs, furniture and lighting and the audience was seated in an auditorium built of scaffolding running through the conifer plantation itself. Words presented by Tom, one of the play's main characters (the terms play and character are only partially valid in the context of Brith Gof's experimental work), were Welsh place names: 'Pentrebanne, Pant-y-fedwen, Sarn Llys, Pretoria, Glanrafon, Glanrhyd, Lluest ucha, Gwar-ffynon, Esger-man, Biwla, Pantresger, Blaenplwyf, Pengelli, Graig-ddu. Esger-ddu, Esger Llanfer, Llether Garw, Llether Brith, Mo'lfryn.'[132] These Welsh sound patterns provided the backbone of the show's linguistic narrative and threw out a challenge concerning the meaning of Welsh language and culture. Each place-name had individual meaning but when linked together literal meaning gave way to a celebration of sound. In this example, Welshness was identified and understood by means of an aural and physical sensibility and receptivity, independent of logical sense but characteristically nostalgic. It seems to me that, at this particular point in the company's history, Brith Gof momentarily secured the future of Welsh culture by a theatricalization of its very essence and the revelation of that essence as global. It may well be that Closs Stephens's prediction that 'the apotheosis of Welsh theatre is to find a theatre language that does not need Welsh'[133] signalled the end of an era in the history of the Welsh national theatre.

From the earliest days of the original call for a Welsh national theatre at the close of the nineteenth century through its various manifestations in the twentieth century, initially appearing in a climate of private patronage and later in one of public patronage, Wales battled with the complexity and contradictions of its rich and diverse national life but it retained one permanent aim – the establishment of a national theatre that would sustain a continuous state of play and never attain a state of rest. However great the sacrifices along the way, an analysis of its history from the closing decade of the nineteenth century to an equivalent period in the twentieth century demonstrates that it can be said to have been wholly and continuously successful in the achievement of this aim.

Conclusion

What is fascinating about twenty-first century Wales is its refusal to be content with the success of the twentieth-century national theatre and its determination to turn anew to an investigation and declaration of Welsh national identity by means of another national theatre – Theatr Genedlaethol Cymru. At this moment of contemporary history, the Welsh nation has devoted its energies anew to the creation of a second Welsh-medium national theatre and it seems that Gwyn Alf Williams's description of modern Wales as 'an artefact which the Welsh produce, if they want to'[1] could well be applied to the Welsh national theatre. How then do we account for the resurrection of Wales's national theatre, in the novel guise of Theatr Genedlaethol Cymru, in defiance of the coming of not only a new century, but a new millennium? David Adams's claim that the return of the great Welsh national theatre debate was 'really about more than theatre ... the state of Wales, about cultural identity, about nationalism and internationalism'[2] throws some light on this perplexing situation. Deborah Parson's examination of questions of European identity illuminates it further. In an essay on the nature of modern European identity, she describes the particular mode of self-awareness and expression promoted by the Single Europe Act of 1987 as 'an identity that is publicly performed, constituted by certain practices of social interaction within a regular territory that strengthens collective identity'.[3] She goes on to argue that this process is articulated in the euro-city itself and whilst this may well be true, her definition might be transferred with ease to a different territory – the arena of national theatre. Surely a national theatre is one of the places in which the public performance of identities by means of certain practices of social interaction that strengthen collective identity is most strikingly and explicitly undertaken. Might the latest stage in the effort to establish and maintain a Welsh national theatre be attributable to the existence of a link between the political and sociological awareness of oneself as a nation-member within a wider European context and participation in this particular kind of national cultural activity?

In *The Yearbook of European Studies,* John Sundholm refers to the modern European writer as one who is alienated from the literary forms available and forced to fashion new modes of expression modelled on his or her own immediate experience. Faced by this dilemma, Sundholm analyses the ways in which the interplay between a nation's cultural spaces and its poetics can mark out a space for identity formation, concluding that the recourse to abstraction in art is often a useful response to the challenges of modern life.[4] It strikes me that theatre is an artistic medium that accomplishes this kind of abstraction at a particularly fundamental level, by virtue of the way in which an audience both recognizes and resists the relationship between their own experience of the fabric and structures of real life and the artistic representation of that reality embodied in the fictional theatrical event. I would argue that the principle of detached engagement with which the audience responds to the presentation of the theatrical event is particularly valuable because it activates a sense of identity that is simultaneous with an awareness of otherness or difference. Furthermore, theatre validates this kind of original and individual expression by facilitating its articulation within the context of community. The physical presence of the audience at the theatrical event, both as individuals and as a common body, enables individual experience to maintain its specific integrity and to function as a means of systematizing and structuring human experience at large in the context of modernity and post-modernity.

In any theatre, cultural activity is the province of the players and their public and the relationship between the two is equal. It is one's own active investment in the debate presented via the theatrical spectacle that dictates the nature and value of the artistic experience discovered therein. However, in the case of national theatre, that debate necessarily has a common relevance to all by virtue of its designation as a national discourse. It is, I believe, the ability of national theatre to play out 'an identity that is publicly performed, constituted by certain practices of social interaction within a regular territory that strengthens collective identity'[5] that makes it a particularly appropriate representative medium for the experience of national identity within the context of a modern

Europe. This argument is based on the idea that theatre is itself an example of a social ritual and, as such, national theatre might function as a statement regarding the nature of relations within the nation, between nation members and both their leaders and their compatriots. This national declaration could then be exported on an international level in a way that maintains both the integrity and individuality of the nation yet offers the possibility of creative interaction with an 'other'. Theatre is by nature a democratic artistic activity in the sense that the relationship between the performers themselves and between the audience and the performance is based on a principle of interpersonal activity. In the case of national theatre, this democratic principle is intensified by the fact that the interpersonal activity instigated by the performance is understood as representative of the real interaction between nation members within the nation itself.

There is always the danger that a national theatre might be used to accomplish a stabilizing task in relation to its political, social and cultural environment. Sundholm touches on this issue when he claims that the rediscovery of a nation's real people is essential to the maintenance of a symbolic economy – the stage on which transactions are carried out according to cultural and moral values with the intent of concealing the driving forces of the material economy. If we transfer this scenario to the realms of national theatre, it becomes evident that the theatrical transaction itself could exploit the national symbolic economy by presenting itself in a national guise whilst it is only really significant in terms of the economic interests of a specific group or individual. It could be argued, however, that the theatrical genre might well escape exploitation of this kind because its formal principles are based on flexibility, experimentation and responsiveness.

Evidently, power relations can be manipulated to achieve different effects but the principle of interactivity itself sustains a basic level of equality and democracy. Ideally, national theatre would be a place in which a moment of action, precipitated towards the future and free from the past is proposed, constantly re-made, but never ultimately fixed. As Lessing would argue, the creativity of the dramatic poet goes beyond the representation of a real or perceived past. He is not a 'historian; he does not relate what was formerly believed to have happened, but makes it happen before our eyes ... he wishes to cause illusion and by illusion to move us'.[6] It is possible, I believe, for a national theatre to function not simply as one of the cultural conduits for the cultivation of modern European public discourse but as an alternative space for the continuation and elaboration of that discussion, truly 'an area without frontiers'.[7]

The idea that a national theatre could clear a space wherein 'private persons'[8] play out representative episodes of life in a manner that manifests what is, in fact, real about human experience in a modern Europe provides a rationale for the vigour of the debate regarding the idea of national theatre in twentieth-century Europe. Although none of the national theatres featured in this study ever actually achieved this ideal, and it may well be that it is, in fact, an impossible task, Wales refuses to end its pursuit of a moment of action, precipitated towards an unknown future and free from a prescribed past – a moment that is constantly in motion, remaking itself and those with whom it comes into contact. Wales's struggle to reassert its national identity by means of a contemporary national theatre – a factor that has characterized the nation's arrival and survival in a new millennium – can be understood as confirmation of Gwyn Alf Williams's claim that whilst a sense of history has been central in 'that Welsh making and remaking of themselves... Wales has always been now'.[9] So too, I would argue, has its pursuit of the idea and the ideal of a Welsh national theatre – a struggle that is all the more rewarding because it never actually achieves completion. As Lord Crowther, the first chairman of the Royal Commission on the Constitution commented, after taking evidence in Wales and Scotland in 1970, 'the difference I see is that the Scots want to do things, the Welsh want to be'.[10] The experience of being in a post-modern Welsh context is inevitably bound up with the task of continuous national creativity – manifest most spectacularly in the nation's relentless wrestling with the idea of a national Welsh theatre. At the close of the twentieth century, Gwyn Alf Williams was somewhat sceptical with regard to the Welsh nation's desire to engage with the 'making and remaking of themselves'.[11] However, I would argue that now, on the threshold of a new millennium, Wales's continuous engagement with the idea and the reality of a Welsh national theatre justifies a more hopeful perspective on its commitment to a continuous process of national invention and re-invention.

Notes

Foreword

1. See *http://www.guardian.co.uk*. Accessed 17 November 2005.
2. Theatr Genedlaethol Cymru is the name for the most recent incarnation of Wales's national theatre.
3. See *http://www.guardian.co.uk*. Accessed 17 November 2005.
4. *Yn Debyg Iawn i Ti a Fi* translates as 'very much like you and me'.
5. The main body of Meic Povey's work is Welsh medium, however, he has published English-medium plays including *Indian Country* and the recent *Life of Ryan and Ronnie*. Both these plays were commissioned by the national body for the promotion of scriptwriting in Wales, *SgriptCymru*.
6. 'Colofn Gareth Miles – Theatr Genedlaethol Cymru', Archif Barn Cyfrol 482, Mawrth 2003, *http://www.theatre-wales.co.uk*. Accessed 20 August 2005:

    - arddull theatr gyffrous a chyfoes wedi ei sylfaenu ar draddodiad theatrig Cymru ac ar ei diwylliant.
    - rhaglenni gwaith yn cynnwys amrywiaeth o genres.
    - darpariaeth o gyfleoedd ar gyfer hyfforddiant a datblygiad gyrfaol.
    - sefydlu enw da i'r cwmni ac i ddrama wedi'i chynhyrchu yng Nghymru ar y llwyfan drama ryngwladol.
    - gwaith newydd yn yr iaith Gymraeg.
    - sicrhau fod y cynyrchiadau yn hygyrch i'r gynulleidfa ehanga bosib.

7. Quoted in Ioan Williams, 'Towards national identities: Welsh theatres', in B. Kershaw (ed.), *The Cambridge History of British Theatre*, vol. 3, (Cambridge, 2004), p. 242.
8. At the time of writing, this was the most recent full-scale production. The company performed a touring production of *Tŷ ar y Tywod* by Gwenlyn Parry in April–May 2005. *Tŷ ar y Tywod* translates as 'house on the sand'.
9. Geraint Talfan Davies and John Osmond, 'Culture and identity', in *The Birth of Welsh Democracy: The First Term of the National Assembly for Wales* (Cardiff, 2003), p. 243.

10   Vicky Featherstone, formerly artistic director of the *Paines Plough Company,* took up her post as the Scottish National Theatre's first director on 1 November 2004. She described her appointment as 'an incredible moment ... for theatre, and for Scotland' and vowed to provide the nation with 'very exciting, epic, state-of-the-nation productions that will make us proud to be alive, let alone Scottish'. See 'Dark horse lands top theatre job', *http://www.news.scotsman.com.* Accessed 15 October 2005.
11   Cwmni Theatr Cymru was the name of Wales's most successful national theatre to date. Chapter 6 of this book gives its history.
12   See *http://www.guardian.co.uk.* Accessed 21 November 2005.

Introduction

1   T. C. W. Blanning, *The Culture of Power and the Power of Culture: Old Regime Europe 1660–1789* (Oxford, 2002).
2   Jürgen Habermas, *The Structural Transformation of the Public Sphere: an Inquiry into a Category of Bourgeois Society,* trans. by Thomas Burger (Cambridge, 1989), p. 27.
3   Blanning, *The Culture of Power and the Power of Culture,* p. 9.
4   Habermas himself argues that the new public sphere that emerged in the closing centuries of the second millennium has by now been infiltrated by the laws of the market governing commodity exchange and social labour. As a result, what he refers to as 'the web of public communication' has fallen apart at the seams and disintegrated into a series of individuated acts of reception. There is no longer a genuinely public sphere, simply an apparently public sphere in which the individual achieves satisfaction of his own needs in the presence of others, but not in conjunction and debate with others.
5   Erika Fischer-Lichte, *History of European Drama and Theatre,* trans. by Jo Riley (London, 2002), p. 2.
6   Ibid.
7   Patrick J. Geary, *The Myth of Nations: the Medieval Origins of Europe* (Princeton, 2002), p. 11.
8   Fischer-Lichte, *History of European Drama and Theatre,* p. 2.
9   Robert Rheinhold Ergang, *Herder and the Foundations of German Nationalism* (London, 1931), p. 86.
10   Ernest Renan, 'What is a nation?', in Stuart Woolf (ed.), *Nationalism in Europe: 1815 to the Present* (London, 1996), p. 57.
11   Ibid., p. 58.
12   See E. J. Hobsbawm, *Nations and Nationalism since 1780: Programme, Myth, Reality* (Cambridge, 1990), p. 104.

13 *The Cambridge Companion to Hegel*, ed. Frederick C. Beiser (Cambridge, 1993), p. 366.
14 Otto Bauer, 'The nation', in Stuart Woolf (ed.), *Nationalism in Europe*, p. 62.
15 See Julie Stone Peters, 'Intercultural performance: theatre anthropology, and the imperialist critique', in J. Ellen Gainor (ed.), *Imperialism and Theatre: Essays on World Theatre, Drama and Performance* (London, 1995), pp. 199–211.
16 Miroslav Hroch, *Social Preconditions of National Revival in Europe: a Comparative Analysis of the Social Composition of Patriotic Groups among the Smaller European Nations*, trans. by Ben Fowkes (Columbia, 2000), p. 3.
17 Renan, 'What is a nation?' in Stuart Woolf (ed.), *Nationalism in Europe*, p. 50.
18 M. Christine Boyer, 'The great frame-up: fantastic appearances in contemporary spatial politics', in Helen Liggett and David C. Perry (eds), *Spatial Practices: Critical Explorations in Social/Spatial Theory* (London, 1995), p. 99.
19 Ibid., p. 100.
20 Anthony D. Smith, 'Modernity and emotions: dating the nation', in Daniele Conversi (ed.), *Ethnonationalism in the Contemporary World: Walker Connor and the Study of Nationalism* (London, 2002), p. 56.
21 Geary, *The Myth of Nations*, p. 156.
22 Ibid., p. 40.
23 Ergang, *Herder and the Foundations of German Nationalism*, p. 90.
24 James Sime, *Lessing*, vol. 2, (London, 1877), p. 34.
25 Gertjan Dijkink, *National Identity and Geopolitical Vision: Maps of Pride and Pain* (London, 1996), p. 11.
26 Ibid., p. 11.
27 Stephen K. White, *The Recent Work of Jürgen Habermas: Reason, Justice and Modernity* (Cambridge, 1989), p. 124.
28 See Robert J. Kaiser, 'Homeland making and the territorialization of national identity', in Daniele Conversi (ed.), *Ethnonationalism in the Contemporary* World, pp. 229–45.
29 Quoted in Kaiser, 'Homeland making and the territorialization of national identity', in Conversi (ed.), *Ethnonationalism in the Contemporary World*, p. 229.
30 Hans-Ulrich Thamer, 'The orchestration of the national community: the Nuremberg rallies of the NSDAP', in Günter Berghaus (ed.), *Fascism and Theatre: Comparative Studies on the Aesthetics and Politics of Performance* (Oxford, 1996), pp. 172–3.
31 George L. Mosse, *The Nationalisation of the Masses: Political*

       Symbolism and Mass Movement in Germany from the Napoleonic Wars through the Third Reich (New York, 1975), p. 4.
32 Thamer, 'The orchestration of the national community: the Nuremberg rallies of the NSDAP', in Berghaus (ed.), *Fascism and Theatre*, p. 173.
33 Renan, 'What is a nation?', in Woolf (ed.), *Nationalism in Europe*, p. 51.
34 Quoted in E. J. Hobsbawm, *Nations and Nationalism since 1780*, p. 101.
35 Alexis de Tocqueville, *Égalité Sociale et Liberté Politique*, ed. Pierre Gibert (Paris, 1977), p. 226. 'Toute passion commune, tout besoin mutuel, toute necessité de s'entendre, toute occasion d'agir ensemble.'
36 See Geary, *The Myth of Nations*, p. 21.
37 Quoted in Hobsbawm, *Nations and Nationalism since 1780*, p. 9.
38 Dijkink, *National Identity and Geopolitical Vision*, p. 11.
39 Strictly speaking, the Globe opened its doors to the public in 1599 but this hardly affects Habermas's point.
40 Habermas, *The Structural Transformation of the Public Sphere*, p. 31.
41 Ibid., p. 39.
42 Peters, 'Intercultural performance', in Gainor (ed.), *Imperialism and Theatre*, p. 200.
43 Ibid.
44 Michael Hays, 'Representing empire: class, culture and the popular theatre in the nineteenth century', in J. Ellen Gainor (ed.), *Imperialism and Theatre: Essays on World Theatre, Drama and Performance* (London, 1995), p. 133.
45 Hroch, *Social Preconditions of National Revival in Europe*, pp. 4–5.
46 Bauer, 'The nation', in Woolf (ed.), *Nationalism in Europe*, p. 76.

Chapter 1: The French national theatre: courting the crowd

1 Jürgen Habermas, *The Structural Transformation of the Public Sphere: an Inquiry into a Category of Bourgeois Society*, trans. by Thomas Burger (Cambridge, 2003), p. 10.
2 Jean-Marie Apostolidès, *Le prince sacrifié: théâtre et politique au temps de Louis XIV* (Paris, 1985), p. 27, 's'approprier l'ensemble des representations du dix-septième siecle, afin qu'elles participent à la mise en scène de l'image du roi'.
3 Pierre Goubert, *The Ancien Régime: French Society 1600–1750*, trans. by Steve Cox (London, 1973), p. 3.
4 Quoted in Pierre Goubert, *The Ancien Régime*, p. 22.

Notes   221

5   This scheme included the establishment of royal academies of dance, music and architecture between 1661 and 1671.
6   David H. Jory, 'The role of Greek tragedy in the search for legitimate authority under the ancien régime', in Magdy Gabriel Badir and David J. Langdon (eds), *Eighteenth-Century French Theatre: Aspects and Contexts* (Alberta, 1988), p. 6.
7   Jan Clarke, *The Guénégaud Theatre in Paris (1673–1680)*, (Lampeter, 1998), vol. 1, p. 2. Clarke is referring to talk of a merger between the members of the Hôtel Guénégaud and the other two Parisian troupes: the Hôtel de Bourgogne and the Théâtre du Marais.
8   Pierre Mélèse, *Le théâtre et le public à Paris sous Louis XIV, 1659–1715* (Paris, 1934), p. 17, 's'adressant à tous et parlant de tout, cette publication devait réussir, et elle réussit'.
9   Ibid., p. 16, 'sans toucher à fond à l'une ni à l'autre, et se préoccupait d'amuser plutôt que d'instruire'.
10 Elizabeth C. Goldsmith, *'Exclusive Conversations'*: *the Art of Interaction in Seventeenth-Century France* (Philadelphia, 1988), p. 148.
11 Apostolidès, *Le prince sacrifié*, p. 48,'le roi prête son corps à la nation qui n'a pas d'existence en dehors de lui, l'acteur donne corps à des images que le prince ne peut plus, ne doit plus être'.
12 Ibid., p. 28.
13 Clarke, *The Guénégaud Theatre in Paris (1673–1680)*, p. 6.
14 Ibid., p. 7.
15 Pierre Mélèse, *Le théâtre et le public à Paris sous Louis XIV, 1659–1715*, p. 167, 'non seulement les comédiens étaient excommuniés, mais l'Eglise englobait dans cette réprobation tous ceux qui touchaient de près ou de loin à leur profession ... Cette sévérité ne désarmait pas devant la mort'.
16 See Hannah Arendt, *On Revolution* (New York, 1963), p. 23.
17 Ibid., p. 24.
18 See Henry Carrington Lancaster, *Sunset: a History of Parisian Drama in the Last Years of Louis XIV, 1701–1715* (London, 1945), p. 5.
19 Mélèse, *Le théâtre et le public à Paris sous Louis XIV, 1659–1715*, p. 4, 'attaquer le théâtre n'est plus s'opposer au goût du roi'.
20 Bert Edward Young and Grace Philputt Young, *Le Registre de la Grange: 1659–1685* (Paris, 1947), vol. 2, p. 43, 'salut du théâtre national'.
21 Apostolidès, *Le prince sacrifié*, p. 32, 'place du roi'.
22 Ibid., p. 33, 'le créateur de la nation, le père du peuple, image de Dieu et soleil dont le rayonnement infini délimite les formes de la société'.
23 See Henry Carrington Lancaster, *Le Mémoire de Mahelot, Laurent*

et d'autres décorateurs de l'hôtel de Bourgogne et de la Comédie-Française au XVIIe siècle (Paris 1920).

24. Fortunat Strowski, 'Le Théâtre de la Foire', in Jean Robiquet (ed.), Le Théâtre à Paris au XVIIIe siècle: Conférences du Musée Carnavalet (Paris, 1930), p. 69, 'il se contente de camper où il peut, aussi longtemps qu'il peut'.
25. Ibid., p. 70. Coudoyés, pressés, pressants, toutes classes mêlées, voilà les gens qui essayent d'avancer, qui piétinent, qui s'arrêtent, et, sécoués par le rire universel provoqué par un 'aboyeur', ou un pitre, ne sentent pas la fatigue de leurs jambes, ou l'âcreté de la poussière. Une baraque s'offre-t-elle où l'on pourra enfin s'asseoir? On y entre; on s'impatiente; on veut du mouvement, des choses excitantes et reposantes, et que tout aille vite, très vite.
26. Ibid., p. 71, 'la petite jeune fille, gracieuse et parée de roses qui dansait sur la corde raide, le héros qui s'y asseyait entre ciel et terre pour installer le fourneau, allumer le feu et battre l'omelette'.
27. See ibid., p. 72.
28. See ibid., p. 76.
29. Ibid., p. 76. Fortunat Strowski labels this kind of duo-monologue, 'the telephone scene', due to the fact that the invention of the telephone normalized the idea of a virtual or one-sided dialogue.
30. See Claude Alasseur, La Comédie-Française au 18e siècle: étude economique (Paris, 1967), p. 11.
31. Quoted in John Lough, Paris Theatre Audiences in the Seventeenth and Eighteenth Centuries (London, 1957), p. 234.
32. See Noelle Guibert and Jacqueline Razgonnikoff, 'En marge d'une chronique de la Comédie-Française pendant la Révolution', Revue de la société d'histoire du théâtre, 161 (1989), p. 8.
33. Alasseur, La Comédie-Française au 18e siècle, p. 15, 'tout évoque la bourgeoisie'.
34. See Young and Young, Le Registre de la Grange, p. 46.
35. See Alasseur, La Comédie-Française au 18e siècle, pp. 11–12.
36. See Stoyan Tzonev, Le Financier dans la Comédie Française sous l'Ancien Régime (Paris, 1977), p. 138.
37. Ibid., 'la classe la plus prospère ... à la faveur de l'expansion de l'industrie et du commerce extérieur au cours de soixante-dix-sept années sans invasion, sans rapine, sans guerre civile'.
38. Alasseur, La Comédie-Française au 18e siècle, p. 15, 'se prend à penser que c'est elle qui, en fait, anime le pays ; qu'elle seule travaille ... et que cela devrait lui donner le droit de participer à la vie politique'.
39. Frederick W. J. Hemmings, Culture and Society in France: 1789–1848 (Leicester, 1987), p. 17.
40. Ibid., p. 21.

[41] Ibid., p. 22.
[42] Ibid., p. 20.
[43] Ibid., p. 30.
[44] See Jacques Boncompain, 'Théâtre et Formation des Consciences: l'Exemple de Charles IX', Revue de la société d'histoire du théâtre 161, (1989), p. 44.
[45] Quoted in Boncompain, 'Théâtre et Formation des Consciences: l'Exemple de Charles IX', p. 46, «Si Figaro a tué la noblesse, Charles IX tuera la royauté.»
[46] Hemmings, Culture and Society in France: 1789–1848 (Leicester, 1987), p. 40.
[47] See Young and Young, Le Registre de la Grange, p. 83.
[48] In this context, the King's gift of many items of attire to the Comédie-Française's wardrobe can be seen as an attempt to sustain the representative style of dressing that told of the theatre's allegiance to its monarchical sponsors.
[49] Christopher Smith, 'French romanticism and the actresses', in Elisabeth Woodrough (ed.), Women in European Theatre (Oxford, 1995), p. 50.
[50] Boncompain, 'Théâtre et Formation des Consciences: l'Exemple de Charles X', p. 44.
[51] Noelle Guibert and Jacqueline Razgonnikoff, 'En marge d'un chronique de la Comédie-Française pendant la Révolution', p. 17, 'ils se sentent abandonnés par la Cour et refusent de se soumettre à la Municipalité-, la moindre blessure d'amour propre prend des allures d'affaire d'état.'
[52] Ibid., p. 16. 'des menaces aux voies de fait, des coups au duel, du duel par les armes à la guerre des gazettes.'
[53] Ibid., p. 8. 'Emanation du pouvoir monarchique, créée par Louis XIV au plus fort de la centralisation, pour son bon plaisir et le divertissement de la société hiérarchisée, qu'il avait su constituer autour de lui.'
[54] Sylvie Chevalley, 'La Civilisation des Comédiens', Revue de la société d'histoire du théâtre, 161, (1989), p. 54. 'Ceux qui ne sont pas exclus sont appelés.'
[55] Guibert and Razgonnikoff, 'En marge d'un chronique de la Comédie-Française pendant la Révolution', p. 11, 'en spectateurs au serment du jeu de paume, à la prise de la Bastille, à la nuit de 4 Août, emportés par la rapidité des événements et sans y participer directement.'
[56] Adam Burgess, Culturally Dividing Europe (London, 1997), p. 83.
[57] Hannah Arendt, On Revolution (New York, 1963), p. 251.
[58] Quoted in Chevalley, 'La Civilisation des Comédiens', p. 54, 'écoles publiques de principes, de bonnes mœurs et de patriotisme.'

59 Hemmings, *Culture and Society in France*, p. 55.
60 Cécile Fridé, 'L'Organisation Spatiale de Trois Fêtes Nationales Révolutionnaires', *Revue de la société d'histoire du théâtre*, 161 (1989), p. 108, 'proclamer l'ordre nouveau et à le consacrer par des actes publics et communautaires'.
61 Arendt, *On Revolution*, p. 13.
62 Ibid., p. 21.
63 Ibid.
64 See Peter Szondi, *Theory of the Modern Drama: a Critical Edition*, trans. by Michael Hays (Cambridge, 1987).
65 Fridé, 'L'Organisation Spatiale de Trois Fêtes Nationales Révolutionnaires', p. 108. 'faire «table rase» de l'ordre ancien'.
66 Hemmings, *Culture and Society in France*, p. 53.
67 Ibid., p. 108, 'le moment va chercher à s'incarner et à investir l'espace'.
68 Ibid., p. 121. 'Comme Louis XVI, Robespierre apparaît au balcon... Comme Louis XVI, Robespierre est en retard... Comme Louis XVI, Robespierre fait son apparition après que le people soit réuni'.
69 Alex Cain and Philip N. Furbank, *A Translation of the Fashion Magazine 'La Dernière Mode', with Commentary* (Oxford, 2004), p. 211.
70 Ibid., p. 215.
71 Ibid.
72 Ibid., p. 177.
73 Phillipe Van Tieghem, *Les Grands Comédiens : 1400–1900* (Paris, 1960), p. 60, 'talents aussi glorieux que ceux qui illustrent la Comédie-Française'.
74 See M Joseph-Isidore Samson, *Mémoires de Samson: de la Comédie-Française* (Paris, 1882), p. 85, 'vieux et cher théâtre qui était pour les anciens une seconde patrie'.
75 Van Tieghem, *Les Grands Comédiens*, p. 71, 'avec un abandon, une passion frémissante'.
76 Ibid., p. 69. 'la simplicité de ses moyens, son absence totale d'emphase et de solennité artificielle'.
77 Samson, *Mémoires de Samson*, p. 79. 'dépourvu de tout moyen d'illusion... une chaise entre les jambes... il était aussi tragique que sur la scène et nous faisait frissonner en nous disons des vers d'*Andromaque* ou de *Phèdre*.'
78 See Helen Krich Chinoy and Toby Cole (eds), *Actors on Acting* (New York, 1970), p. 203.
79 Sarah Bernhardt, *The Art of the Theatre*, trans. by H. J. Stenning (New York, 1969), p. 45.
80 Van Tieghem, *Les Grands Comédiens*, p. 86, 'c'est la femme qui joue... Elle étreint, elle enlace, elle se pâme, elle se tord, elle se meurt.'

81 Susan Bassnett-McGuire, Michael R. Booth and John Stokes, *Bernhardt, Terry, Duse: the Actress in her Time* (Cambridge, 1988), p. 9
82 *Encyclopédie du Théâtre Contemporain: 1850–1914*, ed. by Gilles Quéant (Paris, 1957), vol. 1, p. 112.
83 See Henri Gouhier, *L'Essence du Théâtre* (Sorbonne, 2002), p. 94.
84 H. K. Chinoy and T. Cole (eds), *Actors on Acting* (New York, 1970), p. 203.
85 David A. Bell, *The Cult of the Nation in France: Inventing Nationalism, 1680–1800* (London, 2001), p. 200.
86 See Zeen Sternhell, 'The political culture of nationalism', in R. Toombs (ed.), *Nationhood and Nationalism in France* (London, 1991), pp. 22–37.
87 See Valérie Battaglia, 'Romain Rolland et le Théâtre de la Révolution', *Revue de la société d'histoire du théâtre*, 161 (1989), p. 172.
88 Ibid., p. 194.
89 David Bradby and Annie Sparks, *Mise en Scène: French Theatre Now* (London, 1997), p. 12.
90 Ibid., pp. 152–4.

Chapter 2: The stage of the German nation: twin developments

1 Quoted in W. H. Bruford, *Theatre, Drama and Audience in Goethe's Germany* (London, 1950), p. 107, 'theatralisches Heiligtüm'.
2 *Yeats's Poems*, ed. by A. Norman Jeffares (London, 1991), pp. 471–2.
3 See Bruford, *Theatre*, p. 15.
4 Ibid.
5 Gertrud Rudloff-Hille, *Schiller auf der deutschen Bühne seiner Zeit* (Berlin, 1969), p. 9, 'in Wirtshaussälen, Höfen oder in besonders dafür errichteten Bretterbuden auf freien Plätzen der Orte'.
6 I use the term 'authoritarian' here simply to imply that the predetermined architectural structure of the city was unable, rather than unwilling, to respond to the new spatial demands created by theatre companies and the theatrical genre itself.
7 W. H. Bruford, *Culture and Society in Classical Weimar: 1775–1806* (Cambridge, 1962), p. 57.
8 See Bruford, *Theatre*, pp. 15–16.
9 J. G. Robertson, *Lessing's Dramatic Theory* (London, 1939), p. 14.
10 Bruford, *Culture and Society in Classical Weimar*, p. 38.
11 Bruford, *Theatre*, p. 61.
12 Ibid., p. 55.

13 Ibid., p. 98.
14 *Selected Prose Works of G. E. Lessing*, trans. by E. C. Beasley and H. Zimmern (London, 1890), p. 14.
15 The Duchy of Saxe-Weimar was created in 1741 when Duke Ernest Augustus I, a member of the Ernestine branch of the Wettin dynasty inherited the Duchy of Saxe-Eisenach. He united his new acquisition with the Duchy of Saxe–Weimar, already in his possession. He was succeeded in 1748 by Duke Ernest II who died ten years later leaving his wife, Anna Amalia, and in due course his son and heir, Charles Augustus, in control of the Duchy. Under the influence of mother and son, the Duchy became a cultural centre of some importance and a centre for patronage of art, literature and theatre. The union of the two territories was formally sanctioned by an official merger in 1809 that created the Duchy of Saxe-Weimar-Eisenach, eventually to become a Grand Duchy in 1815.
16 Bruford, *Theatre*, p. 174.
17 Ibid.
18 Robertson, *Lessing's Dramatic Theory*, p. 15.
19 The fact that the repertoire remained more or less the same may be explained by the fact that the company's choice of plays was dependent on the costumes available in the players' wardrobes and the previous parts in which company members had excelled.
20 Robertson, *Lessing's Dramatic Theory*, pp. 18–20.
21 Ibid., p. 18.
22 Bruford, *Theatre*, p. 96.
23 Jürgen Habermas, *The Structural Transformation of the Public Sphere: an Inquiry into a Category of Bourgeois Society*, trans. by Thomas Burger (Cambridge, 2003), p. 39.
24 See Robertson, *Lessing's Dramatic Theory*, pp. 119–21.
25 *Selected Prose Works of G. E. Lessing*, p. 429.
26 Ibid., p. 426.
27 Robertson, *Lessing's Dramatic Theory*, p. 19. 'Ich weiss nicht, was das Wort Nationaltheater bedeuten soll, da es kaum mittelmässig war, und das die Herren Schauspieler seitdem allenthalben zum Scherwenzel gebraucht haben; aber ein sehr vorzügliches Theater zu besitzen, ist Hamburg gewiss der erste Ort in Deutschland.'
28 Rudloff-Hille, *Schiller auf der deutschen Bühne seiner Zeit* (Berlin, 1969), p. 9.
29 Ibid., pp. 11–13.
30 *Selected Prose Works of G. E. Lessing*, p. 430.
31 Ibid., p. 426.
32 Ibid.
33 Ibid., p. 14.
34 Ibid., p. 240.

35 This paper was delivered at the American Society for Theatre Research Conference, 'Accounting for Taste', Las Vegas, Nevada, 18–21 November 2004.
36 See Bruford, *Theatre*, p. 199.
37 Ibid., p. 105.
38 Ibid.
39 Robertson, *Lessing's Dramatic Theory*, p. 124.
40 See Bruford, *Culture and Society in Classical Weimar*, p. 19.
41 Ibid., pp. 19–20.
42 T. J. Reed, *The Classical Centre: Goethe and Weimar, 1775–1832* (Oxford, 1980), p. 57.
43 Ibid., p. 21.
44 Ibid., p. 184.
45 Bruford, *Culture and Society in Classical Weimar*, p. 124.
46 Bruford, *Theatre*, p. 290.
47 Reed, *The Classical Centre*, p. 37.
48 Eric Auerbach, *Mimesis: the Representation of Reality in Western Literature* (New Jersey, 1953), p. 438.
49 The *Sturm und Drang* or Storm and Stress movement flourished in Germany between 1770 and 1784. It was, primarily, a literary movement that investigated and articulated the individual's subjective experience and man's unease in modern society. Many of the works produced during this period, amongst them Goethe's short novel, *The Sorrows of Werther* (1773) and his play, *Götz von Berlichingen* (1773), focused on the themes of youthful genius in rebellion and youthful angst in general. The movement was also characterized by an enthusiasm for nature and a rejection of neo-classical concepts of order and style. Both the *Sturm und Drang* movement and its precursor, Romanticism, have been associated with the development of ideas of nationalism and nationhood in Germany and across Europe.
50 Auerbach, *Mimesis*, p. 439.
51 Ibid., p. 440.
52 Peter Szondi, *Theory of the Modern Drama: a Critical Edition*, trans. by Michael Hays (Cambridge, 1987).
53 Auerbach, *Mimesis*, p. 441.
54 Ibid.
55 Ibid., p. 442.
56 Ibid., p. 443.
57 Ibid., pp. 443–4.
58 Ibid., p. 444.
59 Myfanwy Jones, 'Madness in German drama from Romanticism to Postmodernism: a study of dramatic form in relation to

anti-Enlightenment debate' (unpublished Ph.D. thesis, University of Warwick, 2003), 2.
60. Auerbach, *Mimesis*, pp. 450–1.
61. Ibid., p. 452.
62. Ibid.
63. Ibid., p. 450.
64. Ibid.
65. Bruford, *Culture and Society in Classical Weimar*, p. 41.
66. Ibid., p. 332.
67. Reed, *The Classical Centre*, p. 84.
68. *Correspondence between Schiller and Goethe 1798–1805*, trans. by L. Dora Schmitz (London, 1909) vol. 2, p. 113.
69. See Reed, *The Classical Centre*, p. 173.
70. Ibid., pp. 175–6.
71. *Friedrich Schiller: an Anthology for our Time*, ed. Frederick Ungar (New York, 1959), p. 279.
72. Ibid., pp. 276–7.
73. Peter Jelavich, *Munich and Theatrical Modernism: Politics, Playwriting and Performance, 1890–1914* (Harvard, 1985), p. 16.
74. Ibid., p. 17.
75. See Bruford, *Culture and Society in Classical Weimar*, p. 362.
76. Ibid., p. 125.
77. Larry Eugene Jones, 'Culture and politics in the Weimar Republic', in Gordon Martell (ed.), *Modern Germany Reconsidered: 1870–1945* (London, 1992), pp. 76–7.
78. Ibid., p.76.
79. Habermas, *The Structural Transformation of the Public Sphere*, p. 43.
80. See Bruford, *Culture and Society in Classical Weimar*, p. 388.
81. Karl Marx, *Revolution and Counter-Revolution*, ed. Eleanor Marx Aveling (London, 1971), p. 10.
82. Ibid., p. 14.
83. Ibid., p. 10–18.
84. Mathew S. Seligmann and Roderick R. McLean, *Germany from Reich to Republic: 1871–1918* (London, 2000), p. 15.
85. Nicolaus Sombart, 'The Kaiser in his epoch: some reflexions on Wilhelmine society, sexuality and culture', in *Kaiser Wilhelm II: New Interpretations*, John Rohl and Nicolaus Sombart (eds), (Cambridge, 1982), p. 293.
86. *The Invention of Tradition*, ed. E. Hobsbawm and T. Ranger (Cambridge, 1983), p. 273.
87. William Carr, *A History of Germany: 1815–1945* (London, 1969), p. 23.

88 Richard Taylor, *Richard Wagner: His Life, Art and Thought* (London, 1979), p. 83.
89 Ibid., p. 259.
90 This grand annual festival, at which Wagner staged many of his greatest operatic works, preoccupied him for a great part of his life. It opened in 1876 and continues to date, under the direction of the remaining descendants of the Wagner family. Tickets are generally sold out a long time in advance of productions and the squabbling amongst members of the Wagner family with regard to the festival and their relations with Wagner makes for great entertainment in the German press.
91 Taylor, *Richard Wagner*, p. 221.
92 Ibid., p. 172.
93 Ibid., p. 176.
94 Ibid.
95 Ibid., p. 196.
96 Ibid.
97 Ibid., p. 199.
98 Ibid., p. 256.
99 Ibid., p. 252.
100 Quoted in Stephen Lamb, 'Ernst Toller in the Weimar Republic', in K. Bullivant (ed.), *Culture and Society in the Weimar Republic* (Manchester, 1977), p. 77.
101 Ibid., p. 78.
102 Jones, 'Culture and politics in the Weimar Republic', p. 80.
103 Max Weber, *On Charisma and Institution Building: Selected Papers*, ed. S. N. Eisenstadt (Chicago, 1968), p. 249.
104 Ibid., p. 16.
105 Walter Laqueur, *Weimar: a Cultural History 1918–1933* (London, 1974), p. 125.
106 Ibid.
107 Rudy Koshar, *From Monuments to Traces: Artifacts of German Memory 1870–1990* (London, 2000), p. 18.
108 Ibid., p. 30.
109 Ibid., p. 61. It was not until 1916 that the phrase 'Dem Deutschen Volke' was eventually inscribed on the building.
110 Alon Confino, *The Nation as a Local Metaphor: Württemberg, Imperial Germany, and National Memory, 1871–1918* (London, 1997).
111 *The Theater of the Bauhaus*, ed. W. Gropius and trans. by A. S. Wensinger (London, 1998), p. 17.
112 Ibid., p. 101.
113 Ibid.
114 Laqueur, *Weimar*, p. 112.

115 Ibid., p. 123.
116 Ibid., p. 117.
117 Karl Jaspers, *Man in the Modern Age,* trans. by E. Paul and C. Paul (London, 1951), p. 144.
118 Laqueur, *Weimar,* p. 141.
119 Yvonne Schafer, 'Nazi Berlin and the Großes Schauspielhaus', in Glen W. Gadberry (ed.), *Theatre in the Third Reich: the Prewar Years* (London, 1995), p. 103.
120 Quoted in Lamb, 'Ernst Toller in the Weimar Republic', p. 90.
121 Ibid.
122 Louis L. Snyder, *Roots of German Nationalism* (London, 1978), p. 182.
123 William Grange, 'Ordained hands on the altar of art: Gründgens, Hilpert, and Fehling in Berlin', in Gadberry (ed.), *Theatre in the Third Reich: the Prewar Years* (London, 1995), p. 77.
124 See G. W. Gadberry, 'The first national social theatre festival – Dresden', in Gadberry (ed.), *Theatre in the Third Reich: the Prewar Years* (London, 1995), p. 106.
125 See Schafer, 'Nazi Berlin and the Großes Schauspielhaus', in Gadberry (ed.), *Theatre in the Third Reich: the Prewar Years* (London, 1995), p. 124.
126 Ibid., p. 109. Schiller's play was probably chosen by virtue of its nationalistic sentiment. On close inspection, its thematic may seem somewhat contrary to the officially sanctioned politics of the Nazi period, particularly in view of the fact that both Goethe and Schiller thought of the nation not in terms of 'a politically unified German state, but rather as a body of educated citizens who would employ a common (German) language to maintain a constant public discourse on philosophical, religious, scientific, artistic, social, and political issues'. (Peter Jelavich, *Munich and Theatrical Modernism: Politics, Playwriting and Performance, 1890–1914* (Harvard, 1985), p. 16.)
127 R. A. Pois, 'The National Socialist *Volksgemeinschaft* fantasy and the drama of national rebirth', in Gadberry (ed.), *Theatre in the Third Reich: the Prewar Years* (London, 1995), p. 18.
128 Ibid., p. 19.
129 George. L. Mosse, *The Crisis of German Ideology: Intellectual Origins of the Third Reich* (London, 1966), p. 31.
130 Ibid., p. 81.
131 Schafer, 'Nazi Berlin and the Großes Schauspielhaus', p. 105.
132 Ibid., p. 107.
133 Ibid., p. 108.
134 Pois, 'The National Socialist *Volksgemeinschaft* fantasy and the drama of national rebirth', p. 21.
135 Ibid., p. 23.

136 Michael Patterson, *German Theatre Today: Post-war Theatre in West and East Germany, Austria and Northern Switzerland* (London, 1976), p. 14.
137 Peter Fischer, 'Doing princely sums: structure and subsidy', in Ronald Hayman (ed.), *The German Theatre: a Symposium* (London, 1975), p. 223.
138 See the consensus expressed by Clive Barker and Stuart Parkes in *The German Theatre: a Symposium*, Ronald Hayman (ed.) (London, 1975), pp. 129–51 and pp. 189–201.
139 Klaus Völker, 'The new theatre buildings', in Ronald Hayman (ed.), *The German Theatre: a Symposium* (London, 1975), p. 246.
140 Clive Barker, 'Theatre in east Germany' in Ronald Hayman (ed.), *The German Theatre: a Symposium* (London, 1975), p. 196.
141 Ibid., p. 192.
142 Patterson, *German Theatre Today*, p. 14.
143 Siobhan Kattago, *Ambiguous Memory: the Nazi Past and German National Identity* (London, 2001), p. 118.
144 Ibid., p. 121.
145 http://www.zeit.de, 3/3/2005. Accessed 8 October 2005.

Chapter 3: The English national theatre:
O brave new world, That has such people in't

1 Shakespeare, *The Tempest* (1611), act 5, sc1, l.182.
2 Albrecht Wellmer, *Endgames: the Irreconcilable Nature of Modernity*, trans. by David Midgley (London, 1998), p. 41.
3 Eric Evans 'National Conciousness? The ambivalences of English identity in the eighteenth century' in Claus Bjorn, Alexander Grant and Keith J. Stringer (eds), *Nations, Nationalism and Patriotism in the European Past* (Copenhagen, 1994), p. 153.
4 Ibid.
5 *The Icon Critical Dictionary of Postmodern Thought,* ed. Stuart Sim (London, 1998), p. 268.
6 G. E. Aylmer, 'The peculiarities of the English state', *Journal of Historical Sociology*, 3, 2 (1990), 101.
7 Ibid, p. 128.
8 Ibid., pp. 91–109.
9 George Orwell, *The English People* (London, 1957), p. 7.
10 Tim Goodwin, *Britain's Royal National Theatre: the First 25 Years* (London, 1988), p. 106.
11 Alan Kidd and David Nicholls, 'Introduction: the making of the British middle class?', in Alan Kidd and David Nicholls (eds), *The*

Making of the British Middle Class?: Studies of Regional and Cultural Diversity since the Eighteenth Century (Phoenix Mill, 1998), p. xxv.
12. Ibid., p. xxiv.
13. Loren Kruger, *The National Stage: Theatre and Cultural Legitimation in England, France and America* (London, 1991), p. 85.
14. Keith Stringer, 'Social and political communities in European history: some reflections on recent studies', in *Nations, Nationalism and Patriotism in the European Past*, p. 28.
15. Quoted in Goodwin, *Britain's Royal National Theatre*, pp. 105–6.
16. Henry Arthur Jones, *The Foundations of a National Drama* (London, 1913), p. 94.
17. Matthew Arnold, *English Literature and Irish Politics*, ed. R. H. Super (Michigan, 1973), p. 81.
18. Alfred Emmet, 'The long pre-history of the national theatre', *Theatre Quarterly*, 6, 21 (1976), 55–66.
19. George Orwell was incensed by what he considered as the Englishman's artistic insensibility – a trait that enabled him to pull down ancient monuments or allow them to be swamped by seas of yellow brick whilst applauding the erection of hideous statues to nonentities. Orwell, *The English People*.
20. Arnold, *English Literature and Irish Politics*, p. 65.
21. Jones, *The Foundations of a National Drama*, pp. 158–9.
22. Ibid., p. 159.
23. Quoted in Holbrook Jackson, *The Eighteen Nineties: a Review of Art and Ideas at the Close of the Nineteenth Century* (Dublin, 1976) p. 196
24. J. H. Shennan, 'The rise of patriotism in eighteenth century Europe', *History of European Ideas*, XIII (1991), 159.
25. Quoted in William Archer and Harley Granville Barker, *A National Theatre: Schemes and Estimates* (New York, 1908), pp. 176–7.
26. Arnold, *English Literature and Irish Politics*, p. 78.
27. Jones, *The Foundations of a National Drama*, p. 4.
28. Goodwin, *Britain's Royal National Theatre*, p. 5.
29. 'Drury-Lane Theatre', *The Times*, 1 February 1825.
30. See James Woodfield, *English Theatre in Transition: 1881–1914* (Kent, 1984), p. 94.
31. Ibid., p. 109.
32. Ibid., p. 112.
33. Ibid.
34. Tom Nairn, *Faces of Nationalism* (London, 1999), p. 49.
35. Quoted in Emmet, 'The long pre-history of the national theatre', 56.
36. Archer and Granville Barker, *A National Theatre*, p. vii.

37 Ibid., p. 37.
38 Ibid.
39 Ibid., p. xvii.
40 Ibid., pp. 172–3.
41 Ibid.
42 William Archer, *The Great Analysis: a Plea for a Rational World Order* (London, 1911), p. 65.
43 Nairn, *Faces of Nationalism*, p. 27.
44 Ibid.
45 Ibid., p. 63.
46 Ibid.
47 Geoffrey Barraclough, *History in a Changing World* (Oxford, 1957), p. 31.
48 Archer and Granville Barker, *A National Theatre*, p. xv.
49 Ibid., pp. 171–2.
50 Geoffrey Whitworth, *The Making of a National Theatre* (London, 1951), p. 71.
51 Ibid.
52 Harley Granville Barker, *A National Theatre* (London, 1930), p. 3.
53 Arnold, *English Literature and Irish Politics*, pp. 77–8.
54 Ibid., pp. 78–9.
55 Whitworth, *The Making of a National Theatre*, pp. 232–3.
56 Arnold, *English Literature and Irish Politics*, p. 80.
57 Ibid., p. 85.
58 Archer and Granville Barker, *A National Theatre*, p. xiii.
59 Ibid.
60 Whitworth, *The Making of a National Theatre*, p. 100.
61 Ibid., p. 107.
62 Quoted in John Elsom and Nicholas Tomalin, *The History of the National Theatre* (London, 1978), p. 16.
63 Archer and Granville Barker, *A National Theatre*, p. 1.
64 See Janet Minihan, *The Nationalization of Culture: the Development of State Subsidies to the Arts in Great Britain* (London, 1977), pp. 145–6.
65 Archer and Granville Barker, *A National Theatre*, p. xix.
66 Ibid.
67 Ibid., p. xv.
68 Ibid., p. 6.
69 Ibid., p. 7.
70 Ibid.
71 Ibid., p. 8.
72 Aylmer, 'The peculiarities of the English state', 101.
73 Arnold, *English Literature and Irish Politics*, p. 65.
74 Ibid., p. 67.

75 Whitworth, *The Making of a National Theatre*, p. 58.
76 Archer and Granville Barker, *A National Theatre*, p. 17.
77 Ibid., p. xiii
78 Henry Irving, *The Drama* (London, 1893), p. 7.
79 Gwynedd County Council Archives, Cwmni Theatr Cymru papers, XD68/2/68.
80 Orwell, *The English People*, p. 8.
81 F. C. Burnand, 'TO THE EDITOR OF THE TIMES', *The Times*, 1 March 1905, 12.
82 John Hankin, 'How to run an art theatre in London', *Fortnightly Review*, 82 (1907), p. 815.
83 Ibid., p. 816.
84 Ibid.
85 'Proposed memorial to Shakespeare', *The Times*, 1 March 1905, 12.
86 Whitworth, *The Making of a National Theatre*, p. 76.
87 Ibid., p. 79.
88 'The Shakespeare Memorial Theatre', *The Times*, 23 April 1913, 11.
89 Minihan, *The Nationalization of Culture*, p. 147.
90 Ibid., p. 28.
91 See Nairn, *Faces of Nationalism*, p. 26.
92 Ibid., pp. 26–7.
93 Whitworth, *The Making of a National Theatre*, p. 113.
94 Ibid., p. 168.
95 See *The National Theatre: 'The Architectural Review Guide'*, ed. Colin Amery (London, 1977), p. 65.
96 Minihan, *The Nationalization of Culture*, p. 230.
97 Ibid., p. 237.
98 Whitworth, *The Making of a National Theatre*, p. 266.
99 Helen Dawson, 'The national theatre, London', *Theatre Quarterly*, VI, 22 (1976), 48–9.
100 *The National Theatre: The 'Architectural Review' Guide* ed. Colin Amery (London, 1977), p. 16.
101 Ibid., p. 8.
102 Ibid., p. 56.
103 Ibid.
104 Ibid., p. 8.
105 Ibid., p. 45.
106 Ibid., p. 52.
107 Ibid., p. 25.
108 Ibid., p. 58.
109 Ibid., p. 5.
110 Goodwin, *Britain's Royal National Theatre*, p. 99.

Chapter 4: The National Eisteddfod, the national pageant and the Welsh national theatre: friends or foes?

1. Rhys Davies, *The Story of Wales* (London, 1957), p. 17.
2. Theatr Genedlaethol Cymru is Wales's name for its current national theatre.
3. These are three classes of Welsh poets, prominent in the country's poetical history: the early poets, the poets of the princes and the poets of the gentry.
4. See John Davies, *Hanes Cymru: a History of Wales in Welsh* (London, 1992), p. 401.
5. Kenneth Morgan, *Rebirth of a Nation: a History of Modern Wales* (Oxford, 2002), pp. 3–25.
6. Tom Jones, 'The Welsh drama', *Wales, a National Magazine for the English speaking Parts of Wales,* 1, 8, December 1894, 374. It is likely that the aforementioned Tom Jones was, in fact, the prominent Welsh educationalist, O. M. Edwards. My attention was first drawn to this likelihood by Hazel Walford Davies at a conference held at Aberystwyth, in June 2005, hosted by the Centre for Advanced Welsh and Celtic Studies. The fact that O. M. Edwards, who was the editor of *Wales, a National Magazine for the English speaking Parts of Wales,* wrote another article in the magazine in September 1894, entitled, 'The National Eisteddfod of 1894', in which he quoted from Tom Jones's article on Welsh drama lends credence to this suspicion, as do some of the personal details, offered by Jones in his account of his own interests, upbringing and career, that bear a striking resemblance to the actual life history and experiences of Edwards himself.
7. The Eisteddfod is a cultural festival at which competitive events in poetry, singing and recital feature heavily. The competition culminates in the crowning and the throning of the successful poet. These events occur throughout Wales on regional levels and a week-long annual, national festival is held in August. There are records of eisteddfodau in Wales from the middle of the fifteenth century onwards. These events were originally official assemblies of poets but the Eisteddfod has evolved over the years to include more and more branches of the arts, such as drama, dancing, art, photography, script-writing and the like.
8. J. Kitchener Davies, 'Yr Eisteddfod a'r ddrama', *Heddiw,* V, IV (1939), 170, 'y chwareuaeth Gymreig orau ynôl dull Shakespeare'. 'The Eryri Eisteddfod was not, in fact a National Eisteddfod but a prestigious, local Eisteddford at which a chair was offered for the victorious bard.'
9. Beriah Gwynfe Evans, *Chwareu-gan: Drama yn Null Shakespeare ar 'Owain Glyndwr'* (Llanberis, 1879?). The title of this play is given as

Owain Glyndŵr in later editions. All references in this text, excluding p. 144, are to the *c*.1879 edition where the spelling is as given. See National Library of Wales, Sir John Williams collection, Wb 5850.

[10] Kitchener Davies, 'Yr Eisteddfod a'r ddrama', 170. 'A bod gofyn olhrain y mudiad drama Gymraeg fodern i un dyddiad arbennig, 1879 fyddai hwnnw.'

[11] Jones, 'The Welsh drama', 373–4.

[12] E. Vincent Evans (ed.), *Minutes and Compositions of the Caernarfon Eisteddfod, 1894.*

[13] The Gwyneddigion and the Cymmrodorion societies were London-based groups set up by educated Welsh figures intent on the promotion of Welsh literary culture, mainly by means of sponsorship.

[14] G. J. Williams, 'Eisteddfodau'r Gwyneddigion', *Y Llenor*, 14 (1935), 14.

[15] There is some competition with regard to this issue. Edward Charles was confident that he had pioneered the revival of the Eisteddfod but his claim was contested by Edward Jones, the king's poet, in his *Musical and Poetic Relicks* (1794).

[16] Iolo Morganwg (1747–1826). A charismatic and prolific nineteenth-century Welsh literary figure whose main interest was in resurrecting or, perhaps, in manufacturing and promoting the Glamorgan bardic traditions. There are many informative studies of various aspects of Iolo's work emanating from the University of Wales Centre for Advanced Welsh and Celtic Studies.

[17] For a description of the proposed regulations regarding judges etc. at the Gwyneddigion Eisteddfodau, see G. J. Williams, 'Eisteddfodau'r Gwyneddigion', *Y Llenor*, 14 (1935), 16.

[18] By 1789, the eisteddfodau included competitions for musicians and singers but their scope remained restricted.

[19] Thomas Edwards (1738–1810). The most skilful Welsh interlude writer of his time, Edwards, or, as he was better known, 'Twm o'r Nant', claimed to have written his first interlude at the age of nine. Despite having little formal education he wrote, published and performed in dozens of interludes and pursued an intermittent career as a professional in this field until his death in 1810.

[20] Their regard for respectability is evident from the internal squabbling caused by a senior member of the Gwyneddigion society's insistence on meeting in a particular public house that was considered by other members to be too 'low-down' for them. R. T. Jenkins and Helen M. Ramage, 'A History of the Honourable Society of Cymmrodorion and of the Gwyneddigion and the Cymreigyddion Societies (1751–1951)', in *Y Cymmrodor*, vol. 1 (1951), 116.

21 An account of one of Twm's contributions to the festivities surrounding the Eisteddfod at Bala in September 1789 depicts 'our Welsh Garrick' entertaining the town with an interlude that is set to continue for two or three days longer.
22 See Ceri Lewis, *Iolo Morganwg* (Caernarfon, 1995), p. 233.
23 According to Lewis, this was the name given to Iolo by his English friends and was used as a technical term to designate one who had inherited a wealth of bardic traditions from the past, a man of conviction who cared for the language, literature, culture and morals of his nation.
24 For a full account of Iolo's inventiveness, see Ceri Lewis, *Iolo Morganwg*.
25 The choice of London as the location for this inaugural ceremony may strike the reader as curious in the context of Iolo's vigorous dedication to the promotion of his national and regional culture. It may well be explained by the fact that he considered Primrose Hill to be representative of the centre of the old Brythonic world in Britain.
26 Quoted in Cathryn Charnell-White, *Barbarism and Bardism: North Wales versus South Wales in the Bardic Vision of Iolo Morganwg* (Aberystwyth, 2004), p. 19.
27 See Lewis, *Iolo Morganwg*, p. 232.
28 See R. A. Griffith, 'The prospects of Welsh drama', in the *Transactions of the Honourable Society of Cymmrodorion* (1914), 131.
29 W. Llewelyn Williams, 'The prospects of the drama in Wales', *Transactions of the Honourable Society of Cymmrodorion* (1914), 140–1.
30 'Easter 1916', *Collected Poems of W. B. Yeats* (London, 1952), pp. 202–5.
31 Evans (ed.), *Minutes and Compositions of the Caernarfon Eisteddfod, 1894*, p. 30–1.
32 M. Wynn Thomas, *Internal Difference: Twentieth-Century Writing in Wales* (Cardiff, 1992), p. 13.
33 J. O. Francis, 'A comment from Corwen', *The Welsh Outlook*, VI (1919), 228.
34 Ibid., p. 230.
35 Ibid.
36 Ibid., p. 231.
37 Ibid., p. 228.
38 Ibid., p. 229.
39 The changes expected were due to the deaths of Dyfed, the Archdruid, and Eifionydd, the gorsedd's recorder.
40 See 'Yr Eisteddfod Genedlaethol', *Baner ac Amserau Cymru*, 16 August 1923, 5.

41 For a full discussion of the reputed connection between one particular interlude, *Sherlyn Benchwiban,* and Carmarthenshire, see Huw Walters, *Cynnwrf Canrif: Agweddau ar Ddiwylliant Gwerin* (Llandybïe, 2004), pp. 11–25.
42 See Saunders Lewis, 'Twm o'r Nant II', *Y Faner,* 27 September 1950, 8.
43 D. R. Davies, 'The drama in Wales', *Y Llenor,* 6, 1, (1927), 44, 'o'r ddadl syml'.
44 Full text translates as: 'This great crowd, I believe,/Are listening to the Methodists,/Or watching the playing of an Interlude,/Some dispute of one kind or the other is afoot.' (Translation renders only the literal meaning.)
45 Deborah Parsons, 'Nationalism or continentalism? Representing heritage culture for a new European identity', in *Yearbook of European Studies,* Andy Hollis (ed.), *Beyond Boundaries: Textual Representations of European Identity,* vol. 15 (Amsterdam, 2000), p. 4. Deborah Parsons describes the particular mode of self-awareness and expression promoted by the single Europe Act of 1987 as 'an identity that is publicly performed, constituted by certain practices of social interaction within a regular territory that strengthens collective identity'. She argues that this process is articulated in the Euro-city itself and whilst this may well be true, her definition might be transferred with ease to a different territory – the world of national theatre.
46 Saunders Lewis, 'Twm o'r Nant III', in *Y Faner,* 25 October 1950, 8. 'nyni a gollodd yr allwedd i ddeall ei waith'.
47 Kenneth Morgan, *The Rebirth of a Nation* (Oxford, 2002), p. 92.
48 Ioan Williams, *Y Mudiad Drama yng Nghymru 1880–1940* (Cardiff, 2006), p. 50. 'dathliad o drawsnewidiad rhwng yr hen Gymru Galfinaidd a'r wlad newydd, hyderus yn rhinwedd addysg ddwyieithog a chynnydd cymdeithasol.'
49 Evidence is provided both by reports of the Church's diatribes against that 'ridiculous, immoral custom' of the playing of 'dull, artless' interludes and by Edwards's own decision, as recorded in his bibliography, to throw the cap he wore when playing the miser into the river as a result of his love for a girl of religious tendencies.
50 See Cecil Price, 'Towards a Welsh national theatre for Wales', *The Anglo-Welsh Review,* XII, 29 (1962), 12–25.
51 For a full discussion of the nature of moral and religious suspicion of drama and the theatre in nineteenth-century Wales, including the extent to which this resistance has been mythologized in recent historical accounts, see Williams, *Y Mudiad Drama yng Nghymru 1880–1940.*
52 Joseph Parry was not the first to realize the dramatic potential of

these Welsh subjects. Both *The Maid of Cefn Ydfa* and *Llewelyn ein Llyw Olaf* had appeared as dramas prior to their operatic rendition by Parry. According to Cecil Price, 'Portable theatres in Wales, 1834–1914', *The National Library of Wales Journal*, IX, 1 (1958), 66–92, J. C. Dowd and J. C. Livesey, both members of the Warren and Manges portable theatre company, prior to 1869, had devised dramas carrying the above titles. The former, when performed at Aberdare in April 1870, was billed as an 'entirely new Welsh historical drama, in three acts, placed upon the boards for the first time'. It was also played at Noakes's Star Theatre, Carmarthen, in 1877, where it was billed as 'The Great Welsh drama as performed by this company in English and Welsh'. However, despite this allusion to the Welsh language, I can find no evidence that either drama existed in Welsh. As a result, I suspect that they fell into the category of 'Welsh interest', and as such have limited relevance in the context of the growth of a Welsh national drama movement. I found no evidence either that Parry knew of these plays or that they influenced the creation of his own work in any way.

53 Joseph Parry (1841–1903). He was also the composer of many Welsh arias of a patriotic kind such as *Gwnewch Bopeth yn Gymraeg* (Do everything in Welsh) (1875), *Hoff Wlad fy Ngenedigaeth* (Fond country of my birth) (1894) and *Cymru Fydd* (Wales will Prosper) (1915).

54 *South Wales Daily News*, 16 December 1902, 6.

55 In an essay on the arrival of the drama in Wales, E. Morgan Humphreys makes interesting comment on both the existence of mythological, national descriptors such as the 'Land of Song', and 'Land of the White Gloves', the former referring to the national propensity for song, the latter to the reputed law-keeping of the Welsh, that meant there was rarely any call for the donning of the Justice of the Peace's white gloves. He notes that whilst every thinking man realizes the limitations of such descriptions, yet we, as a nation, have become accustomed to thinking of ourselves in these terms and dislike those who threaten what has become a comforting tradition of national fabrication. In the context of the present argument, it is interesting to note his suggestion that the nation is guilty of compliance in a process of national fabrication.

56 Cecil Price, 'Some Welsh theatres', *The National Library of Wales Journal*, XII, 2 (1961), 163.

57 *Llanelly Star*, 5 November 1910, 1.

58 Quoted in Cecil Price, 'Towards a national theatre for Wales', 12.

59 Jones, 'The Welsh drama', 374.

60 Beriah Evans, *Llewelyn ein Llyw Olaf: Drama Gantata mewn Tair Act i'w Pherfformio gan Bartïon Cymreig* (Llanelly, 1883).

61. W. J. Gruffydd, 'Reviews', *Y Beirniad* (June 1911), 216, '*operetta* a phasiant'.
62. Alaw Ddu, a pseudonym, translates as Black or Morose Harmony.
63. Evans, *Llewelyn ein Llyw Olaf,* 'mae y Ddrama wedi ei hysgrifennu a'i threfnu fel ag i wneud y rhannau adroddiadol yn is-wasanaethgar, ac yn arwain i fyny at y darnau cerddorol', p. 1.
64. John Lloyd Williams and Lewis David Jones, *Aelwyd Angharad: Neu Hwyrnos Lawen Llwyngwern; Chwareugan, yn Dangos Dull ac Arferion Bywyd Gwledig Cymru fu* (Bangor, 1910?).
65. Elidir Sais, 'Welsh folk song', *Y Brython,* 2 December 1909, 5. Evidently, the writer does not know Joseph Parry's work or does not consider it to represent Welsh operatic drama.
66. Ibid.
67. See *Y Darian,* 2 April 1920.
68. T. O. Jones, *A Memorandum on the Recent Drama Movement in North Wales,* p. 3.
69. Williams, *Y Mudiad Drama yng Nghymru.*
70. 'An open Letter to Angharad's tribe', *Y Brython,* 4 December 1913, 4, 'nid golygydd na gohebydd rheolaidd'.
71. The writer actually signs himself, 'AP FFARMWR O FÔN'. This is a play on the Welsh custom of naming the son after his father: 'ap' meaning 'son of'. The term is usually followed by the father's first name, as in the example of Dewi ap Ifan, Dewi son of Ifan, but in this case, the writer identifies himself with one of the most common categories of Welsh citizen, the farmer.
72. Wil Gogerddan, 'Am Angharad a'i thylwyth', *Y Brython,* 11 December 1913, 5. 'Modryb' is translated as aunt.
73. 'More about 'The aelwyd', *Y Brython,* 11 December 1913, 5.
74. 'Hwn, hyn ac arall', *Y Brython,* 6 September 1906, 4. 'Ond y mae i ddrama amcan pellach nag eiddo yr awdl neu'r bryddest – o leiaf pellach na'i chyhoeddi mewn argraff. Bwriedir yr olaf i'w hactio, ac nis gellir barnu ei gwerth yn gyflawn ond yn y goleu hwnnw. Go hwyrfrydig fu Cymru i roi wyneb i ddim ag arno ddelw chwareudy ... Eto, mae'n rhaid symud gyda'r oes, ac ymgyfaddasu i amgylchiadau newyddion, mor bell ag y byddo hynny yn fanteisiol i ddaioni cyffredinol.'
75. E. Derry Evans, 'The evolution of the Welsh drama', *Young Wales,* IV, (1898), 250–1.
76. Evans (ed.), *Minutes and Compositions of the Caernarfon Eisteddfod, 1894,* pp. 31–2.
77. Jones, 'The Welsh drama', 374. He estimates the cost of this theatrical endeavour at £85, a mere trifle in comparison to Badger's offer of £2,500 for the establishment of a memorial to Shakespeare in England just a few years later!

78 Evans (ed.), *Minutes and Compositions of the Caernarfon Eisteddfod, 1894*, p. 64.
79 Hywel Teifi Edwards, *Codi'r Hen Wlad: 1850–1914* (Llandysul, 1989), p. 244. 'Cyfuniad o'r masque, y pasiant canoloesol a'r ddrama ... o'r tair elfen yna y ddrama oedd y bwysicaf.'
80 Kirsti Bohata, *Postcolonialism Revisited: Writing Wales in English* (Cardiff, 2004), p. 74.
81 Evans, 'The evolution of the Welsh drama', 250.
82 Quoted in Edwards, *Codi'r Hen Wlad*, p. 243.
83 Patrick J. Geary, *The Myth of Nations: the Medieval Origins of Europe* (Oxford, 2002), p. 37.
84 For Edwards's account of the way in which Dr James Mullin was inspired to challenge Wales to emulate this feat achieved at the Warwick pageant of 1906, see *Codi'r Hen Wlad*, p. 239.
85 Edwards, *Codi'r Hen Wlad*, pp. 250–1.
86 I heard this argument presented by Andrew Davies at a seminar given in 2005, at the Centre for Advanced Welsh and Celtic Studies, University of Wales, Aberystwyth. I do not know if Davies has articulated it in print.
87 Evans (ed.), *Minutes and Compositions of the Caernarfon Eisteddfod, 1894*, p. 32.
88 Aled Jones and Bill Jones, 'The Welsh world and the British empire', in C. Bridge and K. Fedorowich (eds), *The British World: Diaspora, Culture and Identity* (London, 2003), p. 57.
89 This criticism of the University of Wales's lethargy in relation to the promotion of Welsh national drama is not entirely fair in view of the fact that the Cardiff University players had pioneered a production of W. J. Gruffydd's important play, *Beddau'r Proffwydi*, in March 1913 at the Royal Playhouse, Cardiff. For details see Alban in 'Hybu'r Ddrama', *Y Brython*, 20 March 1913.
90 Elidir Sais, 'The drama', *Y Brython*, 21 July 1910, 5.
91 'National drama', *South Wales Daily News*, 12 May 1914, 4.
92 Owen Rhoscomyl, 'National drama', *Western Mail*, 6 December 1913, 6. It is interesting to note the identity of the writer drawing public attention to the true significance of De Walden's vision. He is Captain Owen Vaughan, our pageant scriptwriter of 1908. Evidently, his was not a voice of the past but for the future.
93 Owen Rhoscomyl, 'National drama', 5.
94 Ibid.
95 Owen Rhoscomyl in *South Wales Daily News*, 31 January 1914, 8.
96 Rhoscomyl in *South Wales Daily News*, 20 January 1914 and 27 March 1914.
97 J. O. Francis, *Change: a Glamorgan Play in Four Acts* (London, n. d.).

98 'Wales and drama', *South Wales Daily News*, 12 May 1914, 5.
99 'The Welsh drama', *South Wales Daily News*, 18 May 1914, 8.
100 Abel Jones, 'Does Wales need the drama?', *The Welsh Outlook* (1914), 254–6.
101 'Welsh Drama Week', *Western Mail*, 16 May 1914, 7.
102 'America's lesson', *Western Mail*, 16 May 1914, 7.
103 Ibid.
104 E. Morgan Humphreys, 'Dyfodiad y ddrama', *Y Beirniad*, IV, 3 (1914), 183. 'i ddarlunio bywyd y genedl iddi hi ei hun neu i egluro a dangos y bywyd hwnnw i'r Saeson'.
105 'Welsh drama week', 7.
106 'Wales and drama', *South Wales Daily News*, 12 May 1914, 5.

Chapter 5: Fragmented reflections and shattered fragments: the mirror image of Welsh national life?

1 See W. A. Humphreys, 'Wales and the drama', *Wales: the National Magazine for the Welsh People*, III, 1 (1913), 21–2.
2 Thomas Richards, 'The Welsh drama', *South Wales News*, 22 September 1927, 10.
3 'Notes of the month: George Bernard Shaw and the Welsh drama', quoted in *The Welsh Outlook* (July 1914), 293.
4 'The Welsh drama', *South Wales Daily News*, 18 May 1914, 7.
5 Quoted in Cecil Price, *The English Theatre in Wales* (Cardiff, 1948), p. 73.
6 E. E., 'Some recent Welsh plays', *The Welsh Outlook* (January 1914), 29.
7 D. Edwin Davies, 'Wales and the drama: a plea for pioneers', *Wales: the National Magazine for the Welsh People*, III, 1, (1911), 139.
8 Quoted in Cecil Price, 'Towards a Welsh national theatre', *The Anglo-Welsh Review*, XII, 29 (1962), p. 17.
9 E. E., 'Some recent Welsh plays', 29.
10 J. Tanad Powell, 'Wales on the stage', *Wales: the National Magazine for the Welsh People*, V (November 1913–February 1914), 97.
11 I focus on Francis's *Change* because it is a striking representation of the nature of the modern Welsh drama emerging at this time. Other contemporary works characterized by similar qualities were D. T. Davies's *Ephraim Harries* and R. G. Berry's *Ar y Groesffordd*.
12 Williams, *Y Mudiad Drama yng Nghymru 1880–1940*, p. 50.
13 J. D. W., 'Change: a successful start to the drama week', *The Cambria Daily Leader*, 30 June 1914, 3.
14 D. T. Davies, *Ble Ma Fa?* (Newtown, 1922).

15 'Mr Lloyd George and Welsh drama', *South Wales Daily News*, 16 May 1914, 7.
16 D. T. Davies, author of *The Poacher, Ephraim Harries* and *Ble Ma Fa?*, and W. J. Gruffydd, author of the important play *Beddau'r Proffwydi*, were the product of modern education and representatives of the new school of humanist thought. They wrote social drama that addressed the difficulties of changing old ways for new ones. D. T. Davies's work was directly instigated by Lord Howard de Walden's Eisteddfod prize offer whilst W. J. Gruffydd's play was written in an attempt to address the rot that he perceived at the heart of Welsh society. Whilst his work was criticized for the stiffness and formality of its language, it set a new standard for playwriting in Wales. It was first produced by the Cardiff University players in the city's Royal Playhouse, 20 March 1913.
17 See E. Morgan Humphreys, 'Dyfodiad y ddrama', *Y Beirniad*, IV, 3 (1914), 189.
18 J. J. Williams, 'Cymru a'r ddrama', *Y Brython*, 16 July 1914, 8, 'tyfiant y dosbarth canol sydd wedi rhoddi bod i rai o gwestiynau mawr yr oes'.
19 Saunders Lewis, 'The new revivalists', *Cambria Daily Leader*, 2 October 1919, 3.
20 Humphreys, 'Dyfodiad y ddrama', 190, 'bywyd nad yw bob amser yn cyrraedd cyhoeddusrwydd y cyngor plwy'.
21 D. T. Davies, *Ephraim Harris: Drama mewn Tair Act yn Nhafodiaith Morgannwg* (Cardiff, 1914).
22 Alban, 'O'r de', *Y Brython*, 4 June 1914, 7. 'y werin sydd fwyaf ymdeimladwy i fudiadau buddiolaf y genedl'. Not everyone is agreed on this point. In 'Chwiw y ddrama', *Y Brython*, 2 September 1914, 3, a different correspondent notes his 'faint suspicion' that the Welsh folk have not yet acquired an interest in the drama. At the same time, he admits that their interest is essential to its success and the success of all cultural phenomena in Wales.
23 Lewis, 'The new revivalists', 3.
24 Glan y Gors, 'Cymru a'r ddrama', *Y Darian*, 18 September 1913, 1, 'afiaeth am ysgubo y lloriau cymdeithasol o bob cyfeiriad'.
25 'Wales and drama', *Cambria Daily Leader*, 15 June 1914, 4.
26 Ibid.
27 'Pioneers. The drama in Wales', *Cambria Daily Leader*, 23 June 1914, 3.
28 'Stage and chapel, prejudice of Swansea', *Cambria Daily Leader*, 10 June 1914, 4.
29 John Colwyn, 'The drama in Wales', *Drama: a Magazine of the Theatre and Allied Arts*, I (2 October 1919), 46.
30 'Notes of the month: a Welsh repertory theatre', *The Welsh Outlook*, February 1914, 8.

Notes

31 See 'Llythyr agored at y Parch W. Morris, D.D., Treorchy ynghylch y Ddrama', *Tarian y Gweithiwr*, 2 July 1914, 4.
32 *Cyfeillachau crefyddol* translates roughly as leagues of religious companionship.
33 An unpatriotic Welshman, 'Welsh drama critic', *Cambria Daily Leader*, 27 June 1914, 3.
34 W. A. Humphreys, 'Wales and the drama', *Wales: the National Magazine for the Welsh People*, III, 1 (1913), 22.
35 'The other side', *Cambria Daily Leader*, 17 June 1914, 5.
36 See 'Symudiad dramodol cenedlaethol Cymru', *Tarian y Gweithiwr*, 18 June 1914, 4. 'llawer ... gormod o helbul a ffwdan'.
37 'The Welsh drama', *Cambria Daily Leader*, 12 June 1914, 6.
38 Owen Rhoscomyl, 'National drama', *The Western Mail*, 20 January 1914, 5.
39 See 'A savage critic!', *Cambria Daily Leader*, 22 June 1914, 5.
40 Ibid.
41 'Chwiw y ddrama', *Y Brython*, 2 July 1914, 3, 'amgylchu tir a môr i chwilio am gefnogwyr'.
42 Ibid. 'peth mor Gymreig â *reception*'.
43 'Wales and drama', *South Wales Daily News*, 12 May 1914, 5.
44 Beriah Gwynfe Evans, 'Welsh national drama: Lord Howard de Walden's mistake, and how it might be rectified, I. – The Mistake', *Wales*, VI, 35 (1914), 44.
45 Abel Jones, 'Does Wales need the drama?', *The Welsh Outlook* (1914), 256.
46 Ibid.
47 'Llythyr agored', 4.
48 Gwynfe Evans, 'Welsh national drama', 98.
49 Gwynfe Evans, 'Welsh national drama, I', 46.
50 Ibid.
51 Ibid., p. 100.
52 'Welsh national drama: some prophets and some critics', *Western Mail*, 27 March 1914, 7. Rhoscomyl's claims that Evans misrepresents the Welsh National Theatre Company's aims by claiming that they intend only to visit the major towns of Wales is fair in view of their intention to purchase a portable theatre capable of travelling to areas of Wales that were not in possession of a theatre of any kind.
53 See 'Nodiadau'r golygydd', *Tarian y Gweithiwr*, 28 May 1914, 4.
54 'A masterpiece coming', *The Cambria Daily Leader*, 24 October 1919, 1. 'Mr. Cadeirydd, Foneddigesau a Boneddigion' translates as 'Mr Chairman, Ladies and Gentlemen'.
55 'Symudiad dramodol cenedlaethol Cymru', 4. The writer actually uses the word *heniaith* that translates rather inadequately as ancient tongue, 'cadw a diogelu yr heniaith'.

56 'Wythnos o ddrama', *Y Darian*, 30 October 1919, 1. 'Ein hawgrym ni i Arglwydd Howard de Walden fyddai hyn: perffeithiad ei Gymraeg, a dechreuad yn y pentrefi o'i gwmpas alw ynghyd rhai a fedrant ffurfio cwmni drama, a cheisio ganddynt ddysgu dramodau Cymraeg, nid rhai Saesneg ac fe gynorthwya drwy hynny i adfer y Gymraeg a bywyd goreu Cymru yn ei ardal. Gallai wneud gwasanaeth gwerthfawr i Gymru pe cymerai y cynllun hwn.'
57 'Ymgais i ddiraddio bechgyn Cymru', *Y Darian*, 30 October 1919, 4. In fairness to W. J. Gruffydd, the report corrects many misrepresentations of his actual address and notes that he is very ready to acknowledge the existence of another quite different and much more sympathetic English presence in Wales.
58 Ibid.
59 Ibid.
60 See 'Welsh drama week', *Western Mail*, 3 March 1920, 8.
61 J. O. Francis, *Cross Currents: A Play of Welsh Politics* (Cardiff, 1922?), p. 8.
62 Rhys Puw, 'Cannoedd o gwmnïau'n chwilio am ddrama', *Y Ford Gron*, vol. 1 (November 1930), 20.
63 J. O. Francis, 'The deacon and the dramatist', *The Welsh Outlook* (June, 1919), 159.
64 Ibid.
65 W. C. Elvet Thomas, 'Thoughts on Welsh drama', *The Welsh Outlook* (November 1930), 306.
66 Puw, 'Cannoedd o gwmnïau yn chwilio am ddrama', (November 1930), 20, 'rhywbeth â blas pridd Cymru arno'.
67 T. Rowland Hughes, 'Chwi ddramawyr Cymreig!', *Y Ford Gron*, vol. 3, 7 (1933), 149, 'dan ei sang am fod drama ar y llwyfan; ar y diwedd tyrrau o bobl frwdfrydig yn casglu at ei gilydd ar yr heol i feirniadu, i ganmol, i ddadlau yn chwyrn ac yn ddiarwybod bron, i geisio darganfod anghenion ac anhepgorion y gelfyddyd, – dyna'r olygfa a welir yn aml yng Nghymru heddiw'.
68 D. T. Davies, 'Welsh folk drama: its future', *Anglo-Welsh Review* (January 1920), 65.
69 Ibid.
70 Quoted in Cecil Price, 'Towards a national theatre for Wales', *Anglo-Welsh Review*, XII, 29 (1962), 21.
71 See J. J. Williams, 'Cymru a'r ddrama', *Y Brython*, 30 July 1914, 3.
72 D. T. Davies, 'Welsh folk drama', 66.
73 D. T. Davies, 'The Welsh drama', *Western Mail*, 17 March 1920, 10.
74 Davies, 'Welsh folk drama', 66.
75 Davies's article refers to the writing of Welsh folk drama, in particular, as opposed to the more mature writing of the modern drama movement of which he himself was a primary exponent.

76 Davies, 'Welsh folk drama', 66. *Dadl ddirwestol* translates as temperance debate.
77 Ibid.
78 Saunders Lewis, 'Drama week: a retrospect', *Cambria Daily Leader*, 25 October 1919, 4.
79 R. G. Berry, *Ar y Groesffordd: Drama Gymraeg mewn Pedair Act* (Cardiff, 1914?).
80 D. T. Davies, 'Welsh drama week', *Western Mail*, 6 March 1920, 10.
81 D. T. Davies, 'The Welsh drama: important aspects of production', *Western Mail*, 12 March 1920, 8.
82 Saunders Lewis, 'Welsh drama: a speech and a play', *Cambria Daily Leader*, 24 October 1919, 5.
83 D. T. Davies, *Y Dieithryn: Drama mewn Un Act* (Cardiff, n. d.).
84 Saunders Lewis, *Gwaed yr Uchelwyr (Drama mewn Tair Act)* (Cardiff, 1922).
85 'Welsh drama at Cardiff', *Western Mail*, 15 May 1922, 6.
86 Ibid.
87 W. J. Gruffydd, *Beddau'r Proffwydi: Drama mewn Pedair Act* (Cardiff, 1914). *Beddau'r Proffwydi* translates as the graves of the prophets.
88 J. O. Francis, 'The new Welsh drama', *Wales: the National Magazine for the Welsh People*, V, 31, (1913), 7.
89 'Welsh drama at Cardiff', *South Wales Daily News*, 15 May 1922, 10.
90 'Llawr dyrnu', *Y Brython*, 1 November 1923, 7, 'yr unig feddyginiaeth all ddiogelu y ddrama, a'i chadw a'i pherffeithio'.
91 See *Y Darian*, 'Undeb y ddrama Gymreig', 22 September 1927, 5.
92 Gwernydd Morgan, 'Title', *Y Brython*, 1 November 1923, 7. 'Bu llawer o siarad beth amser yn ôl am gael Chwaraeudy Cenedlaethol i Gymru, ond mae'r peth fel pebai wedi ei anghofio erbyn hyn. Mynnai eraill i'r Ddrama Gymreig aros yn ei heiddilwch. Dywedant mai 'drama'r pentref' ydoedd y ddrama Gymreig i fod. Credwn ninnau y dylasai'r pentre gael y ddrama ar ei goreu, ac yn sicr trwy gymorth y chwaraeudy y ceir hynny. Pe ceid Undeb Genedlaethol holl gwmnïau a dramodwyr y wlad, gwelid yng Nghymru, Chwaraeudy Cenedlaethol yn y dyfodol agos.'
93 For a thorough analysis of the union's influence on the development of Welsh drama, see Williams, *Y Mudiad Drama yng Nghymru*, (2006).
94 Ifan Kyrle Fletcher, D. R. Davies and J. Eddie Parry, 'Adroddiad ar y gystadleuaeth ddrama',*Y Llwyfan*, II, 1 (1928), 19.
95 Ifan Kyrle Fletcher, 'Welsh plays in English', *Y Llwyfan*, I, 1 (1927), 4.
96 Michael Hechter, *The Celtic Fringe in British National Devolution: Internal Colonialism* (New Jersey, 1999).

97 Idwal Jones, 'Y ddrama yng Nghymru', *Cambria*, I, 7 (1932), 31. 'Nid oes modd i'r dramäwr a fynn roddi mynegiant i'r bywyd Cymreig ... ledaenu ei adenydd, oherwydd fod rhannau helaeth o'r bywyd cymdeithasol allan o'i gyrraedd. Gweinyddir ein Deddf Gwlad yn Saesneg; mae'r system addysg yn Seisnig, a chynhelir y rhan bwysicaf o'n masnach yn Saesneg. Y mae rhan helaeth o'n moddion difyrrwch yn Seisnig ei ddiwyg, ac y mae tuedd i droi i'r iaith Saesneg yn ein ymdrafodaeth boliticaidd. Saesneg a siaredir gan ein Uchelwyr a chan adran 'Gymreig' y Fyddin a'r Llynges. Yn wir, ni fedrir yn hawdd fynegi gwrthdaro cenedlaethol rhwng y Cymro a'r Saes ond yn iaith yr estron.'
98 George Moore, *Confessions of a Young Man* (London, 1928), p. 291.
99 Moore, *Confessions*, p. 293.
100 'Editorial notes', *Y Llwyfan*, I, 1 (1927), 8.
101 Evan D. Jones, 'Pwy sy'n siarad dros Gymru heddiw?', *Y Brython*, 15 July 1937, 5, 'arweiniad teg a boneddigaidd ar gwestiynau pwysig i Gymru'.
102 Ibid. 'Nid yw Cymru Gymreig wedi cymryd cwestiwn ei chynrychiolaeth o ddifrif eto, ac nid yw'r cynrychiolwyr yn ymdeimlo digon â'r angen am hunan-baratoi ar gyfer gwasanaeth cyhoeddus yng Nghymru.'
103 D. Gwenallt Jones notes, in his *Memoir to Idwal Jones* (Aberystwyth, 1958), that it was established as a monthly publication in December 1927 but reduced to two monthly from January 1928 and only produced eight issues in total.
104 *Y Faner*, 20 January 1931, 5.
105 *Y Darian*, 19 February 1931, and 5 March 1931.
106 J. E. Williams, 'Trwyddedu dramâu Cymraeg', *Y Darian*, 5 March 1931, 2, 'sy'n gorfodi awdur o Gymro i gael trwydded swyddog o Saes cyn gallu perfformio Drama Gymraeg yng Nghymru ... Y mae'r dull hurt presennol yn union fel petai meddyg yn ceisio dyfalu a oes clefyd mewn dyn trwy edrych ar size ei het.'
107 J. E. Williams, *Inc yn fy Ngwaed* (Llandybïe, 1963).
108 This venture was arranged by Lord Howard de Walden. A note in Theatr Genedlaethol Cymru, 'Clifford Evans papers, 6' says that whilst undertaking the major role in the Reinhardt 1934 National Eisteddfod production, Clifford Evans was asked by Lord de Walden to take control of a national theatre organization under his patronage. He declined due to his desire to acquire more professional experience before undertaking such a task but was later to become the driving force behind the St David's Trust campaign to establish a Welsh national theatre at Cardiff.

[109] O. Llewelyn Owain, *Hanes y Ddrama yn Nghymru* (Liverpool, 1948), p. 180.
[110] Kitchener Davies, *Cwm Glo* (Cardiff, 1994)
[111] Despite the play's technical excellence, National Eisteddfod adjudicators refused to reward it on the basis that 'not a single man in this tent would like to see his sister play the part of the heroine'. (*Y Brython*, 13 September 1934, 5.) Sybil Thorndike fuelled the controversy surrounding the play with the observation that the ability of drama to reveal 'life in its true guise is beneficial though not always popular and sometimes irreverent'. (*Y Brython*, 5 December 1933, 5).
[112] 'Eisiau Cymraeg', *Y Faner*, 14 January 1936, 5. 'Rhag cywilydd na alwer lle o'r fath yn "Genedlaethol" nac yn "Gymreig". Pa rhyfedd na fynn y mwyafrif mawr o'n cwmïau Cymraeg ddim ag ef? Pa rhyfedd fod eu noddwyr haelionus yn ddiweddar wedi gorfod yn gyhoeddus ddatgan eu siom na fyddai iddo gefnogaeth y genedl? Y mae'n rhy hwyr ar y dydd i unrhyw sefydliad "cenedlaethol" dalu'r ffordd yng Nghymru ac yntau yn diystyru'r Gymraeg.'
[113] 'A ydyw'r chwareudŷ cenedlaethol yn Gymreig?', *Y Brython*, 23 January 1936, 4. Cyfarfod digri oedd hwn, a dysgais i, beth bynnag, na fynn y Chwareudŷ Cenedlaethol fod yn Gymreig. Nid trwy gael cwmni o Gymry a Saeson i chwarae drama Almaenaidd dan gyfarwyddyd Awstriad (er bod y boneddwr hwnnw yn well Cymro ... na lluaws o Gymry Lerpwl – yn ôl pob golwg) y gyrrir y ddrama Gymraeg ymlaen.

Chapter 6: Changing old lamps for new: private patronage gives way to public subsidy

[1] Elidir Sais, 'The Drama', *Brython*, 21 July 1910, 4.
[2] The twentieth annual report of the Arts Council of Great Britain, 1964–5, p. 56.
[3] The eighth annual report of the Arts Council of Great Britan, 1952–3, p. 53.
[4] The fifteenth annual report of the Arts Council for Great Britain, 1959–60, p. 71.
[5] The seventeenth annual report of the Arts Council for Great Britain, 1961–2, p. 70.
[6] The eighteenth annual report of the Arts Council for Great Britain, 1962–3, p. 87.
[7] The twenty-fourth annual report of the Arts Council for Great Britain for the year ending March 1969, p. 55.
[8] The eighteenth annual report of the Arts Council, p. 69.
[9] Tom Jones, 'The Welsh drama', *Wales*, 1, 8, December 1894, 374.

Notes

10 See Owen Rhoscomyl, 'The presentation of Welsh plays: a travelling theatre', *South Wales Daily News*, 20 January 1914, 4.
11 See J. J. Williams, 'Rhodder cartref cysyrus i'n drama', *Y Brython*, 3 March 1932, 5.
12 Idwal Jones, 'Y ddrama yng Nghymru', *Cambria*, 1, 7 (1932), 32. '[M]erlyn mynydd, ifanc, hoyw yn methu tynnu ei gerbyd ymlaen oherwydd ei fod ef a'i gerbyd yn ceisio croesi cors'. '[N]id oes ganolbwynt dinesig, na chwareudy, na chwareuwyr chwaith – heb ddim arall ond y ddrama yn brif ddiddordeb eu bywyd.'
13 The Arts Council's Welsh Committee does not appear to have been capable of applying any standards other than English ones to the situation in Wales at this point in its history.
14 The fifteenth annual report of the Arts Council, p. 71.
15 The thirteenth annual report of the Arts Council for Great Britain, 1957–8, p. 74.
16 W. C. Elvet Thomas, 'Thoughts on Welsh drama', *Welsh Outlook*, (November, 1930), 306.
17 'Pioneers', *Cambria Daily Leader*, 23 May 1914, 5.
18 The Trust secured support from illustrious figures such as Dame Sybil Thorndike, Richard Burton, Elizabeth Taylor, Emlyn Williams, Harry Secombe, Hugh Griffith and Siân Phillips. For full details of all those present at the Trust's inaugural meeting November 1959, see Theatr Genedlaethol Cymru, Clifford Evans Papers, 6.
19 Williams, 'Rhodder cartref cysyrus i'n drama', 5. 'Mae dyfodol y Ddrama Gymraeg yng nghlwm wrth broblem brics a mortar.'
20 At the time, Elidir Davies ran his architectural business, Elidir L. W. Davies and Partners from 100 Wigmore St., London. It was he who had designed the Mermaid Theatre in which the founding meeting of the St David's Trust took place. Bernard Miles, the founder of the Mermaid Theatre was one of the St David's Trust's trustees.
21 Theatr Genedlaethol Cymru, Clifford Evans papers, 6.
22 Theatr Genedlaethol Cymru, Clifford Evans papers, 8.
23 See D. T. Davies, 'Drama', *Welsh Outlook* (December 1933), 331.
24 Theatr Genedlaethol Cymru, Clifford Evans papers, 12.
25 Gwynedd County Council Archive, Cwmni Theatr Cymru papers, XD68/2/307.
26 Elan Clos Stephens, 'Drama', in M. Stephens (ed.), *The Arts in Wales 1950–1975* (Cardiff, 1979), p. 253.
27 The eighth annual report of the Arts Council, p. 51.
28 Emyr Edwards, 'Blwyddyn o ddrama', *Baner ac Amserau Cymru*, 18 January 1962, 7.
29 Theatr Genedlaethol Cymru, Clifford Evans papers, 7.
30 Theatr Genedlaethol Cymru, Clifford Evans papers, 8.
31 The seventeeth annual report of the Arts Council, p. 86.

32. Ibid.
33. For full details of these ambitious plans, see Theatr Genedlaethol Cymru, Clifford Evans papers, 15.
34. Ifan Kyrle Fletcher, 'Plays and playhouses', *Welsh Outlook* (February 1926), 48.
35. The seventh annual report of the Arts Council for Great Britain, 1951–2, p. 22.
36. Stephens, 'Drama', p. 253.
37. Ioan Williams, 'Towards national identities: Welsh theatres', in B. Kershaw (ed.), *The Cambridge History of British Theatre*, vol. 3, (Cambridge, 2004), p. 242.
38. The sixth annual report of the Arts Council for Great Britain, 1950–1, p. 34.
39. Enid R. Morgan, 'Theatr Fach Llangefni yn dyfod i oed', *Y Llwyfan*, 3, (1969), 8–9. 'Theatr Fach Llangefni translates as the Llangefni Little Theatre.
40. The thirteenth annual report of the Arts Council, p. 81.
41. M. O. Roberts, 'Theatr Fach Llangefni', *Cymro*, 15 December 1960, 11.
42. Morgan, 'Theatr Fach Llangefni yn dyfod i oed', 9, 'grŵp o bobl sydd er yn amaturiaid, yn anelu at y safonau uchaf posibl. Y maent felly yn sefyll rhwng y theatr gwbl broffesiynol sy'n gofyn gan y gymdeithas leol ddim ond gwrandawyr a gwerthwyr tocynnau, a'r cwmni bach lleol sy'n cynhyrchu un ddrama dros dymor y gaeaf ac yn ei chyflwyno yn aml dan amodau echrydus mewn neuaddau pentref a festrïoedd capel.'
43. See H. Pierce Jones, 'Drama newydd Saunders Lewis: beirniadu'r cyngor celfyddydau mewn seiat', *Baner ac Amserau Cymru*, 28 September 1955, 1.
44. Garthewin was a manor house on the estate of the Wynne Family at Llanfair Talhaearn in Clwyd. It has now passed out of the family's possession.
45. R. O. F. Wynne, 'The Garthewin little theatre', *Dock Leaves* (1953), 5.
46. 'Cartref i'r ddrama', *Cymro*, 1 September 1959, 6, 'drwy borth llydan o dan hen glochdy, ... nes cyrraedd pen pellaf cwrt eang'.
47. Roger Owen, 'Theatr fach Garthewin'. An unpublished essay. (1993).
48. The production in question combined T. Gwynn Jones's *Y Gainc Olaf* with a nativity play in mime.
49. See Saunders Lewis, 'Drama Gymraeg', *Empire News*, 6 February 1955.
50. Roger Owen notes that the festival's move to Theatr Tywysog Cymru, Colwyn Bay after 1968 was an indication of its waning

significance in Wales's national life. See R. Owen, 'Y ddefod golledig?: Theatr, cymdeithas a Chymreictod yn y Gymru Gymraeg, 1945–1990' (unpublished Ph.D. thesis, University of Wales, Aberystwyth, 1999), 93.
51 National Library of Wales, Garthewin papers, G14.
52 Quoted in Roger Owen, 'Theatr fach Garthewin'.
53 See 'Cartref i'r ddrama', *Cymro*, 1 September 1959, 6.
54 Roger Owen, 'Theatr fach Garthewin'.
55 This is a reference to Ioan Williams, *A Straitened Stage: a Study of the Theatre of John Saunders Lewis* (Bridgend, 1991).
56 Geraint T. Davies, 'Lewis shows harsh facts of Wales', *Western Mail*, 9 August 1967, 7.
57 Roger Owen, 'Theatr fach Garthewin'.
58 The seventeenth report of the Arts Council, 1961–2.
59 Gwynedd County Council Archive, Cwmni Theatr Cymru papers, XD68/5/1.
60 Ibid.
61 Ibid.
62 Ibid.
63 Gwynedd County Council Archive, Cwmni Theatr Cymru papers, XD68/5/1 1965.
64 From 1974 onwards, the Welsh Theatre Company was amalgamated with the Welsh National Opera and Arts Council subsidy thereafter appears as a joint item.
65 The Casson Studio Theatre, Cardiff, accommodated an audience of eighty at this stage in its history.
66 The Welsh Arts Council's annual report for the year ending 31 March 1971.
67 Gwynedd County Council Archive, Cwmni Theatr Cymru papers, XD68/2/307. I suspect that this report, although unsigned, was written by Wilbert Lloyd Roberts himself.
68 This radio play was initially broadcast on St David's Day, 1937. At the time, its author was undergoing a period of incarceration at Wormwood Scrubs as a result of his part in the arson at the military site at Penyberth, an area of historical importance to the nation.
69 Gwynedd County Council Archive, Cwmni Theatr Cymru papers, XD68/2/307.
70 Stephens, 'Drama', p. 249.
71 Gwynedd County Council Archive, Cwmni Theatr Cymru papers, XD68/2/307.
72 Ibid.
73 The Welsh Arts Council's annual report for the year ending 31 March 1974.
74 Ibid.

75 The Welsh Arts Council annual report for the year ending 31 March 1972.
76 Saunders Lewis, *Gymerwch chi Sigaret?* (Llandybie, 1956).
77 Gwynedd County Council Archive, Cwmni Theatr Cymru papers, XD68/2/307.
78 Ibid.
79 Ibid. The sentence formed part of a press-release and stated that the newly registered company proposed to 'administer the affairs of the Welsh Theatre company' out on tour at the time.
80 Welsh Arts Council report for year ending 31 March 1973.
81 Gwynedd County Council Archive, Cwmni Theatr Cymru papers, XD68/2/6.
82 Gwynedd County Council Archive, Cwmni Theatr Cymru papers, XD68/2/307.
83 Cefin Roberts is the director of the current Welsh national theatre, Theatr Genedlaethol Cymru, established in 2004.
84 Gwynedd County Council Archive, Cwmni Theatr Cymru papers, XD68/2/6, 'cael eu cipio yma a thraw ac y collir felly elfen hynod o werthfawr i'r theatr Gymraeg'.
85 Ibid.
86 See Gwynedd County Council Archive, Cwmni Theatr Cymru papers, XD68/2/6.
87 The *cynghanedd* is a highly stylized form of Welsh versification involving a complicated paralleling of sound patterns.
88 Stephens, 'Drama', p. 294.
89 Gwynedd County Council Archive, Cwmni Theatr Cymru papers, XD68/2/6.
90 Ibid.
91 Gwynedd County Council Archive, Cwmni Theatr Cymru papers, XD68/2/304.
92 Theatr yr Ifanc translates as youth theatre or literally theatre of the young.
93 Gwynedd County Council Archive, Cwmni Theatr Cymru papers, XD68/2/133, 'egwyddor ac o awydd'.
94 Ibid., 'heb unrhyw ymrwymiad o'r naill du na'r llall'.
95 See Gwynedd County Council Archive, Cwmni Theatr Cymru papers, XD68/2/304.
96 Gwynedd County Council Archive, Cwmni Theatr Cymru papers, XD/68/2/128, 'clebran di-ben-draw a di-gyfeiriad', 'elfennol eu iaith a'u crefft a'u syniadau'.
97 Gwynedd County Council Archive, Cwmni Theatr Cymru papers, XD68/2/134. 'amser elusengarol'.

98 Gwynedd County Council Archive, Cwmni Theatr Cymru papers, XD/68/2/133.
99 See Gwynedd County Council Archive, Cwmni Theatr Cymru papers, XD/68/2/148.
100 Gwynedd County Council Archive, Cwmni Theatr Cymru papers, XD68/2/6.
101 See Eleanor Dwyryd, 'Anghytuno yng nghylch y theatr genedlaethol', *Baner ac Amserau Cymru*, 2 February 1967, 1.
102 Stephens, 'Drama', p. 262.
103 Gwynedd County Council Archive, Cwmni Theatr Cymru papers, XD68/2/133.
104 Welsh Arts Council report for year ending 31 March 1973.
105 Welsh Arts Council report for year ending 31 March 1975.
106 See Welsh Arts Council report for year ending 31 March 1974.
107 Cymdeithas Theatr Cymru translates as the Welsh Theatre Society. The society had been in existence for some time in 1974, but it was then that it was organized into this efficient network of regional committees.
108 The Cwmni Theatr Cymru papers include a discussion paper from Lynn Owen Rees dated 15 October 1974 to Wilbert Lloyd Roberts detailing plans for this society but there are also some undated notes by Wilbert himself outlining a similar scheme that seem to have been used as a draft for the scheme submitted by Rees. It was probably a collaborative effort.
109 Gwynedd County Council Archive, Cwmni Theatr Cymru papers, XD68/2/89, 'fod eu cenhadu'n hanfodol i ddyfodol y Cwmni'.
110 Ibid.
111 Gwynedd County Council Archive, Cwmni Theatr Cymru papers, XD68/2/307.
112 The fact that his style of management had some shortcomings is manifest in a request by Bill Dufton on behalf of the Welsh Arts Council on 2 July 1973 that the company's affairs should be put in order, its administration streamlined, regular budgetary reports prepared and produced and its overdependence on the small Bangor committee reduced.
113 *Adran Antur* translates as adventure section.
114 See 'Antur newydd Theatr Cymru', *Y Cymro*, 2 December 1975 in Gwynedd County Council Archive, Cwmni Theatr Cymru papers, XD68/8/16.
115 Stephens, 'Drama', p. 267.
116 Welsh Arts Council report for year ending March 31 1972.
117 Williams, 'Towards national identities: Welsh theatres', p. 243.
118 Bara Caws translates as Bread and Cheese.

119 See Roger Owen, *Ar Wasgar: Theatr a Chenedligrwydd yn y Gymru Gymraeg, 1979–1997* (Cardiff, 2003), p. 4.
120 *Byw yn y Wlad* translates as Living in the Country.
121 This company was wound up in 1981 and replaced by Theatr Crwban and Cwmni Cyfri Tri, eventually to become Arad Goch, the successful Theatre in Education and Youth Theatre Company that still thrives in the town.
122 Quoted in Gill Ogden, 'A history of theatre in education in Wales', in Anna Marie Taylor (ed.), *Staging Wales: Welsh Theatre 1979–1997* (Cardiff, 1997), p. 51.
123 Welsh Arts Council report for year ending 31 March 1981.
124 Brith Gof was an internationally acclaimed Welsh-language company founded in 1981 by Mike Pearson and Liz Hughes Jones. Brith Gof can be roughly translated as either Distant or Pied Memory.
125 Charmian Savill, 'A critical study of the history of the Welsh theatre company Brith Gof', (unpublished M.Phil thesis, University of Wales, Aberystwyth, 1993), p.1.
126 Williams, *Towards New Identities: Welsh Theatres*, p. 265.
127 Cliff McLucas was one of Brith Gof's most influential members in the sense that his thought on the architecture of theatrical space shaped much of the company's ideology from the 1990s onwards.
128 Quoted in Savill, 'A critical study of the history of the Welsh theatre company Brith Goth', p. 7.
129 See Gwynedd County Council Archives, Cwmni Theatr Cymru papers, XD68/2/307.
130 Savill, 'A critical study of the history of the Welsh theatre company Brith Gof', p. 7.
131 David Adams, *Stage Welsh: Nation, Nationalism and Theatre: the Search for Cultural Identity,* (Llandysul, 1996), p. 57.
132 See programme.
133 Elan Clos Stephens, 'A century of Welsh drama', in Dafydd Johnston (ed.), *A Guide to Welsh Literature: 1900–1996*, vol. 6 (Cardiff, 1979), p. 95.

Conclusion

1 Gwyn A. Williams, *When was Wales?* (London, 1985), p. 304.
2 David Adams, *Stage Welsh: Nation, Nationalism and Theatre: the Search for Cultural Identity* (Llandysul, 1996), p. 5.
3 Deborah Parsons, 'Nationalism or continentalism: representing heritage culture for a new Europe', in *Yearbook of European*

Studies, Andy Hollis (ed), *Beyond Boundaries: Textual Representations of European Identity,* vol. 15 (Amsterdam, 2000), p. 4.

4 John Sundholm, 'The non-place of identity: on the poetics of a minority culture', in *Yearbook of European Studies,* Andy Hollis (ed.), *Beyond Boundaries: Textual Representations of European Identity,* vol. 15 (Amsterdam, 2000), pp. 165–81.
5 Parsons, 'Nationalism or continentalism', p. 4.
6 James Sime, *Lessing* (London, 1877), p. 41.
7 Parsons, 'Nationalism or continentalism', p. 1.
8 T. C. W. Blanning, *The Culture of Power and the Power of Culture: Old Regime Europe 1660–1789* (Oxford, 2002), p. 8.
9 Williams, *When was Wales?,* p. 304.
10 Geraint Talfan Davies and John Osmond, 'Culture and identity', in *The Birth of Welsh Democracy: the First Term of the National Assembly for Wales* (Cardiff, 2003), p. 243.
11 Williams, *When was Wales?,* p. 304.

Index

Abbey Theatre 161
Aberdare, Lord *see* Lord Aberdare
Ackermann, Konrad 48, 50, 53, 54, 56, 57
Action Française 44
Adams, David 213
Adran Antur 207, 208
Alasseur, Claude 26, 27
Alaw Ddu 144
Albanians 7
Albert Hall 167
Allies 87
Anderson, Benedict 2, 13
Anna Amelia *see* Duchess Anna Amelia
Antoine, André 45
Apostolidès, Jean-Marie 15, 18, 22, 27
Archer, William 55, 94, 95, 98, 103, 104, 105, 106, 108, 109, 111, 112, 114, 116, 119, 164, 185, 186
Arendt, Hannah 20, 21, 25, 34, 35, 36, 37
Arnold, Matthew 95, 97, 98, 107, 108, 109, 111, 112, 180
Arons, Wendy 61
Arts Council of Great Britain 120, 182, 187, 189, 193, 197 *see also* Welsh Arts Council and Welsh Committee of the Arts Council of Great Britain
Arts Theatre 178
Ast 56
Athens 171
Aubignac, François d' 15
Auerbach, Eric 65, 66, 67, 68
Austria 48, 73
Austro-Prussian War (1866) 48

Avignon Festival 45
Aylmer, G. E. 92, 111

Badger, Richard 101, 102, 114
Bara Caws 208, 209
Barraclough, Geoffrey 105
Bastille 38
Battaglia, Valérie 44, 45
Bauer, Otto 4, 5, 6, 13, 97
Bauhaus 81
Bayliss, Lilian 121, 122
Bayreuth Festival 75, 76
BBC Wales 197
Beaumarchais, Pierre-Augustin Caron de 26, 27
Beirdd yr Uchelwyr 129
Belgium 48
Bell, David A. 43
Berlin Wall 88
Bernhardt, Sarah 41, 42, 112
Berry, R. G. 171
Bevin, Ernest 107
Billington, Michael xi
Bismarck, Otto von 48, 73, 74, 75, 77, 93
Biwla 211
Blaenplwyf 211
Blanning, T. C. W. 1
Bogdanov, Michael vii
Bohata, Kirsty 148
Borrow, George 157
Boulangism 44
Boursault, Edmé 18
Bowen, Evelyn 178, 179
Bozonnet, Marcel 127
Brandenburg Gate 87
Brecht, Bertolt 82, 88
Brith Gof 209, 210, 211

British Drama Festival 174, 175
British Drama League 175
British Empire 149
British Empire Exhibition 119
British Museum 96, 118
Bruford, W. H. 48, 53, 54, 57, 62, 69
Bubbers, J. 57
Büchner, Georg 74, 75
Burgess, Adam 34, 35
Burnand, F. C. 114, 115
Bute, Lady see Lady Bute
Bryant, A. T. 12

Caerleon 174, 175
Caernarfon Eisteddfod (1894) 131, 135
Cain, Alex 40
Cambridge University 111
Cardiff 184
Cardiff Castle 149
Cardiff City Council 186, 188, 189
Cardiff College of Music and Drama 201, 202
Cardiff Drama Week (June 1914) 152, 159
Cardinal Richelieu 15, 16, 26, 29
Carmarthen Eisteddfod (1819) 134
Carpenter, Edward 117
Carr, W. H. 74
Casson, Lewis 153
Casson Studio Theatre 197
Chappuzeau, Samuel 19
Charlemagne 48
Charles, Edward 132
Charles IX 29, 30, 42
Charles Augustus 63, 64, 67
Charnell-White, Cathryn 134
Chénier, Marie-Joseph 29, 30, 31
Chesterfield, Lord see Lord Chesterfield
Chevally, Sylvie 29
Churchill, Winston 112
Clairon, Mlle 26
Clarke, Jan 19
Cleopatra 198
Clouet, François 30
Clwyd 207

Clwydfardd see Griffith, David
Coleg Harlech 205
Collège des Quatre-Nations 21
Colletet, Guillaume 17
Colwyn, John 161
Comédie-Française x, 11, 15, 16, 19, 21, 24, 26, 28, 29, 30, 31, 32, 34, 35, 36, 37, 39, 41, 44, 45, 46, 47, 51, 91, 93, 107, 122, 127, 180
Committee of Provincial Diets 73
Commune of Paris 29, 32, 34
Comte de Mirabeau 31
Confino, Alon 80
Connor, Walker 5, 117
Conservatoire 41
Copeau, Jacques 45
Corneille, Pierre 28
Cottesloe Theatre 123
Council for the Encouragement of Music and the Arts 120
Crowther, Lord see Lord Crowther
Curtis, William 124, 125
Cwmni Drama Llangefni 190
Cwmni Môn 190
Cwmni Theatr Cymru ix, 183, 186, 196, 198, 199, 200, 202, 203, 204, 206, 207, 209, 210
Cwmni Theatr y Werin 208 see also Theatr y Werin
Cymdeithas Theatr Cymru 205
Cymmrodorion, Honourable Society of 133, 164, 172, 173
Cynan see Evans-Jones, Albert
Cynfeirdd 129
Czech Republic 48

Dadaism 82
Danton 29
David, Louis 27, 33, 38
David Lewis Theatre 145
Davies, Andrew 150
Davies, Bryn 171
Davies, Conrad 174
Davies, D. R. 139
Davies, D. T. 158, 159, 169, 170, 171, 172, 173, 186
Davies, Elidir 184, 185

Davies, Emily 209
Davies, J. Kitchener 130, 179
Davies, Sharon 207
Debussy, Claude 77
Declaration of the Rights of Man (1789) 33
Department of Continuing Education 174
Deutsche Schaubühne 88
Dickens, Charles 97, 98
Dodsley and Company 62, 63
Donneau, Jean 17, 63
Dorval, Marie 41
Drama League 119
Dresden 84
Dreyfus 44
Dubois 26
Duchess Anna Amelia 53, 63
Dufton, Bill 201, 202
Duke of Kent 114
Duke of Westminster 118

Edwards, Hywel Teifi 148, 149
Edwards, O. M. 147
Edwards, Thomas (Twm o'r Nant) 133, 139, 140, 141, 182, 184
Ekhof, Konrad 57, 61
Elidir Sais *see* Jones, William Hughes
Eliot, George 97, 98
Eliot, T. S. 191
Emmet, Alfred 97, 102
Engels, Friedrich 76, 129
England *see* chapter 3
English National Theatre x, 45, 46, 94, 97, 117, 123, 124, 126, 127, 128, 185, 196, 204
Enlightenment 59
Ernest Augustus II 2, 63
Esger-ddu 211
Esger Llanfer 211
Esger-man 211
Esher, Lord *see* Lord Esher
Evans, Beriah Gwynfe 130, 143, 145, 165, 166, 169
Evans, Caradoc 168
Evans, Clifford 184, 185, 186, 187, 188, 189
Evans, E. Derry 147, 148

Evans, Eric 90
Evans, Grey 207
Evans-Jones, Albert (Cynan) 179, 180
expressionism 82

Fawkes, Richard 198
Featherstone, Vicky ix
Federal German Republic 87
Fête de la Féderation (1790) 37, 38
Fielding, Henry 101
First German Reich 48
Fischer, Peter 87
Fischer-Lichte, Erika 2
Fisher, George 191
Fletcher, Ifan Kyrle 175, 176
France *see* chapter 1
Francis, J. O. 137, 138, 152, 158, 159, 168
Frankfurt 74
Frederick William IV 73
French Revolution (1789) x, 9, 26, 33, 35, 36, 43, 70, 74, 78, 91, 98, 150
Fridé, Cécile 37, 38
Frisch, Efraim 80

Galsworthy, John 106, 126
Garlick, Iestyn 207
Garmon, Owen 202
Garrick, David 97, 99
Garthewin *see* Theatr Fach Garthewin
Geary, Patrick J. 2, 4, 5, 7, 9, 12, 13, 129, 149
Gellner, Ernest 9, 10, 11, 12, 13
German Democratic Republic 87
German Labour Front 86
Germany *see* chapter 2
Girouard, Marc 125
Glamorgan 135
Glanrhyd 211
Globe Theatre 111
Glyn, Gwyneth viii
Goebbels, Joseph 84, 86
Goethe, Johann Wolfgang von 53, 63, 64, 65, 66, 67, 68, 69, 70, 72, 78, 80, 86, 103, 170

Gogynfeirdd 129
Goldsmith, Elizabeth 18
Goodwin, Tim 126
Gordon, Martell 72
Göring, Herman 84
Gorsedd y Beirdd 134
Gotha court theatre 54
Gottsched, Johann 57, 58, 60
Graig-ddu 211
Grand Theatre, Swansea 197
Granville Barker, Harley 55, 94, 102, 105, 108, 113, 114, 119, 160, 164
Greek city states 20, 25
Greek mythology 72
Griffith, David (Clwydfardd) 136
Griffiths, Bruce 191
Gruffydd, W. J. 143, 159, 167, 173
Guibert, Noelle 25, 31
Gwar-ffynon 211
Gwynedd 207
Gwynedd County Council Archive 197
Gwyneddigion Society 132, 133

Habermas, Jürgen ix, x, 1, 6, 8, 10, 11, 16, 17, 34, 41, 46, 54, 57, 65, 72, 86, 90, 91, 105, 111, 115, 124, 125, 126, 128, 129, 130, 137
Haggar, William 143
Hall, Owen 102
Hall, Peter 125, 126
Hamburg 47, 50, 53, 57, 58
Hamburg National Theatre 54, 55, 56, 58, 131
Hand, Terry vii
Hankin, John 115, 116
Hanseatic League 55
Hanslick, Eduard 76
Hardy, Thomas 111
Harrison, Tony 126
Harz 85
Hauptmann, Carl 82
Hawtrey, G. P. 149
Hechter, Michael 176
Hefin, John 203
Hegel, Georg Friedrich Wilhelm 9

Hemmings, Frederick 27, 30, 35, 37
Herder, Johann Gottfried von 3, 5, 6
Hickling, Alfred vii
High Sheriff of Glamorgan 164
Hitler, Adolf 7, 8, 38, 39, 84, 85, 87
Hobsbawm, E. J. 3, 9, 10, 73
Hock, Stefan 178, 180
Hoffmanstahl, Hugo von 178, 180
Holy Roman Empire 48, 67 *see also* Roman Empire
Horace 28
Hôtel de Bourgogne 15
House of Commons 92, 116, 118
Hroch, Miroslav 4, 12, 13
Hudson, W. H. 101
Hughes, Richard 178
Hughes, T. Rowland 169
Hugo, Victor 77
Humphreys, E. Morgan 154
Humphreys, Emyr 203, 204
Humphreys, W. A. 156, 162
Hwfa Môn *see* Williams, Rowland

Ibsen, Henrik viii, 191
Illyrians 7
Inland Revenue 119
Iolo Morganwg *see* Williams, Edward
Irving, Henry 109, 113

Jelavich, Peter 71
Jenkins, Warren 195, 196
Jessner, Leopold 82
Jones, Abel 153, 165
Jones, Aled 150
Jones, G. R. 177
Jones, Gwyn 186
Jones, Henry Arthur 94, 95, 96, 97, 98, 99
Jones, Idwal 176, 183
Jones, J. Tywi 168, 170
Jones, Larry Eugene 78
Jones, Lewis David 144
Jones, Morris 193
Jones, Myfanwy 67

Jones, T. Gwynn 178, 180
Jones, T. O. 145
Jones, Tom 167, 183
Jones, Valmai 207
Jones, W. S. 197
Jones, William Hughes (Elidir Sais) 144, 146, 151, 161
Jory, David 15
Joseph II 53

Kaiser, Robert J. 6, 7, 117
Kattago, Siobhan 89
Kean, Edmund 99, 100
Kenny, Sean 204
Kidd, Alan 95
Koch, Gottlieb Heinrich 52, 53, 63
Koshar, Rudy 80
Kosovo 7
Kotzebue, August von 70
Kruger, Loren 95

La Grange, Charles de 22, 25, 30
Labour government vii
Labour Party 121
Lady Bute 148
Lagarde, Paul Anton de 85
Lamb, Stephen 83
Lampeter 211
Lancaster, Henry Carrington 21
Langbehn, Julius 85
Laqueur, Walter 80, 82
Las Vegas 127
Lasdun, Denys 123, 125, 126
Laurent, Michel 22
Leipzig 50, 53
Leland, John 134
Lemaître, Jules 42
Lenin, V. I. 117
Leon, Mechele 127
Lessing, Gottfried Ephraim 6, 48, 49, 53, 57, 58, 60, 61, 62, 63, 67, 70, 71, 103, 215
Lessing, Nicolai 59
Lewis, Ceri 133, 135
Lewis, Saunders 139, 140, 159, 171, 172, 173, 175, 176, 184, 188, 190, 191, 192, 193, 197, 199
Ley, Robert 86

Licensing Act (1737) 100
Lichtenstein 48
Liebknecht, Karl 77
List, Friedrich 9
Little Theatre Guild of Great Britain 191
Liverpool 159, 180
Llanelli 143
Llanberis 130
Llanfair Clydogau 211
Llanfairfechan 174
Llangefni Drama Festival 192
Llether Brith 211
Llether Garw 211
Lloyd George, David 131, 148, 151, 152, 153, 158, 178
Lluest Ucha 211
London City Council 120, 121
London County Council 111
London University 111
Longueville, Mlle de 17
Lord Aberdare 184, 188, 200
Lord Chamberlain 100, 177
Lord Chesterfield 100, 101
Lord Crowther 216
Lord Esher 94
Lord Howard de Walden ix, 151, 153, 154, 156, 160, 164, 165, 167, 168, 172, 173, 174, 178, 180, 182, 183, 193
Lord Lytton 116
Lord Mostyn 150
Lord Plymouth 116
Loret, Jean 17, 24, 145
Louis XIV 15, 16, 18, 19, 21, 26, 32, 47
Louis XV 15, 25
Louis XVI 34, 38
Löwen, Johann Friedrich 47, 56, 57, 59
Ludwig II 76
Lukács, George 82
Lully, Jean Baptiste 21
Lustiana Medal 84
Lutyens, Edward 119, 121, 124
Lyceum Theatre 109, 116, 117, 118
Lynch, Mr 108

Lyotard, Jean François 91
Lyttleton, Alfred 116
Lyttleton, Oliver 122
Lyttleton Theatre 123
Lytton, Lord *see* Lord Lytton

MacKinder, H. J. 108, 116
McLucas, Cliff 210
Mahelot 22
Mallarmé, Stéphane 40
Mann, Thomas 76, 80, 85
Mannheim 54
Mansion House, London 114, 115
Marcos, Emelda 39
Mars, Mlle 41
Marx, Karl 73
Marxist theories 6
Masey, Cecil 121
Mathews, Dan 172
Mélèse, Pierre 17, 20
Mercier, Louis Sébastien 25
Mermaid Theatre 184
Merthyr Tydfil 166
Methodism 171
Meyer, Carl 116
Middle Ages 6, 10, 23, 55
Mill, John Stuart 102
Miller, Arthur 191
Milošević, Slobodan 7
Minihan, Janet 120, 121
Mirabeau *see* Comte de Mirabeau
Moeller van den Bruck 85
Mo'lfryn 211
Molière, Jean Baptiste 16, 21, 41, 127, 191, 193
Moody, John 193
Moody-Manners Opera Company 142
Moore, George 176
Morgan, Enid R. 191, 192
Morgan, Gwernydd 174
Morgan, Kenneth O. 129, 140
Morris, Lewis 136
Morris, W. 161
Mosse, George 85
Mostyn, Lord *see* Lord Mostyn
Mounet-Sully, Jean 42
Müller, J. F. 52, 56

Munich 54, 76

Nairn, Tom 102, 104, 117
Napoleon 39
National Assembly for Wales vii
National Culture/National Identity Research Group 127
National Dramatic Union 174
National Eisteddfod 185, 201, 202, 203 *see also* chapter 4
National Eisteddfod (1858) 133
National Gallery 96
National Playhouse for Wales 175
National Socialism 85, 87, 89
National Theatre Bill (1973) 124
National Theatre Board 122, 123
National Theatre Company 187, 191
National Theatre Festival (1934) 84
Naudet, Émile-Contat 31
Nazi Germany 127
Nazis x, 7
Nazism 83, 84, 86
Netherlands 48
Neuber, Caroline 48, 50, 51, 52, 56
Neue Wache 89
Neumann, Franz 78
New Theatre, Cardiff 153, 155, 187, 197
Nicholl, Allardyce 122
Nicholls, David 95
Nietsche, Friedrich 77, 82
Normal College, Bangor 201
North Wales Arts Association 201
Nuremberg rallies 7, 8, 38, 39, 85

Odéon Theatre 46
Offa's Dyke 149, 207
Ogden, Gill 208
Old Vic Theatre 121, 122
Olivier, Laurence 122, 123
Olivier Theatre 123, 196
Orwell, George 93, 101, 106, 114, 124
Ottoman Turks 7
Owain, O. Llewelyn 178
Owen, Goronwy 134
Owen, Myra 190

Index

Owen, Roger 193, 194, 195, 208
Owen-Rees, Lynn 206
Owen Rhoscomyl *see* Vaughan, Owen
Oxford University 111

Palais Royal 21
Pant-y-fedwen 211
Pantresger 211
Paris 5, 28
Parker, Louis Napoleon 148
Parry, Gwenlyn 203
Parry, Joseph 141, 142, 143
Parry, Mendy 142
Parry, Thomas 193
Parson, Deborah 213
Patterson, Michael 87
Pengelli 211
Pentrebanne 211
Peters, Julie Stone 4, 11
Pfistermeister, Franz von 76
Phillipines 39
Phillips, John 172
Phillips, Siân 192
Piscator, Erwin 83
Plas Newydd, Llangollen 178, 179
Playhouses Act (1843) 177
Plymouth, Lord *see* Lord Plymouth
Pois, R. A. 86
Povey, Meic vii
Powell, J. Tanad 158
Pretoria 211
Price, Cecil J. 141, 143, 157
Primrose Hill 134
Privy Purse 2
Puleston, John 136
Puw, Rhys 168, 169

Racine, Jean 41
Raine, Allen 157
Razgonnikoff, Jacqueline 25, 31
Red Dragon Company 145
Reed, J. T. 61, 64, 70
Reichard, H. A. O. 62
Reichstag 80
Reinhardt, Max 83, 86
Renaissance 22, 65
Renan, Ernest 3, 4, 8

Renner, K. 9
Richard and Morris, solicitors 152
Richards, Thomas 156
Richelieu *see* Cardinal Richelieu
Roberts, Cefin 201
Roberts, Dyfan 207
Roberts, Eigra Lewis 203
Roberts, Wilbert Lloyd 196, 198, 201, 202, 203, 205, 207, 208, 209, 210
Robertson, J. G. 50, 54, 55, 56
Robespierre, Maximilien de 33, 35, 36, 38
Rockerfeller Trustees 118
Rolland, Romain 44, 45, 75
Roman Empire 5 *see also* Holy Roman Empire
Romans 110
Rome 28
Royal Academy of Dramatic Art 111, 118
Royal Commission on the Constitution 216
Royal National Opera 45
Rudloff-Hille, Gertrud 48, 59

St David's Trust 184, 185, 187, 188, 189, 196, 199, 200, 205
Sarcey, Francisque 41
Samson, M. Joseph-Isidore 41
Sardou, Victorien 40
Sarn Llys 211
Savill, Charmian 208
Savoy Hotel 122
Schafer, Yvonne 83
Scheidemann, Philip 77
Schönemann, Johann Friedrich 48, 58
Schiller, Friedrich von 53, 63, 64, 65, 66, 67, 69, 70, 71, 72, 78, 80, 85, 103
Schlemmer, Oscar 81
Schröter, Corona 72
Scott, Walter 150
Scotland ix, 187
Second German Reich (1871) 48, 73
Serbia 7

264 Index

Seyler, Abel 54, 57
SgriptCymru vii
Shakespeare, William viii, 42, 66, 70, 96, 97, 99, 100, 106, 108, 114, 115, 189
Shakespeare National Memorial Trust 118, 121
Shaw, George Bernard viii, 94, 96, 98, 127, 156
Shennan, J. H. 98, 114
Siegesallee 80
Single European Act (1987) 213
Slovenia 48
Smith, Anthony 5
Smith, H. W. 117
Snyder, Louis 84
Society for the Rights of Authors (1777) 26
Sombart, Nicolaus 73
Sophocles 64
South Bank 113, 120
Soviet Russia 87
Springer, Keith 96
Staatliche Schauspielhaus 82
Starcke 63
Stein, Peter 88
Stephens, Elan Closs 187, 190, 197, 198, 201, 204, 211
Sternhell, Zeen 43
Strasbourg Theatre 46
Strength through Joy 86
Strowski, F. 23, 24
Stubbs, William 92
Sundholm, John 214, 215
Swansea 160, 162, 163, 172
Switzerland 48
Synge, J. F. 161
Szondi, Peter 36, 65

Taig, Thomas 192
Taliesin 135
Talma, François 30, 32, 40, 41, 43
Talysarn Drama Company 177
Terry, Ellen 112, 174
Thamer, Hans-Ulrich 7, 8
Thatcher, Margaret 127
Thatcherism 209

Theater der Nation 85
Theater des Volkes 85, 86
Theatr Clwyd vii
Theatr Fach Garthewin 191, 192, 193, 194, 195
Theatr Genedlaethol Cymru vii, viii, 129, 213
Theatr Gwynedd 204, 205
Theatr y Werin 202, 205 *see also* Cwmni Theatr y Werin
Theatr yr Ifanc 202
Theatr yr Ymylon 202
Théâtre de la Colline 46
Théâtre de la Foire 23, 24
Théâtre de l'Oeuvre 45
Théâtre de la Révolution 75
Théâtre du Vieux Colombier 45
Théâtre Guénegaud 15, 16
Théâtre Libre 45
Théâtre National de Chaillot 46
Theodor, Karl 54
Thomas, D. J. 193, 202
Thomas, John Stradling 189
Thomas, W. C. Elvet 184
Thorndike, Sybil 154
Tocqueville, Alexis de 9, 33, 44, 57, 106
Toller, Ernst 83
Traherne, Cennydd G. 184
Tree, Beerbohm 116
Trewin, J. C. 193
Tudur, Gwenllian 191
Tuileries 25
Twm o'r Nant *see* Edwards, Thomas
Tzonev, Stoyan 26

Unified Theatre Law (1934) 84
Union of Welsh Drama 174, 176, 177
United States of America 120
University College, Cardiff 205
University College of North Wales, Bangor 204
University College of Wales, Aberystwyth 141, 205
University of Wales 151

Index

Vaughan, Owen (Owen Rhoscomyl) 149
Vienna 53, 54
Vigny, Alfred de 41
Vilar, Jean 45
Voltaire (François Marie Arouet) 29, 58

Wachler, Ernst 85
Wagner, Richard 75, 76, 77
Wahrman, Dror 95
Walden, Lord Howard de *see* Lord Howard de Walden
Wales Theatre Company vii, 183, 195, 197, 198
Walpole, Horace 101
Watts-Dunton, Theodore 157
Weber, Max 79
Webster, Roger 186
Weimar 53, 63, 64, 67, 69
Weimar Republic 78, 79, 81, 82, 103
Wekwerth, Manfred 88
Welsh Arts Council vii, 198, 199, 200, 203, 205, 207, 209 *see also* Arts Council of Great Britain and Welsh Committee of the Arts Council of Great Britain
Welsh Committee of the Arts Council of Great Britain 182, 183, 184, 186, 188, 198, 190, 191, 192, 195, 199, 204 *see also* Arts Council of Great Britain and Welsh Arts Council
Welsh Drama Union 179
Welsh Joint Education Committee 202
Welsh National Drama Company (Welsh Players) 152, 158, 159
Welsh National Opera 198
Welsh National Opera Company 187

Welsh National Pageant (1909) 148, 149
Welsh National Theatre 155, 192
Welsh National Theatre Company 160, 166, 167, 196
Welsh Office 209
Welsh Players *see* Welsh National Drama Company
Westminster Abbey 96
Whitworth, Geoffrey 116, 118, 175
Wieland, Christoph Martin 69
Wilhelm I 48, 73, 75, 76
Wilhelm II 80
Wilhelmsburg 63
Williams, Edward (Iolo Morganwg) 132, 133, 135, 136, 139, 141
Williams, G. J. 132
Williams, Gwyn A. 213, 216
Williams, Ioan 140, 142, 143, 145, 190, 208
Williams, J. D. 161
Williams, J. J. 159, 183, 184, 191
Williams, John Ellis 177, 178
Williams, John Lloyd 144
Williams, Llewelyn 156
Williams, Meriel 179
Williams, Rowland (Hwfa Môn) 135
Williams, Taliesin 134
Wilson, Effingham 95, 99, 100
Woodfield, James 100
Workers' Education Movement 174
Wynne, R. O. F. 192, 193

Yeats, W. B. 47

Zollverein 73
Zoten's Hof 50
Zulus 12